Awaken Your Potency

a practical guide to Law of Attraction, Ayurveda & Meditation

Kimberly Beekman

April 2019

Lois,
It's been an
to journey
with you!
love,
Kim ♡

First edition
This book is very much like its author: Deep, reflective, and
perfectly imperfect. Please be patient with this first edition as
it may have imperfections, just like each of us.

Table of Contents

Gratitude

My growth in consciousness, and therefore this book, would not have been possible without the many people who have contributed to my life's path.

Matt Beekman, my husband, my biggest supporter, my mirror, my love … Your consistent loving presence in my life is the foundation upon which I have built this brighter version of who I am. Thank you for always loving and supporting me, and shining your beautiful Light back to me … always. I love you.

Mirabai Devi, thank you dear teacher for your guidance in this whole enLIGHTenment process. You showed up in my town at the moment I was ready for deep awakening, and you have held my hand through every step in the process. You model such Divine Love and Grace and continue to show me what it looks like to walk this path in full Divine consciousness. Thank you for doing your work in the world so that we all can awaken to the truth of who we are. I hope I have reflected your teachings with care and purity. I love you.

My daughters—**Ava, Lillian,** and **Juliet**—you always inspire me to be the best version of myself. Thank you for reflecting back everything within me that needed to be transformed, and teaching me how to love. I'm so blessed to be your mom. I love you three more than you can imagine.

I extend reverence and honor to my mother, **Joyce Locks**, who did an incredible job creating the perfect environment for me to become a fiery spark of Light. She always held the vision of my creativity and success, which built the foundation for me to step into my truth. Thank you, mom. I love you.

I'm deeply moved by my friendships that have held me throughout my life—**Jen DeVincenzo** for guiding me during my teenage years through now, **Sally Drew** for being my loving rock, **Kim Marks** for your spiritual wisdom and fellowship, and **Anna Kaganer** and **Sara Madakour** for holding 5D with me.

Deep gratitude to **Abraham, Esther Hicks,** and **Jerry Hicks** for the wisdom on Law of Attraction weaved throughout this book. (*I strongly recommend their books, recordings and YouTube* *teachings that so effectively raise the vibration of the planet.*) **Neale Donald Walsch**, thank you for your Conversations With God books that resonated so deeply when I was in my twenties.

So much gratitude goes to Bridgette Shea for introducing me to my breath and Ayurveda, **Sivananda Ashram** and **Swami Sitaramananda** for the Yogic wisdom, to **Durga Leela** and **Dr. David Frawley** for the Ayurveda wisdom, and **Saratoga Regional YMCA** and **Skidmore College** for the opportunity to serve authentically.

Deep gratitude to those who contributed directly to this book: **Endre Balogh** (www.EndresArt.com), for the amazing cover photo; **Elettra Cudignotto** (www.elettracudignotto.com), for this book's interior artwork; and **Carrie White** for the skillful editing.

Awaken and Align

We spend most of our lives on the hamster wheel of our unruly minds, running around and around the wheel unconsciously. We're just trying to keep things going, keep things moving. Work, family, commitments, obligations—our lives are filled with the minutia of daily living. Most of the time we are just operating on autopilot.

And really, life doesn't feel satisfying. We are not deeply joyful. We don't feel fulfilled. We're depleting ourselves by keeping the hamster wheel moving most of our lives. We are not creating the life of our dreams. We are not consciously manifesting our greatest potential. We are just reacting to what life serves up.

If we are lucky, life presents us with a life-changing situation that makes it impossible to stay on the hamster wheel. Perhaps a traumatic event shakes us up. When we land, we either go into self-pity and fear … or we awaken to who we really are. We may look around and realize that we don't have much in our lives that reflects our passion for life. We either go back to sleep, or we commit to staying awake. If we stay awake, we have lots of changes to make in our external reality, because things veered away from our joy. While it takes some work to shift our life into one that is more fitting, this journey back to who we really are doesn't feel like angst. The shift is exciting, and we start to taste the sweet nectar of alignment with our Heart and Soul. Nothing feels better than having this alignment. Nothing.

As we align with our Heart, our life becomes a reflection of what we love—work feels purposeful, relationships are nourishing, and everything flows with more ease. Life becomes everything we dreamed … and more.

And so begins a spiritual journey to the TRUTH of who we are. An alignment between the outer and the inner. An alignment of our thoughts to our Soul, our relationships to our inner being, and our life to the truest expression of who we are. When we have that alignment, life is enjoyable. Fulfilling. Meaningful. Fun.

That doesn't mean that everything is easy. There are still challenges, but the challenges now bring more truth. And truth feels good when we are in the Light.

This is a journey to the Light of who we are. A journey to the truth of who we are. This book will give you the platform for that discovery. This process will wake you up. **It will be impossible to remain ignorant about how amazing you are.** It will be impossible to keep sleepwalking. You will develop compassion for your struggle, and start to understand why you haven't been able to find joy. You will begin to shift your perspective on life. You will undoubtedly be able create the life you always wanted.

This is a journey of getting more of what you want out of life … and less of what you don't want. By systematically getting clearer about what you want, desiring to feel better, and trusting your worthiness, you will achieve more alignment and life will change dramatically. I have seen it happen over and over again. It's inevitable.

In early 2015, I facilitated a group of students through a two-month journey of the process outlined in the chapters that follow. They were given recorded teachings and guided meditations, and had several one-on-one mentoring sessions with me. This recorded Law of Attraction program set the basis for the material in this book, which was co-created with that amazing group, all of whom had extraordinary experiences with the Law of Attraction over that two-month period. A few of their experiences are highlighted in the last chapter.

YOUR journey through this book will be a process through the steps to work the Law of Attraction to ultimately attain joy, peace and freedom. While you may begin by finding a new partner, or a new job, this will be just the beginning of your journey in working with the Universe to find your potency. Because, after you've mastered the ability to manifest what you want in life, you will begin to unravel your true purpose on this earth.

Enjoy the ride, my friends! BRING IT ON!

Set Your Intentions

You aim for what you want,
and if you don't get it, you don't get it,
but if you don't aim, you don't get anything.
–Francine Prose

WAKE UP! It's time to wake up and start enjoying life! We can't enjoy life if we are sleepwalking through the negativity of our daily lives! But how do we wake up? And what do we DO once we wake up? How do we live a more joyful existence?

For many, life isn't engaging, or it doesn't feel good to stay awake. There's too much negativity, or life may not feel satisfying. If life isn't how you want it to be, then ask yourself: What could life look like, ideally? How would it feel? Who would (and wouldn't!) be in it?

Our ticket out of the mundane, out of the stress and negativity, is to start thinking about how we would *like* to feel and experience life. Once we have a sense for how we would like life to look and feel, we have the power to change it.

Law of Attraction

The Law of Attraction is the universal law that states that every person is always attracting their circumstances and life situations based on their thoughts, emotional vibrations, and actions. Negative thoughts, emotions, and actions will attract negative circumstances. Positive thoughts, emotions, and actions will attract positive circumstances.

If we build mindful awareness in life, and start to witness what we do and say each day, we can begin to change how we participate. Even better, we begin to *feel* like we have the potential to shift things, which allows us to work more proactively with the Law of Attraction.

Nothing that occurs in life is by accident. We are responsible for attracting everything! This sounds pretty daunting if you consider that you have attracted all the negativity that you're now trying to get rid of! However, this is very empowering if you consider that you have the potency to change your life circumstances very quickly!

So, if we know that what we think, feel, and do *causes* our life situations, and we have an awareness about what we're doing to attract what we're currently attracting, then we can use mindful intention and self-awareness to change things for the better. Et voila, we're living a more purposeful, intentional life, in no time!

My Early Encounters with the Law of Attraction

In 1997, I was in graduate school at Syracuse University. It was winter break, and I was sitting at the library, miserably working on my resume. (While my graduate school friends had landed their jobs, I had no clue what I was going to do.) I was chatting with an older man who was making photocopies nearby, and before he left, he handed me the booklet he'd been copying for his friends and family. I tucked it away in my bag, went back home, and opened it up. It said something like,

Anything you want in your life, you can have it. Here are the three steps to make that happen:

> **Step 1:** *Write down the most detailed list of what you want to create in your life. If you want a spouse, write down specific qualities of that person. If you'd like a job, come up with all the aspects you want in that job.*

> **Step 2:** *Read this list three times a day.*

> **Step 3:** [Something like…] *Poof, all your dreams will come true!*

I don't remember what Step 3 was exactly, but I do remember sitting down and making a very detailed list of every single thing that I wanted in my life. I knew what I wanted because I had experienced a lot of what I *didn't* want in life. I didn't want abusive family situations like I grew up with. I didn't want the terrible body image. I didn't want to be alone anymore. I didn't want to be jobless and directionless. I knew what I didn't want, and I used that to create a detailed list of what I *did* want.

I started with the man I wanted to manifest. I had just dated someone who always sat in front of the TV watching hockey, and I realized that didn't work for me. On my list was a man who was athletic but not *too* into sports, nurturing and maternal (because God knew I didn't have a maternal instinct), kind, and successful … plus many other uncommon qualities.

I wrote all the things that I wanted to manifest in my own body, too: health, vibrance, my ideal size, how strong I wanted to be, and how I wanted to feel energetically.

I wrote a long list of the qualities I wanted in my job: my ideal salary, what skills I wanted to use, what type of environment I wanted to work in, and how successful I wanted to feel at that time.

I wrote on and had about two pages before I was done. I was just starting two weeks of holiday vacation, so three times each day, I looked at the list and read it just as the pamphlet had directed. When school break was over, I stuck the list in my nightstand and forgot about it.

A year later, while visiting home with my fiancé, I opened that nightstand drawer and found that **everything I had written on that list had come to fruition in my life**. EVERY SINGLE THING—every last detail—had occurred over the one-year period.

And that, my friends, was my first experience with the Law of Attraction. I didn't have a label for it because the movie *The Secret* hadn't come out yet. I didn't know what it was, but I did know that if I seriously thought about what I wanted in my life, I could somehow create it. I didn't know how it worked. I didn't know the mechanics of it, but I knew I had to get real clarity on what I wanted in life.

I wrote up that list with desire, and passion, and creativity, and really connected to my Heart; but then, I released the list, and completely forgot about it until I found it again. That level of detachment from my deepest desires was also critical.

So by my early twenties, I knew that **going into detail about my desires, creating a level of passion**, and **letting go** were three principles that could create the life I wanted. And now, after almost 20 years of exploration and introspection, it is with great pleasure that I add the energetic and spiritual aspects to my understanding of the Law of Attraction. When you bring your Soul connection into your desires, and lean on your Higher Self, things can get *very* juicy!

Setting Intentions

You can't get to a destination if you haven't decided where you want to go.

The Law of Attraction is the underlying law of the Universe that dictates what we get in our lives. To proactively work with Law of Attraction, we need to develop clear, focused and positive intentions to guide the Universe to give us what we want! Setting intentions and systematically vibrating the positive feelings associated with the intentions creates a ripe environment for us to attract that situation to ourselves.

We can operate *without* any intentional direction and reactively respond to the chaos that life serves us. This will take us in the circle around where we are, never really accomplishing our dreams or getting to our potential (see below: B, C, D, E). Or we can take command and start putting in our order to the Universe so we can eventually start manifesting what we desire (Z)! When we live with intention, we set the stage for a more purposeful existence. We begin to use our will, our desires, to direct us to our destination.

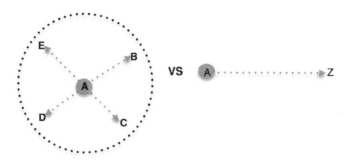

So, what DO you want? Most of us have clarity about what we *don't* want in life, but very few of us know what we *do* want. And here's the thing: It is impossible to create a more fulfilling life if we don't know what that life might look or feel like! Crazy, right? We spend so much time focusing on what doesn't work in life, and very little time defining what would work, so we have trouble moving forward at all.

Why do we avoid defining what we want? Maybe we're scared that we'd never get what we want, so we'd rather not define it. Maybe it never occurred to us to define what we want. Maybe we're lazy and want it to just plop in our lap, so we don't have to figure it out. It takes time and brainpower to figure out what our ideal life would be. It takes creativity and vision to develop intentions. And it takes focus to maintain that vision.

Many of us haven't developed the skills necessary to create the life we want. Creating the life you want isn't magic; it's a set of skills. We aren't taught those skills as children, so we have to learn them. This takes practice and trust—in both ourselves and in something bigger!

What does your Heart Desire?

Have you ever seriously considered what your Heart desires? Do you know what that voice deep within is yearning for? Close your eyes to ask yourself, *What does my Heart desire? What do I yearn for most in life?*

It may take time to listen, REALLY listen, to what you want most in your life. And it's important not to swat the ideas out of your mind because they don't seem practical. Send yourself on a mini-exploration of the desires that don't seem practical. Let it be a dream that you surf through for a few days to identify the seeds of some new intentions.

As you attempt to explore your Heart's deepest desires, you may encounter a lot of fear. Push through the fear and do it anyway. Don't be afraid to ask yourself what you desire, even if life would look radically different from the life you're living right now. Just let yourself dream a little to consider what you desire. Yes, it may scare you to even think about it, but do it anyway. Try not to let your mind convince you that you have to jump ship on your current life to live the life you want. Jumping ship is probably not necessary. Just give yourself the chance to explore it, to let the dream live a little.

Letting your Heart speak about what it wants will unlock something within you. It will allow you to access some good-feeling energetic momentum that will feed your intentions in the most incredible way. Once you've felt this momentum, you will know what type of feeling, vibration, and excitement is required to attract what you want into your life.

Develop Intentions that Feel Good

When you are first learning to work with Law of Attraction, it's important to choose intentions that feel good. We attract based on how we feel, so if you come up with an intention that you have heavy dread or fear around, it will be difficult to attract a joyful situation because dread attracts more dread.

It MUST feel GOOD to think about the intention. If it doesn't feel good, look for another intention that does feel good while you are still learning how to use Law of Attraction. What is one thing that your Heart desires? What do you long for? Write it down now. Write ALL of it down. Don't wait. And if you don't know, start writing. Write until you figure out what you want. It doesn't matter if it's not articulate. Let it pour onto paper, without reservation.

Can't think of anything? Have you blocked yourself from your desires? Feeling perfectionistic with your list? Then start with all the areas in your life where you are NOT happy. What is not going well? Write it down in the first column. Then, in the second column, define how you would want things to be. Shift the negative into a statement or vision of how you DO want the situation or relationship to work. Write the details down with clarity and positivity, and in present tense. For example:

My body is unhealthy can turn into:
  - I'm eating healthy foods
  - I have lots of energy
  - I'm an ideal size 8
  - I feel comfortable in my skin
  - I'm confident
  - I move my body often, exercise regularly
  - I feel good in my clothes; my jeans and bathing suit are my favorites!

I'm lonely because I don't have deep relationships can turn into:

- I make friends easily
- My friendships are meaningful
- I see my friends often and we spend quality time together
- I feel their love even when I'm alone
- I feel ease and comfort when I'm alone
- I like to be with myself

My job doesn't pay enough and is not fulfilling can turn into:

- I have clarity on what I love to do
- My work is becoming more purposeful and aligned with my preferences
- My income increases by $15k in the next six months

Keep It Positive and Focused on the Destination

Recognizing that we always attract things based on what we say and feel, keep the intention stated in the positive sense, and happening in the present moment. *I see myself living in my dream home filled with loving friends and family*, versus *I want a home that's not cramped*. See the difference?

Make sure you keep your intentions focused on the ultimate expression of your intention. For example, *to be happily married*, versus *meet a good guy*, or *have a successful bestselling book* versus *write a book*.

Keep the intention on the final destination, rather than *how* you might get to the destination. You don't need to know *how* you will achieve the intention … that is up to the wisdom of the Universe. For example, if you want to be happier at work and make more money, you may not be creative enough to figure out *where* you would work or what type of situation would make that happen. But perhaps you know you want to be in a field that you're passionate about. If so, that's your answer. If you don't know what you're passionate about, then start with an intention of gaining clarity on what you feel passionate about.

Build Possibility Around Your Intention

Do you believe the intention is possible? Is it attainable? If this intention were easy, then you would've attracted it already. Somewhere within you, it will be important to access a new sense of possibility. If it doesn't seem remotely possible, start with an intention that feels more possible. No need to climb Mt. Everest before you know how to hike! Learn to use Law of Attraction with intentions that you believe are possible, and then use the hindsight of success to inform your future intentions.

Now, here's a secret: If you have the ability to create the intention, then it's within your realm of possibility to manifest it. You simply cannot come up with something without the ability to fulfill the potential for it! Isn't that incredible? You wouldn't develop an intention if it didn't come accompanied by the energies to create it. (There is an energetic reason for that, but that's the topic of many other quantum physics books!)

It will take time for you to build TRUST that your intentions are possible, and that the Universe has your back. Consistently working with the Universe to co-create desires will build the trust that you need to live your life with these new belief systems:

What I want is possible.

The Universe has my back.

I am a potent creator.

This sounds like an easy exercise, but it can be very challenging for some, so take your time and allow the list to evolve as you go through. Allow it to be fun and exciting, like you are building your Christmas list!

Practice the Manifested State of Your Intention

Once you have your intention, you feel like it's possible, and it feels good, it's time to **start practicing the feeling of the intention as if it has <u>already occurred</u>**. As you will learn in later chapters, how you feel will dictate what you attract. If you feel like you don't have what you want, or you are soaked in the feeling of *wanting*, you will continue to want. If you want to manifest the feeling of *having*, then you have to feel like you have your intention already. This is different from how we typically go about life … we sit in the feeling of not having what we want, we suffer about it, and stay in a state of deprivation, and that keeps us exactly where we started. But if you learn to practice feeling like you *already* have what you want, then you are setting yourself up to attract it!

When you have an intention that feels possible and achievable, it's critical to explore how it would feel when this intention occurs. We call this the **manifested state**. What emotions would you feel? What sounds and smells would you experience? What would be your thoughts? Can you try on, in your body, what that might be like? Here's an example:

In my late twenties, I had my first experience of losing those extra 20 pounds. I had to work hard to clean up my diet, and I suffered through the slow and excruciating process of two pounds down, and one pound up. Eventually, I made it to my goal weight and I felt good about it. I enjoyed every sensation of the weight loss—how my jeans felt with less muffin top, how my arms felt against my sides, how little time I thought about my body, how much ease I felt overall. I didn't take the experience for granted after a lifetime of body rejection.

Within about a year of that, I started having babies. And I gained <u>60 pounds</u> during each of my three pregnancies! After my first daughter was born, I was back to that uncomfortable feeling with myself and I was anxious to get the weight off. I decided to use Law of Attraction this time, so I developed a body vision drawing. I drew the perfect size, and all the qualities of my body that I wanted to feel, and every night I would look at that drawing and close my eyes and remember back to when I was that size and weight. I remembered how my arms and belly felt. I remembered how I moved with ease. I remembered how I naturally ate what was nourishing. Most importantly, **I actually tried on the feeling in my body**. I made up the feeling of less puff on my belly (of course I had to take off my tight jeans to do this!). I felt the sensation of feeling strong. I imagined vibrance and energy radiating out of my body until I felt like that. My imagination created the feeling of what I wanted to manifest. Within about 6 months, I was back down to my goal weight and it was much easier using Law of Attraction (vs suffering and self-deprivation!).

This was my ultimate Law of Attraction experience because it taught me the mechanics of trying on what we call the **manifested state**. And when I gained the 60 pounds for baby number two, it worked again. And again, for baby number three.

In Summary...

If you want to change something in your life, you must decide how you would like it to be and begin to feel that intention in the present moment. There's no way around this very important step toward your transformation.

Journaling Practice: Set Your Intention NOW!

Before going any further in this book, I encourage you to develop at least one intention. Big or small—doesn't matter. Perhaps you want to go through every aspect of your life to define how you want it to look and feel. Perhaps you want to start with something very small. Choose something that excites you; something that will drive you to take that next step. Find that one thing you desire and feel it with every cell of your body. Do the following:

1. Write down your intention(s) stated in the **positive** (e.g., feel good about myself, manifest a life partner).

2. Begin to work yourself into feeling your intention is **possible** (or even inevitable!). Surround yourself by people who think it's possible. And practice feeling the *possibility* of your intention.

3. Practice the feelings of your intention in the **manifested state**. Feel it in your emotions, in your body, and see if you can hold that throughout the day (at least three times a day!)

This practice is critical in manifesting your intentions, so spend some time developing your intentions and practicing them!

Master Your Mind and Emotions

Common sense is nothing more than a deposit of
prejudices laid down by the mind
before you reach eighteen.
-Albert Einstein

We have heard that our thoughts create our reality, and that if we want our lives to change, we must change our thoughts. But for many of us, that hasn't helped us much because our thoughts seem to have a life of their own! They drive themselves straight into negativity every chance they get! Sometimes it feels impossible to stop the negative thoughts when the hamster wheel of the mind gains negative momentum!

The things we focus our minds on create patterns in our brains, and the patterns create our autopilot. Since we don't spend time consciously focusing our mind, our mind focuses itself on mostly negative circumstances, so our brain patterns have developed deep grooves of negative thinking!

Our thoughts create energetic momentum, setting the energetic vibrations of our body. Our emotions are an effect of these vibrations. Negative thoughts create negative energy which results in negative emotions. And these vibrations and emotions attract our future circumstances through the Law of Attraction. It's a self-perpetuating cycle—one that we need to learn how to navigate more skillfully.

Self-awareness is critical in attracting more of what we want in life. We must watch our unruly mind to see where it goes, and we must develop more positive thought patterns so we can replace negative thought with intentional and more purposeful thought. That way, we can mindfully decide where the mind spends its time, what vibrations the mind creates, and ultimately what future will come of our present thoughts.

The Madness of the Mind

We don't learn about our minds in school, but in the Eastern philosophies, it is well known that we must develop mindfulness if we want to be happy. **It is important to control the mind, so the mind doesn't control you.** We must be in the driver's seat so the negative autopilot doesn't take over. The mind has a mind of its own, if you will, and those conditioned thought patterns will continue on autopilot if we don't learn to practice a state of present AWARENESS about where our thoughts are going. In fact, simply bringing ourselves into a state of awareness, or observation, will allow us to take back the steering wheel.

When we catch ourselves in the negative hamster wheel, we immediately trigger awareness, bringing ourselves into a state of consciousness. In that state of consciousness, we can literally *change our mind* by practicing a more positive thought pattern until we have rebuilt the neural pathways of our brain into a more positive path. It's simple, but it takes practice.

Layers of the Mind: Subconscious (Ego), Conscious, and Superconscious

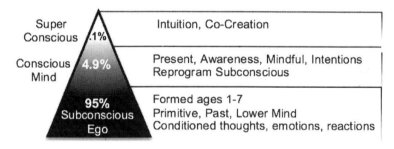

There are three layers of the mind (see diagram above):

The **subconscious mind**, or the ego, operates from the past, steers toward negative thought patterns, and serves as our autopilot. It keeps the hamster wheel running toward the negative. We spend 95-99% of our time in the pre-programed thoughts, emotions, and reactions of the subconscious.

The **conscious mind** lives in the present moment and requires our mindful awareness to keep it engaged. This is where we can evaluate that which occurs on autopilot, set intentions, and develop more positive patterns and grooves in our minds. We spend about 1-5% of our time in conscious awareness.

The **superconscious mind** is a mindful connection to Soul/Source that provides us with a higher perspective through intuitive wisdom based in Light, love, unity, and interconnectedness. Most people spend about .01% of life here, but by raising our consciousness we can strengthen our superconscious and intentionally create a more purposeful existence. This can also be referred to as Higher Consciousness.

Subconscious Mind

Between the ages of 0-7, our subconscious mind was programmed through our senses (sound, touch, taste, smell, sight) during our life experiences. The subconscious was therefore programmed before we understood cause-and-effect, rational thinking, right versus wrong, how relationships and families worked, who we are, and how the Universe works! We didn't have the capacity to fully understand the dynamics of life at that age, but that is when much of our thought patterns were programmed in.

Our neural pathways were set early in life, and 95-99% of our lives has been spent replaying or triggering all of these programmed thoughts, emotions, and patterns. We just trigger them and replay them over and over. In fact, we have over 60,000 thoughts per day and over 90% of them are the same thoughts we had the day before. How can we manifest something new if we are running the same program from one day to the next?

We can see this repetition throughout our lives, right? We can see the repeated patterns in our relationships, in our emotional reactions, in the thoughts that consume the space of our mind. We're just triggering our subconscious mind and churning the same thought processes and emotions that we downloaded in our formative years ... running them over and over and over. It's just the way the mind is wired.

For example, let's say that at the age of 5, your parents fought about how to raise you, and ultimately decided to divorce. You thought it was your fault because you didn't understand adult dynamics. You programmed your subconscious to believe that if you were never born, your parents would've stayed together, and life would be better if you didn't exist. So you filter your whole life on that limiting belief.

Or let's say that you were the fourth child, and your mom was pretty wiped out when you were a toddler, so she criticized everything you did. You couldn't do anything *right* in her eyes. You programmed your subconscious to believe that you were unworthy of your mom's approval, and you couldn't do anything *right*. So you now filter your whole life through that limiting belief of needing to be *right*, or doing things the *right way* to get others' approval.

Do you see how the subconscious can get us stuck in negative patterns? The work in raising our consciousness out of the hamster wheel of the subconscious mind is to stop this autopilot process and bring awareness to our thoughts, emotions, and actions. We have to re-evaluate the subconscious thoughts with our conscious *adult mind* to reprogram the limiting beliefs that have been running on autopilot for so long. It is a process of surfacing the wackiness out of the subconscious by observing it, and then allowing the Light of awareness to shine in. Shifting the subconscious into conscious to stop the madness! This process is like unraveling an onion, layer by layer, until we get to the truth of who we are.

Conscious Mind

We only spend about 1-5% of our time in the conscious mind, where we have a sense of presence, awareness, and mindfulness. It's where we evaluate our thoughts and emotions, and set intentions for change and transformation. It's where we experience happiness, playfulness, and calming peace. All joy exists in the present moment.

Shifting into the conscious mind requires coming into the present moment. It is here that we can dig through our subconscious and bring up to awareness that which we want to shift and change. The way off the hamster wheel of the subconscious is through present awareness, watching the madness, and knowing we are not our madness! We change it by watching it in the present moment.

Working with this awareness is a lot like building a muscle through practice. At first, that muscle of observation may not be built, but in time and with practice throughout this book, you will be able to surface the subconscious confusions. You begin to figure out what untrue irrational thoughts and patterns your mind consistently serves you up. You become familiar with the emotions that you *don't* want to manifest more of, and you will gain clarity on that which you *do* want to manifest.

In time, with the help of the conscious mind, you will begin to challenge the untrue thoughts of the autopilot mind and retrain yourself in the present moment to think more positively. This consists of:

- catching yourself in the act of negativity and subconscious programming,
- challenging the validity of those negative thoughts,
- creating more reality-based thoughts, and
- practicing those new thoughts until they become your go-to thought programs.

Using the example about being *right* … If I know that I have this need to be right, I can watch myself doing the whole *right/wrong* thing every day. I can sit with each instance and talk to myself from the conscious mind about how *there's really no need to be right*, and *I'm not going to die if I'm wrong*. Then I can create more reality-based thoughts like, *I'm valuable even if I'm incorrect*, *I can be compassionate with myself around my need to be right* and *I can create more softness around situations*, or *I'm good and worthy despite whether I do things according to my/other's expectations*. As time goes on, and I practice these more flexible thoughts around right-ness, I'm able to keep replacing the rigid *If I'm right, I'm good* and *If I'm wrong, I'm bad* thoughts with *it's totally okay whether I'm correct or incorrect*, and *life doesn't need to be defined by perfect or imperfect* and *I have so much value outside of my actions*. After time, I find myself releasing the need to be right because I'm creating new thought patterns and brain synapses around being right.

Practicing new thought patterns is critical for lasting change in thoughts, feeling and behaviors. The brain will build new synaptic pathways with new thought patterns, but without continued practice of these new thoughts, the brain will truncate the new synaptic pathways within a few days. In this *being right* example, having the initial new awareness that *I don't need to be right* may not be enough to make significant change in thought patterns. These new *right/wrong* thoughts need to be practiced for them to be fully wired into the brain. Without daily conscious practice, the thought synapses around *I don't need to be right* will be truncated within days of having the new awareness.

When we read a new book about life patterns and changing our thoughts about ourselves, we may have awareness about our behaviors, but without working at the conscious level repetitively, we will forget what we learned and continue the old behavior. Changing the mind takes awareness and new pattern repetition until the brain synapses are fully programed toward a more positive way of thinking.

When we set our intentions toward new desires, they too need to be practiced in the conscious mind so that we can build the new thought patterns and brain synapses, which then create the hormones and body chemistry to match and support the thoughts and desires. Daily practice of our intentions rewires the brain toward our desires, and sets the chemistry of our body to positively vibrate with the new desires. This leads to our new intentions feeling good in our bodies, which wires them into our bodies in a way that supports further repetition because when something feels good, we naturally want more of it!

The conscious mind is critical to stop negative thought patterns, rewire the brain toward our intentions, and change our behavior.

Superconscious Mind

The third and most critical layer of your mind is superconsciousness, which is connection to Source energy, a grid of interconnectedness and higher wisdom. Through the Heart, we have access to this universal wisdom and bliss. However, most people don't know the opportunity for this connection exists, and if they do, they haven't consistently practiced accessing this part of their consciousness. To do so requires us to raise our consciousness past the present moment, by connecting into the Theta wave state of the brain, to attain an elusive state of peace, creativity and bliss. This is why meditation is a great tool to hook us into that brain wave state of feeling good.

If we are made up of a Soul, and there is a bigger Source of energy out there for us to connect or plug into, then that's where our true potency comes from. Once we bring ourselves into a state of present moment consciousness through the practice of mindfulness, we can shift into the connection with Source energy, which can transform us into alignment. This alignment sets the vibration for what we attract to us. Connection with superconsciousness is super useful in manifesting our desires!

Ego

We will refer to the autopilot of the subconscious mind as the ego. We have this subconscious programming and it is regurgitated throughout the day, taking up about 95% of our waking hours. Yikes! While this is not ideal, it's important not to judge the ego as good or bad. It's just part of the human condition to have an aspect of the mind that takes over the steering wheel, but we don't need to get stuck on the hamster wheel.

The ego tells us that we are not enough—that to find true happiness and feel good, we must find it from the outside world. But we never can find our happiness in the external world because it comes from within. The constant chasing outside of ourselves is the basis for the never-ending hamster wheel.

For example, the ego tells us that, *If I can just find that romantic partner or that perfect job, THEN I will be happy,* but then you get the partner, and you're still not happy. Or you get the perfect job and there's a problem elsewhere. We keep chasing happiness outside of ourselves because the ego tells us that: Happiness is OUT THERE; Feeling good is the RESULT of something happening; Feeling good happens TO us. The ego always keeps our positive, feel-good experience of life at arms-length away. In reality, happiness is a vibration that is created and maintained from WITHIN. It has little to do with the external world.

Our goal is to shift out of ego, out of autopilot, off the hamster wheel … and into a state of conscious thought so that we can be the driver of our lives. (In time, we will let the superconscious mind take the steering wheel! That's when life gets juicy!)

Limiting Belief Systems

Since the subconscious mind is programmed at such an early age, there are many confused or irrational thoughts that get past the filter of the conscious mind before we can use our rational mind to reevaluate them. Once we have these irrational thoughts a few times, and filter our world through them, they become our operating belief systems ... a thought matrix of how we think the world works. We assume that these thought matrices are reality and we surround ourselves with people who share the same or complementary belief systems to confirm our reality.

Since these belief systems were built by the ego, they are based in FEAR and are therefore completely limiting in our quest to experience more joy, peace and expansiveness in life. They tend to *feel* limiting and imprisoning. We can feel that they lack truth, and Light, and the realness of who we really are.

Because this is a common limitation of the human mind, there are many irrational belief systems that get handed down from generation-to-generation, and become *fact* or *truth*—but in fact, they have no basis in reality. Here are a few common erroneous belief systems that are deeply engrained in society:

Scarcity Mentality (vs Abundance):

Many people have a fear that there's not enough, they are not enough, or there will never be what they need or want: *There's not enough time; we don't have enough money; this job isn't enough; my contribution isn't enough; I'M not enough.* If we feel like there's not enough, what do we create through Law of Attraction? Situations that prove this scarcity belief system.

Scarcity mindset creates an *every man for himself* experience of life and leaves almost everyone involved feeling like nothing is ever enough. Even in the presence of abundance, our scarcity mentality will take over and we will project *not enough* into the future, or we will suffer about how short lasting the abundance is. This belief system can suck the life out of people and create a perspective of suffering that can make you feel like you are always underwater.

In reality, the Universe is abundant. There is enough of everything! Love, *yup, plenty to go around*. Food, *yes lots of it*. Success, *everyone can have it!* Really, with an abundance mentality, the world is your oyster. You can attract whatever you have the courage to desire!

Victimhood Mentality (vs Potency):

Many of us are walking around with the feeling that we can't get what we want in situations, relationships, jobs, with our bodies ... you name it. *I am powerless in the presence of this illness*, or *My work life is miserable because of my boss*, or *My marriage sucks because my husband doesn't do for me*, or maybe *I'm stuck in a situation and it's someone else's fault.* We feel disempowered and unable to shift situations in our lives, and we feel like a victim of it. The more disempowered we feel, the more we attract disempowering situations in life.

This belief system is also based in fear and lack of understanding of responsibility and empowerment. It makes us completely powerless because we take our own responsibility and potency out of the equation of our lives.

In reality, we have the potency to change every single aspect of our lives, especially the ones that don't work for us. We attract everything. We choose our emotions and vibrations that we hold in our bodies. The Universe is responding to what we are putting out there, so if we don't like what we are attracting, we must first realize that we have attracted it in the first place— RESPONSIBILITY! Then we can begin to shift our vibrations and desires, to attract something new. Whether it's an illness, a partner, or an unfortunate situation, there is always an internal shift we can make to find joy, peace, happiness, and empowerment in the situation. We are never a victim.

Entitlement Mentality (vs Earning):

Due to patterns we set up when we were young, many people feel entitled for life to work out a certain way. We don't see how we are an active player in everything, co-creating with the Universe, exerting our will with precise action to earn what we want in life. Instead, we feel jealous or angry that life isn't working out. This belief system is based on others or the Universe meeting our needs without our having put in the proper effort to attract what we desire. Instead of seeing and doing what it takes to earn what we want, we believe that others should accommodate our needs.

Again, this is a belief system based in fear and lack, which attracts more fear and lack. When we take ourselves and our responsibility out of the equation, and set up expectations for the world to meet us, then we lose our power to attract, and we shift from Entitlement mentality straight into Victim mentality.

In reality, we must earn what we want in life through right vibration, effort, willpower, action ... and acceptance of what the Universe is providing in response to our vibration. We are not entitled to our children behaving 24/7 because they are children and children aren't perfect. We are not entitled to an effortless job situation, especially if we chose to throw our life purpose out the window. We are not entitled to a happy marriage if we married for fear-based reasons or we haven't done the work to create good communication and relationship skills. Life takes presence, engagement, mindfulness, and a consistent effort to evaluate what we want versus what we are getting, and adjusting accordingly.

Control and Knowing Mentality (vs Acceptance):

Many of us want to feel in control of the situations in our lives. Our control can be exerted through our circumstances, needing to *know*, setting expectations and being controlling over our life situations. If I can just control the *outcome of my kids' grades in school*, or *the way this presentation will be pulled off*, or *how this person will react to a situation*, then I can alleviate the fear I have around it.

The reality is that the only thing we can control is our reaction and response to external circumstances. We can do our best and roll with what life serves us ... accepting what is. And we never really *know* anything. The need to control or *know* is just our mind's way of trying to feel safe because of the deep fears that are hanging out beneath the surface. Control is an illusion.

Negative Thought Momentum ~ Judgement

The ego has a bad habit of driving us straight into negative thought, using judgment to prove us unworthy in some way, *I'm bad, not valuable, unloved*. If we let our ego drive for too long, we get stuck in those negative thoughts, which gain momentum and start to form our belief systems, thought patterns, and behaviors. And because our thoughts dictate our emotions, vibrations, and ultimately our circumstances, our negative ego's thoughts can be destructive in our lives.

It only takes sixty-eight seconds to create thought momentum, which then creates our reality. Just one minute of autopilot negative thought can create negative vibration and circumstances.

When the subconscious wackiness (that was patterned into us before the age of seven!) reveals itself in our lives, we typically go straight into self-judgment and lose all potential for conscious awareness. It can go something like this:

When I was young, I was terrible in Math. So I've walked around life feeling dumb. And it just so happens that in adulthood, I manage million dollar contracts at work and I make mistakes when budgeting...often...which creates tension with my boss and snowballs into all kinds of interpersonal issues. Because I have so much old subconscious baggage about the fact that I'm bad at Math, I can't even look at the issue. It just feels terrible, and I feel bad about myself, and I can't even break down the issue at work because there are so many layers of self-judgement and fear. So I call it 'work stress' and live a scattered life.

When we judge ourselves, we don't want to look at the underlying issue because it makes us feel bad. We form BLIND SPOTS, where we don't acknowledge parts of ourselves, and we cover them up with whatever we can.

We must be on top of our negative self-defeating thoughts so that we can shift our awareness and become more mindful of what takes up space in our heads. This is a critical step in aligning with our Soul and our potency. To clear out the subconscious madness, we must open up the issue to examine the negative thought processes that are going on in our head. The simple act of bringing awareness to the negative thoughts, vibrations, and emotions will allow them to shift. You're taking them out of the darkness and bringing them into the Light. When you do, they have the opportunity to shift from subconscious thought to consciousness so you can re-evaluate your thoughts from the adult mind.

Our judgments keep us from taking the negative out of the darkness and into the Light. Judgement keeps us completely disempowered and in the shadow. If you find yourself going into judgment at any point in this book, stop yourself, come back to your breath and observe what you're thinking. **Ten breaths will shift you out of judgment and negativity.**

Projection

Sigmund Freud said that people have a tendency to project their subconscious negativity onto others. The ego uses psychological projection as a coping mechanism to deal with the negative emotions that lurk in the subconscious mind. We all do this. We feel an emotion and projectively believe instead that *others* are feeling that way about *us*. Freud gives an example of a woman who is having a marital affair and accuses her husband of having an affair; or a man who has a bad habit of stealing, and assumes that others are always trying to steal from him.

The process can be even more subtle than that. For example, *If I have low self-esteem and I don't like myself, then I can project that you don't like me either.* Or, *If I don't look people in the eyes, that means I'm mad at them, so I assume you are mad at me if you don't look me in the eyes.*

On the path Law of Attraction and shifting off the hamster wheel, we have to be careful not to feed into our mind's projections. We must stay focused on our own stuff to avoid making things up about what's going on for other people. If we maintain communication with others, we can find out what's going on in their heads, rather than making it up based on our fears and projections.

Personally, the understanding of projection changed my life. I started to challenge my assumptions that I KNEW what was going on for other people. How could I know? I was just making it up based on what was going on in MY mind! They had a different family, different experiences, and a completely different life, so it's impossible for their thoughts to be the same subconscious thoughts as mine! Think about that. We often think we know what's going on for other people because we project based on how we feel. But we have absolutely NO CLUE.

Our mind has a desperate need to KNOW: We know what others are thinking and feeling; we know what we should be doing; we know what the best approach is; we know why things happen. Or maybe we tell ourselves that we DON'T KNOW, and we spend our lives searching for the way to finally know. In this perspective, life is dualistic—black or white, right or wrong, good or bad—and our thoughts are rigid. These rigid thoughts lead to stress, and doomsday thinking, which can make it difficult to manifest positive situations on the path of Law of Attraction.

Byron Katie's technique, called The Work, approaches projections and rigid stressful thinking with a set of introspective questions. She suggests that when you are struggling with a situation, and you can't get past your thoughts and emotions, ask the following for each stressful thought you have:

1. Is this true?

2. Can I absolutely know it's true?

3. How do I react—what happens—when I think that thought? (How do I feel? How do I act toward self and others?)

4. Who would I be without that thought? (How would life be different if I didn't think this thought? Which do I prefer—life with this thought, or without it?)

5. Turn the thought around (How can the opposite of this thought be true in my life?)

The Work can help you begin to loosen your thoughts and belief systems to bring yourself into a more mindful, conscious state of mind.

As you can imagine, the habits of projection can feed right into our negative thoughts, judgments, fears, and anger—and keep the negative autopilot on! Our job is to be mindful of it, so our conscious mind can take over.

Navigating Vibrations and Emotions

We are vibrational beings. We are made of energy, and the energy vibrates based on our thoughts and emotions. We are walking vibrations set into motion by our thoughts.

The Law of Attraction operates on the basis of vibration—we attract that which we vibrate. We are attracting more of what we are currently vibrating. If I'm in a positive vibration, then I attract positivity. If I'm in a negative vibration, I attract negativity. If I'm in a negative vibration and I want to attract positivity, what do I need to do? I need to vibrate more positively so I can attract what I want! If I am in a negative vibration, suffering all day long and consumed by negative thoughts—*I don't get what I want, my relationships aren't the way I want them to be, things don't really end up the way I want them*—then my vibration of suffering will attract more situations where I will suffer. Suffering attracts more suffering. Negativity attracts negativity. That's the Law of Attraction.

Wherever we are, wherever we're vibrating, whatever thoughts are consuming our head will dictate what we will get more of in our lives.

Our thoughts seed our vibration, which set our emotions, which dictate what we manifest. Remember, the thought synapses in our brain trigger corresponding hormones and chemicals within our bodies, which dictate how our vibration FEELS in our bodies. Negative thoughts trigger a body chemistry that doesn't feel good. Positive thoughts trigger body chemistry that feels really good. If we can catch a thought BEFORE it seeds our vibration and emotions, then we can change our trajectory by practicing a more positive set of thoughts to build more positive synaptic pathways and body chemistry. Do you see how critical it is to harness the unruly mind?

As discussed, our subconscious negative thoughts are like an autopilot hamster wheel inside of our heads. The negative thoughts go on and on and on, replaying all the old conditioning. They trigger old vibrations and instantaneously churn up fear, doubt, anger and sadness (or whatever your go-to negative emotion is). There are all kinds of stories attached to these thoughts which anchor the thought's vibrations and trigger all kinds of emotion. And we wonder why we are stuck with the same external circumstances in our lives! How can we manifest our intentions if the same old thoughts, vibrations and emotions are running the show, right? The answer lies in interrupting the pattern in the conscious present moment by following our inner emotional guidance system.

Emotional Guidance System

If our thoughts set our vibration, then our emotions (*energy-in-motion*) are indicators of how we are vibrating, and therefore whether our thinking is in alignment with our Heart. Our emotions can tell us immediately what we are attracting into our lives. We are either vibrating positively, with positive thoughts that are aligned with the vibrational resonance of our Heart, in which case we are feeling positive emotions. Or we are vibrating negatively, and our emotions are negative, which means we are not aligning with the truest part of who we are.

Our Heart is guiding us back to ourselves through our emotions. Our emotional guidance system tells us when we're close to Source-Soul-Self, and when we're getting separate and further from ourselves. It's like that game of Hot-and-Cold that we played when we were little. *Oh, you're getting warmer. You're getting closer. You're hot. You're hotter! You're so hot! You're burning hot!* Those are our positive emotions. They tell when we're getting so hot and so close to our Soul. When we start to get further from our Soul, we're getting colder: *You're colder. Oh my God, you're freezing cold. You're so cold!* Those are negative emotions. It shows we're separate from our Soul. We're getting disconnected from ourselves.

Our emotional guidance system shows us the way back into alignment with our inner self if we can stop ignoring and judging the negative emotions. There is no need to judge our emotions! There is no right emotion or wrong emotion. They are indicators. Messengers! They are here to tell us what's going on in the hamster wheel. Don't wish them away! Invite them in to have a seat so they can tell you what's going on behind the scenes. We must not make the judgement that *only* positive emotions are good and negative emotions are always bad. Even though it doesn't feel good to have negative emotions, it is critical for us to have them, feel them, acknowledge them, and determine what they are here to teach us. A lot of our judgment comes up around our emotions and what we're feeling—we decide it's acceptable to have some emotions, and not acceptable to have others. For the emotions we deem unacceptable, we separate from ourselves and stuff those emotions down below the surface.

When we judge and separate from our emotions, we separate from ourselves and the messages from the Heart, which keeps us from growth, transformation, and true joyfulness in life. Our emotions are simply showing us our base vibration. They are the messengers to alert us that we've veered away from our highest expression of ourselves. Judging the messengers makes no sense. It's like ignoring your car's low gas alert. If a negative emotion has shown up to tell you that your direction has a pattern that isn't aligned with your Heart, celebrate the message and act quickly to identify where you veered.

Where Vibrations Reside in the Body

Many people don't realize that our emotions and vibrations reside deep within our bodies. I'll never forget teaching this material to a large group for five weeks and halfway through the session, a man raises his hand to say, *Uh, I have no idea what you're talking about when you refer to these 'vibrations'*. As someone who has walked this earth feeling like a raw nerve, I hadn't realized that not everyone could feel every single experience so deeply.

John Barnes teaches a bodywork technique to Physical and Occupational Therapists, called myofascial release. He says that when we go into our fight-or-flight response in daily life, we store these vibrations in our body because we haven't given ourselves the opportunity to release them. When animals go into fight-or-flight, they'll shake the response out of their vibrational body. We don't shake it out. We don't release it from our bodies so the response gets stored vibrationally deep within the layers of the body. We need to connect with these vibrations to release them.

We will be talking about the yogic and Ayurvedic perspective of the body later, but for now, here are some cliff notes on some yogic wisdom of the mind/body connection. Depending on which paradigm or system you look at, there are 4-5 overlapping layers of the body: **Physical** (body), **Energetic** (pranic and elemental layer), **Mental** (thoughts and emotions), and **Spiritual** (consciousness and Soul-bliss).

These layers of the Physical, Energetic, Mental, and Spiritual bodies meet up at the seven major **chakras**, or energy centers, of the body. Associated with each chakra are: specific organs and glands (physical), energy flows and vibrations (energetic), thoughts, emotions and life lessons (mental), and conscious connection to Source energy (spiritual). Each chakra is related to a certain set of vibrations and energetic frequencies. There are specific colors of Light associated with each chakra—starting from the bottom, the colors span the rainbow with the lower frequency of red at the base of the spine, ending in purple at the top of the head.

As you can imagine, this is a pretty complex network layered within our bodies. Most of us have no idea that all this is interwoven into who we are, and because this is so, we can't decode what the different vibrations are telling us about what's going on in our bodies!

There are many signs that we can receive from our bodies before issues manifest as physical ailments. An issue can start as a seed of energetic/spiritual blockage that permeates into the vibrational body, then to the thoughts and emotions, which creates a physical blockage. If we can listen to the vibrations and energies that happen at a subtle level in our bodies, we can prevent all kinds of unnecessary emotional and physical issues. To listen to the subtle messages, we must slow down and learn to decode what the different vibrations are telling us. By setting the intention to have more self-connection, we can naturally develop the attunement required to get the messages while they are still whispers, before they turn into sirens!

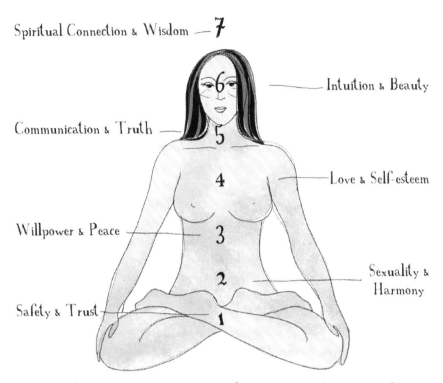

Spiritual Connection & Wisdom — 7

Intuition & Beauty

Communication & Truth —

Love & Self-esteem

Willpower & Peace

Sexuality & Harmony

Safety & Trust

Here are the general energetic, life themes and colors around each chakra:

1. **Root Chakra (red)**—at the lower base of our spine down to our legs—lessons can be about security (e.g., financial, physical, relationship), safety, foundation, belonging to our tribe, and the right to exist in this world. This is where we feel our right to exist.

2. **Sacral Chakra (orange)**—at the low belly / back—lessons can be about harmony, intimacy, and closeness with others; to find balance. This is where we feel our right to feel.

3. **Solar Plexus Chakra (yellow)**—at the upper belly and mid back—lessons can be about strength, action and responsibility, and self-worth. This is where we feel our right to act.

4. **Heart Chakra (green)**—in the chest—lessons can be about love, compassion and abundance around self and other. This is where we feel our right to love.

5. **Throat Chakra (turquoise)**—in the neck—lessons can be about communication, truth and purpose. This is where we feel the right to speak and be heard.

6. **Third Eye Chakra (indigo)**—between the eyebrows— lessons can be about inner wisdom, beauty and vision. This is where we feel the right to see clearly and intuit.

7. **Crown Chakra (purple)**—at the top of the head—lessons can be about connection to Source and enLightenment. This is where we feel the right to know.

When you learn more about the energy centers of the body, and feel into the vibrations that you feel within your body, you can create a deeper inner listening to figure out what's going on in the mind/body connection. **Learning to listen to our emotions and deeper vibrations within the body can give us cues for what is happening at the subconscious level.**

Most of us don't know how we're feeling much of the time. We think it's not important, or we decide that how we're feeling at that moment doesn't make any sense. It's critical to watch your emotions and vibrations within the body, because they are the true indicators of where your vibration settles. They alert you when you need to make a change.

Vibrations and Attraction

By setting intentions and gaining clarity on what we want in life, we bring awareness to how we are feeling. We start to observe the difference between the vibration of <u>what we want</u> versus <u>where we are at</u>. *I want to feel happy, but right now I feel miserable.* Intentional living magnifies our awareness of our vibration.

If we have Heart-based intentions that take us toward a more joyful expression of who we are, then we need to work our vibration up to resonate with those Heart-based intentions. For example, if I want to manifest my future husband—who is handsome, successful, kind, and has a good sense of humor— then I need to get out of my suffering, woe-is-me pity party and get my vibration to a place where I feel beautiful, worthy, good, and playful. I simply can't attract a person with vibrant qualities if I'm in a low vibration. I must feel complete and whole BEFORE I attract him into my life.

If we want to attract more of what we want in our lives, we must work ourselves into a more positive vibration. We must mindfully check in with how we are feeling before we can work our vibration higher. We simply can't attract a more beneficial situation if we are not vibrating in a more beneficial way. If I want a better job, then I must find the vibration of how it would feel to *have* that better job. A bit challenging if I'm in a negative vibration, right? I have to really imagine how it would feel to have that better job in my life in the present moment. I must create the vibration of me enjoying a better job. That will attract the better job into my life.

We can't create something better if we are having negative emotions, so we must set the intention and work our vibration into a better place. Then we can create the better situation.

Vibrational Ladder

If we want to up-level our vibration to feel better, we need to find a vibration that we can easily reach from our current feeling. As Abraham-Hicks says, it is like climbing up a ladder, with each rung being a higher vibration. We can't move from the first rung to the seventh in one jump. We can do it gradually. For example, if I am feeling sad and depressed, I won't be able to access the feeling of blissed-out love. In fact, blissed-out love may feel terribly uncomfortable from my current vibration of feeling of sad and depressed.

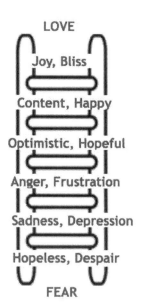

We must reach for the next rung on the vibrational ladder, and find vibrations that are not too much of a stretch from our current vibration.

We do this unconsciously all the time, because we are wired to want to feel better. If someone feels sad and lonely, they may unconsciously choose to blame others and be angry at the world. This anger can create a little fire and motivation for them to be able to envision having a better situation. It may be a gateway to hopefulness, which is the next rung up on the ladder.

People unconsciously use anger to overcome fear and sadness all the time, but when we are mindful about our emotions, we recognize that anger is not necessarily the ultimate choice. It may feel better than fear or sadness, but there are higher rungs on the ladder—ones that will make us feel even better. The destination is the highest vibrational emotions of love and joy.

Perhaps going from anger to joy is too much of a jump, though. If you are angry, then you can think about the potential for feeling better. You can picture yourself being content or think about things that are better than your dissatisfied state, and that may get you into a more optimistic state. From there, you can start to open up to the possibility of feeling happy.

Once we shift our vibrations a bit higher, we develop intentions that will shift us into an even higher state, and in small steps that leads us right to the top.

We must develop a practice of staying awake and aware of how we're feeling in the present moment to determine whether we need to raise our vibrations. We can manage this by setting a reminder on our phone, three times a day, to check in with ourselves. *How I'm I feeling? Where is my vibration? Oh wow, I got stuck three hours ago, I didn't even notice. Let me work my vibration back up. Let me think of something that feels good. Let me get my body feeling good.*

As we practice mindful positive vibration, and get the momentum flowing in that direction, that will become our default. So when we go negative, it will be like, *Oh wow, how did I get here? This doesn't feel good. I've been here for like ten minutes. How can I shift this?* We don't have to lose three days to a negative vibration. Soon, the negative vibration turns into the exception, the odd vibration.

It's not difficult—we're just thinking of things that feel good. We don't have to make it a big chore: *Oh man, now I have to make myself feel good.* We don't have to put a bunch of rules or guilt or *shoulds* around it. You're just taking time out of your day to feel good. It should feel good to feel good, and in the meantime, we're retraining our vibration so that the positive becomes the default and the negative stands out as odd.

With time, we gain confidence that, *I am the master of my own vibration.* We start to see the results of our positive vibration, and things start to line up. Life begins to feel like a bizarre series of things that work out in our favor.

Changing to a Positive Vibration Momentum

We've established that it's important to practice positive thoughts to build new synapses and pathways toward positivity, but how do we do this on a daily basis? I find that the vibration of *appreciation* is a vibration I can attach to quite easily from any of the states I get into. My life has a lot of good in it, so I can focus on just about anything to start the gratitude momentum. The gratitude momentum will usually help me get out of negativity and into a more positive vibration.

If we can focus on four positive thoughts or feelings for 68 seconds (17 seconds each), we can get a positive vibration momentum going. We need four segments of 17 seconds to give us 68 seconds of focus on positive thought. A positive vibration momentum will begin in that time period. Once we develop that positive vibration momentum, it will start a new trajectory of thought and vibration. A general positive vibration momentum may look something like this: *Connecting to my breath...*

1. *I am grateful for my dog* (focus for 17 seconds).

2. *I have so many supportive people in my life* (17 seconds).

3. *Each day I'm equipped to be more joyful* (17 seconds).

4. *My life is so abundant* (17 seconds).

Then we let the mind wander to more related positive thoughts and vibrations to allow for a positive thought trajectory.

A more specific positive vibration momentum around an intention of launching a bestselling book might look like: *Connecting to my breath...*

I am a potent lightworker in the world (17 seconds) > *I am here to awaken humanity* (17 seconds) > *The Divine has imparted important wisdom into my book* (17 seconds). > *I see my book in the hands of millions, awakening humanity* (17 seconds). Then more thoughts and visualizations and vibrations related to the potency of my work.

If you are in a negative vibration and find your thoughts getting more specific in a negative vibration momentum, Abraham-Hicks suggests to simply **get more general** and neutral with your thoughts. For example, if you are stuck on *I hate this job* and all the specific details about what you hate about your job, try:

My job pays all my bills > I am lucky that I have a job > My days keep getting better > I have a beautiful life

It is recommended that you do a positive vibration momentum in the morning when you first wake up. The sleep that we get at night allows us to slow down negative thought momentum and reset our vibration. Sleep heals on many levels! Unfortunately, we often wake up the next morning and import the negative thoughts and vibration from the day before. Let's end that pattern and give ourselves a clean slate every day! Doing a positive session in the morning will help you to get on the right track.

Through the duration of this book, I recommend that you wake up and do your positive vibration momentum every morning so you can start your day in the highest vibration, and attract positivity for the best possible trajectory. Throughout the day, you can be more mindful and conscious of what you're vibrating, and set your vibration consciously, so that you are lifting and Lightening your vibration. To start your positive vibration momentum:

1. **Identify four separate thoughts** that build on each other for your positive vibration momentum. They can be general thoughts to raise your vibration. Or you can choose four thoughts that are closely aligned with your intentions.

2. Find your phone's **stopwatch** to keep time on each thought.

3. **Come into your breath**. Feel the breath in your chest and bring awareness to the energy of your body. Notice how good you feel as you breathe.

4. **Spend about 17 seconds on each thought**. Think the thought. Feel the positive vibrations and emotions with the thought.

5. After the fourth thought, allow yourself to add more thoughts until you **start feeling really good**.

In Summary...

The key to manifesting your intentions is to cultivate the positive thoughts AND feelings you imagine you would experience upon successfully attracting your intention. It is that simple. Walk around thinking and feeling like you have already manifested your intention.

Even if you read no further in this book, you have plenty of *knowledge* to get you started in transforming your life. What's left is the *practice* required to implement change. Simply practice the following 14-minute meditation once a day and you will watch your life begin to transform.

14 MINUTES PER DAY CAN CHANGE THE TRAJECTORY OF YOUR LIFE. Who can't spare 14 minutes? If you do nothing else, just do this.

Recorded Meditation Practice: Manifested Intention

The following is a 14-minute daily meditation that will guide you through practicing a Positive Vibration Momentum and the manifested state of your intention. You can access the guided meditation at: www.enLIGHTenWithKim.com. Click on **Community Resources** and **Book Meditations**, log in for free, and find the meditation called **#1 Manifested Intention Meditation**

Tune Into Your Heart

It is only with the heart that one can see rightly;
what is essential is invisible to the eye.
-Antoine De Saint-Exupéry

The purpose of this book is to help you create a more joyful life by releasing the patterns of the mind, raising your vibration, manifesting what you desire, and creating alignment in yourself. Alignment of your thoughts with the truest part of your mind, alignment of your emotions with your highest joy, alignment of your body with the most vibrant expression of your energy, and alignment of your desires with the truest purpose of yourself. The *truest and highest part of who you are* is accessible from the space within your HEART; this is where your highest qualities reside.

The vibration of the Heart is one of LOVE, truth, peace, safety, harmony, beauty, oneness and wisdom. When we look to raise our vibration, we are connecting with that part of ourselves that is closest to these qualities. While the human mind will autopilot to the vibrations that feel bad, such as fear, scarcity, judgement, disharmony and separation, the Heart aligns us back to the vibrations that feel good. Shifting off the hamster wheel is the act of handing the steering wheel back to the Heart, and since the Heart always *feels* good, our emotional guidance system can show us the way back into the Heart.

Last chapter, we looked at the three aspects of the mind: the *subconscious* mind or ego, the *conscious* mind, and the *superconscious* mind. Well, the Heart is the space that links present moment *consciousness* with *superconsciousness*. The Heartspace is where the Heart meets the Universal Energy, where the Soul meets Source energy. There is abundant power, wisdom, and love—super high vibration—when we can hook into the energy of the Heart.

A well-developed relationship to your Heart/Soul and Universe/Source can help with your mastery of Law of Attraction. We manifest situations that are resilient and matched with our life's purpose when we do so from the place of the Heart, when we are in alignment with the vibration of Source. In fact, our manifestations are incredibly potent and resilient when they originate from our Heart.

We are More than our Bodies and Thoughts

What are we beyond our mind and bodies? What is the Soul and the energy of the Heart? What is Divine or Source energy? While it's important to honor your personal belief systems around Soul/Source, perhaps it's also good to continue to build onto your belief system, especially now that science is producing more evidence on quantum physics, consciousness, and the electromagnetic energy of the Heart.

Most people can agree that within our physical heart resides some mysterious energy that has yet to be fully understood by science. Did you know the Heart beats before the brain is formed in utero? Since that's true, then what mechanism allows the Heart to beat before the brain is there to regulate it? Can you consider that Source energy feeds the miraculous energy of the Heart? In this book, we shall refer to this energy that feeds the Heart as Source, Divine, Universe, or Universal energy. It's what exists beyond the physical body, and continues when we leave the body.

The HeartMath Institute (heartmath.org) has conducted experiments (repeated many times) on the function of the Heart energy in our lives. In one experiment, the participants had no idea what image was about to come up on the computer screen. They would click the mouse and there was a delay. If there was going to be a highly emotional picture coming up on the screen, *before* the image appeared, the Heart would decelerate to prepare for the emotional image. The Heart could get the information of what was going to be on the screen *before* the actual picture popped up! **The more we connect with our Heartspace, the more connected we will be with our intuition.**

We are energetically receiving information through the electromagnetic field of the Heart. The brain receives signals AFTER the Heart. HeartMath has proven that the electromagnetic frequencies of the Heart are picking up on the energy outside of us before brain cognition. They have also proven that the body's energetic field can pick up the energy of another person before they walk in the room, from up to six feet away. So what is this Heart consciousness? Where does it come from? These are questions worth exploring to clarify your beliefs.

Play with me for a minute here ... Imagine that you were in "heaven" and decided to take a body. You chose your parents and flowed into your physical vessel. But your whole spiritual self couldn't *fit* into your small body container, so you have a good part of yourself on the other side of the veil, still in the spiritual world. The Heartspace is the point through which you can access this non-physical energy on the other side. **Your Higher self. Your Source. Your peeps. Your spiritual entourage.** That part of you has access to all kinds of information, energy, and wisdom.

Because you have free will, this part of yourself won't interfere in your life unless you call upon it—with your intentions—for assistance, guidance, and wisdom. It's important to engage with that part of yourself when you are setting Heart-based intentions for your life.

When you access this part of yourself through your Heart—your Source, your Higher self, your angels, your guides, your PEEPS, your ENTOURAGE—you are connected to infinite wisdom and potency.

Everything and everyone is connected to this Universal Energy Source, and so **we are all connected**. We are all a drop from the same ocean. We can view the Heart as our unique flavor or drop of Source energy. We all have a spark of Light within our Heart, which is pure and aligned with the vibration of love. **The vibration of love is our Source energy.**

We may not have the same word for our Heart, Soul, or Higher Consciousness, and we may not share the same word for

Universe or Source energy. Some people call it God, or project the energy onto a Divine Master such as Jesus, Buddha, Krishna. It is Divine Light projected in different forms—Divine water frozen as different forms of ice. We may all see it formed differently, but the essence is of the same spiritual energy: Heart connects to Universal Source. Soul connects with Source. Individual Light connects with Divine Light. (I will use all these terms interchangeably because I believe it all to be the same.)

If we can buy into the fact that we are not solely a physical body on a very separate journey than others, that **we are all connected to the same Universal Source Energy**, that we are all sipping from the same well, then we begin to shift the way we experience ourselves and each other. While most of society confuses who they are with their physical body and mind, our mind and body are just a tiny fraction of who we are. We are way more than *just* physical bodies doing physical things, producing physical results. We are more than our thoughts, our opinions, our failures and successes. Often we make up our beliefs based on what our physical five senses can bring in, but our sense of intuition is the sense that is attuned to the Heart, to the energetic and spiritual world, and therefore connected to truth.

Personally, a huge trigger for my spiritual awakening was being at my 45-year-old friend's wake. As I approached her casket, I looked at her and realized that while her body was there, SHE wasn't there. It was the first time I was able to distinguish the body from the Soul, and it made me realize how much of us is energy. Our bodies are simply sacred vessels for the energy of the Heart, our own drop of the Universal ocean.

We are spiritual beings having some playtime on this physical planet. We came in for the purpose of feeling a wide spectrum of emotions and experiences. We were just Light beings floating in the cosmos before, but took a contract to come into these physical bodies, **accepting the complete spiritual amnesia of our magnificence, and taking on the challenge of finding our way back to the Light**. We're playing with this duality of Light and dark here on the planet, watching the dance of Light and dark play out. Emotionally and spiritually, the duality plays out as the dance of Fear and Love. In order to truly understand the qualities of Love, we explore the lower vibrations of Fear. The contrast of the dark of the world provides us with the ability to understand the qualities of our Light. The contrast draws forth our appreciation and honor for both qualities.

We can gain a sense that we're much more than just these physical bodies, despite the fact that we have amnesia that has made us forget our Light and Love. We sense and intuit that there is a greater Source energy connected to us, and that the physical body is just small percentage of who or what we are. We are spiritual beings having a physical experience.

No matter your belief system, what's important is that it allows you to connect to love and helps you feel better. If you believe *I'm a sinner and I'm going to hell*, that is a belief system that has a lot of resistance and fear around it. If you can believe *I am pure Love and Light* and *I'm here on Earth simply to have a human experience, and there's really no right or wrong in the experience*, then you can have more Lightness, creativity, and playfulness on the journey with a Heart-based belief system of the spiritual realm.

The Way into the Heart

An effective way to tune into our Heart or Source energy is through stillness, quiet, breath, and connection within … meditation. There are different paths of meditation, but most originate with the breath and a connection to the Heart.

I have studied so many different types of meditation, and the consistent thread among all of them is that they help you: develop a deep internalized and inward state, raise your vibration, create focus, clear your mind, and connect with your Heart. The physical, mental, and emotional benefits of meditation have been researched and demonstrated in many studies. Meditation reduces stress, heals the body, and promotes happiness. While it takes effort and practice, there is a high Return on Investment (ROI), and it is well worth your time!

Meditation rewires the brain to help us bring our vibration into resonance with Source energy. From the perspective of the brain, meditation is the shift from Beta (externalized thought), to Alpha (present moment calm state), to Theta (expansive mind) brain wave state. Mindfully shifting out of Beta wave to Theta wave can help you access your superconscious and connect to more of yourself for Higher states of consciousness.

As we start to develop our consciousness—move from *subconscious* autopilot to a more present moment *conscious* state of mind to *superconscious*ness—and build a Heart-based intention in our lives, we can bring meditation and introspection into our journey. This connects the meditation state to a state of examining our lives, so we can shine Light on how we do things, how we feel about things, and what Divine inspiration we can assimilate. Introspective meditation brings the mind into a state of witnessing so that we can begin to see ourselves as the observer of the thoughts and life ... while actively listening for inspiration (In-Spirit-ation) to bring Light and consciousness to our daily life.

Meditation Practice: Introspective Meditation

To do Introspective Mindfulness Meditation, simply:

1. Create some time in your day or week to spend some time in stillness. Don't stress over it. Just schedule and carve out twenty to thirty minutes when you can sit without people or distractions around you.

2. Sit down and make sure you are comfortable. Maybe grab a cup of tea or something that feels nourishing.

3. Begin to feel your breath pulsing through your body. Feel it in your back and belly, and just follow it for a while. Notice whether it feels like a wave coming in and out of your body. This will help you connect to yourself and even feel yourself. (Don't worry if this is uncomfortable and difficult; it is for most people!)

4. Notice where your mind is going, and watch what is taking up space in your head. See if you can observe the thoughts like you are just taking note of what consumes you. *You are not your thoughts.* Keep redirecting your mind to your breath.

5. Feel what's going on in your body physically. Any pain? Tension? Simply direct your breath into those areas. Feel how the tension dissipates.

6. Feel your emotions. This is important! What are they? *Good? Bad? Happy? Sad? Angry? Irritated?* See if you can observe them without thought or judgment. Just feel it

and know you're not going to die. Continue until those emotions start to release.

7. Now talk to yourself and/or your Divine Source. Strike up a conversation. Ask a question and wait for an answer. Or simply listen.

Breath + Gratitude = Gateway to the Heart

In raising our consciousness, we are simply creating a more intimate relationship with our breath. Breath carries Light, prana, chi, life force energy, love, relaxation, and nourishment. It is a very powerful tool that you can use to heal yourself. The breath is like a fast track connection to the energetic layer of your body.

The breath is the one function of the autonomic nervous system that is both voluntary and involuntary. We can control it when we want, but 95% of the time, the body breathes without our awareness. When we bring awareness to the breath we take the steering wheel from the unconscious and hand it over the conscious mind. Bringing awareness to the breath pulls in prana more effectively, and serves as a physical/pranic bridge connecting our somatic nervous system (conscious and voluntary) and autonomic nervous system (unconscious and automatic), therefore bridging our unconscious and conscious selves. Virtually every meditation practice in existence consists of focusing on the breath consciously and continuously, which is tantamount to *crossing the bridge* into what would otherwise be unconscious behavior. Breath helps us move from the mind to the Heart very quickly.

Just three minutes of consistent conscious breathing will trigger a relaxation response in the nervous system. Doing this consistently for longer periods of time rewires the brain, creates a more positive chemistry in the body, develops emotional and physical resilience, and positively affects the neuroplasticity of the brain.

I invite you to come into your breath as you journey through this section, so that you can experience it from the place of the Heart as universal truth, and automatically assimilate the material into your life because *you know this*. That's why spiritual truth is invigorating—because our Heart knows it. We know it to be true, and we just need to be reminded so that we can remember who we really are. When we hear about the Light, and when we see the Light, we're reminded we are Light.

All we have to do is take our mind back into the attention of the breath at the Heart. Once we develop this as a practice, once we start listening through the ears of the Heart (instead of the ego), we see life through a totally different filter. We see life for what it truly is, a more meaningful experience.

When I first arrived in California for a two month stay, my husband and I were at the beach. As we were walking on the beach we found ourselves talking about how beautiful it was to be in California. Our conversation quickly digressed into, *Should we live here? Do we have the money to live here? Where would we want to live? It's too bad we don't live here. It's too bad we don't have this ALL the time. Why don't we have this all the time? Wouldn't it be great? I wonder if this would work. What would we miss about the Northeast? What would we be missing? What we would be afraid of? What would be preventing us from being happy?* (Can you feel that fear and negative momentum?) We spent a good part of our walk focused on the what-ifs, the fears and what we *didn't* have. All the while, here we were in paradise taking a beautiful walk on the beach with beaming sunlight.

Because I was preparing to write this book, and that's what my mind was focused on 24 hours a day, I stopped us. *Oh, honey. Look, we are completely focused on what we don't have when we're actually experiencing the thing that we are wishing for!* We were focused on how we don't have it **forever,** and we were projecting that into the future with some suffering. Scarcity Mentality! By focusing on lack, we immediately took ourselves out of our two-month experience of sunlight, beaches, and freedom. We focused on the part of our lives where we *wouldn't* be in CA ... which was two months into the future.

This is what we all do. We spend much of our time focused on the fear, the lack, and the scarcity in our lives when we are sitting in abundance in the present moment. **The mind distracts us to the past and the future, and keeps us completely out of the present moment.**

From that point forward, every time we walked on the beach, we brought ourselves *back to our breath* to carry us back into the present moment. We focused on our breathing and all of our senses—seeing the sun, hearing the ocean, smelling the air, feeling the water and sand—which guided us into a place of appreciation and presence ... straight back into the vibration of the Heart. We knew that if we could just appreciate where we were at, we'd create more of it from the positive vibration. More experience of appreciation, more experience of blissfulness. We worked to mindfully practice a higher vibration and stay in the present moment of the Heart. So simple but so challenging to practice, isn't it?

While staying connected to the breath and Heart, we can mindfully keep ourselves in *appreciation* of what we *do* have. Appreciation or gratitude keeps our focus on the base vibration of the Universe—the vibration of love, abundance, and appreciation. That's all our Source knows. Every time we go into an easily accessible vibration like appreciation for the present moment, we connect with Source and align with our Heart.

In every experience, we can focus on not having what we want OR we can focus on appreciating currently having what we want. Right? I can think about how blessed I am to have three amazing daughters, or I can focus on how doomed I am when they are teenagers. She can focus on how she doesn't have a boyfriend OR she can focus on appreciating all the special people she has in her life. You can focus on how you don't like your job, OR you can appreciate *having* a job. Doesn't every experience have two sides of the coin?

We have habits, belief systems, and well-worn neural pathways with years of focus on what we *don't* want. How do we shift that focus? How do we shift into the focus of abundance, satisfaction, and appreciation? The path is through the breath and gratitude. **Mindful breathing accompanied by gratitude is the fast track into the Heart.** Try it. You will see.

Breathless Life

The problem is that most of us are barely breathing, so you can begin to watch your *lack of* breath to help you remember to consciously breathe. Being mindful and aware of our breath is an act of self-love and self-care. Your mindful breath says, *I care about myself enough to give myself life.* As you care for yourself in that way, in that simple non-time-consuming way, you're shifting focus into self-affirmation, self-love, self-care, and self-nourishment. As you take your attention into that self-nourishment place, you then attract more nourishment.

For many, life throws us challenges that often feel jarring and negative, so we shut down and stop wanting to feel. Then we cut ourselves off from the very thing that directs our connection to our Heart. We stop breathing. We lose the connection to our potency. We numb out and just continue on the hamster wheel, with our ego leading the way.

People live a numb, breathless life to avoid negative feelings. Breathing through the negative vibrations leads the way back to the Heart.

Most of society is living an externally focused life. Living vicariously through others (Facebook, TV, movies, video games) is not the way toward potency. It is often an escape. We watch the lives of other people and project onto their lives so we can feel the range of emotions in a safe, detached way, where we intellectually know that the emotions we are experiencing have nothing to do with us. The reality is that we don't truly feel good when we cover up the underlying negative vibrations with distractions, computer, or TV; that's externally focused, temporary feeling good. The purpose of life is to feel into the goodness and the nourishment of *our own lives*!

Many of us are walking around asleep and numb. The idea of living a more conscious life, being connected to our breath, and feeling good and nourished is foreign because we don't even know where to start.

Connecting into our Heart—and letting that beam out into every cell of our body—is the path to feeling good. The more mindful we can be in creating that positive flow in our body, the more we can create more of that in our external manifestations through Law of Attraction. We just need to get to a place of feeling good and create a wave, an avalanche, or some fire around that feeling.

The point of life becomes feeling good. It's not about achieving a result or getting a product or getting anything out of anybody. We realize that the more we feel good, the more we *want* to feel good, and the more attentive we can be to how we feel. Then, when the negative emotion arises, it's like, *Red alert, there's something underneath here that doesn't feel good. Let's work through that so we can feel good again quickly!* That's where our negative emotions come in as the indicator that something is not aligned. We may not be able to see it, but if we are breath-centered, we can feel it, and once we can feel it, we can use it to navigate back to what feels aligned, what feels good.

Breathing Practice: Created by HeartMath Institute

1. **Bring awareness** to your breath to switch on the parasympathetic nervous system which calms the body. Bring awareness to the chest at the heart to bring focus to the electromagnetic field of the heart.

2. **Engage in patterned breathing:** Through the nose, inhale at the count of 5, and exhale at the count of 5.

3. Bring up the **feeling of caring, appreciation or gratitude**. Use a thought or memory to trigger the positive emotion. Focus on the feeling of the positive emotion in the chest and work to maintain the feeling as you continue patterned breathing for 15-20 minutes.

You can go to www.HeartMath.org to learn more about the breath and the Heart. Also, check out the book *Living in the Heart* by Drunvalo Melchizedek for more info about the following guided meditation.

Recorded Meditation Practice: Journey Into the Heart

You can access a guided meditation that will bring you into the Heart at: www.enLIGHTenWithKim.com. Click on **Community Resources** and **Book Meditations**, log in for free, and find the meditation called #**2 Heart Meditation.**

Bhakti Yoga of Devotion

Bhakti Yoga is a practice of devotion toward Divine Source that opens the Heart and brings practitioners into alignment. The devotion vibration is an offering of love to your personal Divine Source, and in return, through the offering, you *receive* love from your personal Divine Source. In Bhakti, the relationship is between a Soul and Divine Source, but the *nature* of your relationship with Source can be similar to relationships between humans, such as lovers, friends, family; for example, Divine is teacher and you are student, or Divine is Beloved and you are lover, or Divine is father/mother and you are son/daughter.

Bhakti yoga, like any other form of yoga, is a path to self-realization, to having an experience of oneness with everything. The practice brings you straight into your Heart, and when done regularly with clarity of intent, can keep you in high vibration.

Bhakti Yoga is practiced by chanting the names of the Divine (most often in Sanskrit). The ancient chants are thousands of years old and the vibration of the Sanskrit words vibrates that which you want to attract. This helps the typical "recovering Christian" who flinches at the word "God" but hasn't yet re-established a loving relationship and reunion with Source. As you can imagine, when you establish a relationship of Soul-to-Source chanting, it vibrates through your energetic centers, the chakras, connects you deep into your Heart, and provides a deep connection with Source ... straight into the vibration of love. This bypasses the mind and subconscious because it is a vibrational experience.

There are chants for anything you want to shift energetically, and for any energetic cleansing you might desire. A mantra can be chanted 108 times, on a mala (a strand of 108 beads), twice a day.

Mantra Meditation Practice: Bhakti Sanskrit Chants

The following mantras are provided by Nama Deva and Mirabai Devi; pronunciation and recordings can be found by Deva Premal on iTunes and YouTube. Use a mala with 108 beads to chant a mantra 108 times and shift into the heart of devotion:

Om Gum Ganapatayei Namaha (Removes obstacles)

Om Shree Dhanvantre Namaha (Provides healing)

Om Namo Bhagavate Vasudevaya (Liberation, open Heart)

Om Shreem Mahalakshmiyei Namaha (Abundance)

Aham Prema (I am Divine Love)

Om Dum Durgayei Namaha (Divine protection; dispels negativity)

Om Namah Shivaya (I bow to the Divinity within)

In Summary...

The breath pulls us out of our subconscious, reactive, hamster wheel mind. It connects us to our conscious awareness to observe our thoughts, emotions, and subtle vibrations. This gives us the opportunity to step off the hamster wheel and choose a different, more positive feeling or thought. Mindful breath is our most potent tool to create awareness and change in our lives.

The breath bridges our Heart to Universal energy, our Soul to Source energy. If we practice using our breath to consciously shift back to the place of the Heart, we can learn to feel good by retraining our habits of negative emotions and thoughts back to the vibration of love. Attuning with the Heart works us back into alignment to the vibration of the Soul. When we spend time in the Heart, we gain access to Universal wisdom, superconscious thoughts, vibrations and experiences.

This state of conscious awareness at the Heart takes practice so that it becomes a new habit, our new normal. And why not? It feels so good to be in that space and all it takes is a reminder to breathe. We're breathing anyway, so bringing awareness is a super easy way to feel good and literally rewire the brain to make positive, feel-good chemicals.

Allow the Universe to Fulfill Your Desires

The Universe is saying: "Allow me to flow through you unrestricted, and you will see the greatest magic you have ever seen."
-Klaus Joehle

At this point, we know that we need a solid Heart-based intention, a good grasp on what our mind is doing on autopilot, and mindfulness around our emotions and vibration so that we can focus our thoughts and vibration on our intention. Spending time with our breath, in the present moment, focused in the Heartspace is our best chance for being able to stay aligned toward the manifestation of our intention. With this base understanding of the mind and the Heart, we can now dive into some of the deeper aspects of Law of Attraction!

We are on this earth to CREATE, and to create, we must move past the mind's programming of limitation. We do this by accessing our imagination to shift us to the new paradigm of our future selves. Once we make that shift, we must ASK for what we desire and RECEIVE from the Universe. This is the potency that's available to us.

We Are Creators

Eckhart Tolle talks about the Power of Now and staying in the present moment. When we go into our breath, we bring ourselves back into the present moment. That's where we have access to our ability to create—and the Law of Attraction is our energetic tool to do just that. This is our birthright. This is what we're meant to do. We're meant to consciously CREATE our intentions and our desires. We're wired for it. It is our right to have a vision, align our energy to the vision, and manifest it to fruition. Creation!

Many people believe that it's a luxury to be able to create a life that you want. It's not a luxury! It's our purpose. Creating and manifesting our Heart-based desires is critical to leading potent lives! **It is our birthright to manifest our dreams!**

My husband and I manifested the ability to leave the Northeast for two winter months, with our three daughters, to live in CA. We simply wanted to get out of the cold for the winter, and didn't want to wait until we were retired to enjoy January and February in the warmth. The reaction from others was often, *Wow, I wish I could do that!* As if the option wasn't accessible to them! And to that I would respond, *Well actually you CAN do it. You just have to be able to commit to your desire and put the energy behind it, believe it's possible, detach from the need for it to happen, and let go of the fears. Et voila!* There's a process around creating the life you want: intentional creation and manifestation.

Some people would get jealous and angry at my ability to create what I wanted in my life. That showed me that they were pushing their desire's vibrations and potential away from themselves. If you can't support someone who is manifesting that which she wants, then you're not in a state of allowing that for yourself. You're not willing to accept your potency and allow it into your own life.

Upon looking at our winter away, some people said, *Well I could never do that.* Right, you can't do it if you don't believe that what you want is possible.

The Law of Attraction allows us to clarify our intentions, identify the energy and pure desire behind the intention, and then align our thoughts, emotions, and vibrations. We create from the Now, and our breath is the path to get into the Now and focus on our desire's thoughts and vibrations.

Imagination Is Our Ticket to Transformation

When we work the Law of Attraction, we are guiding our mind to think about things in a more positive way. We are guiding our emotions to a more positive emotion. We are working our vibration up to the next level. In doing so, our imagination is our most potent tool in raising our vibration and setting the stage for our intentions to manifest.

Our imagination allows us to visualize the manifested state of our intention so we can easily access all the vibrations necessary to attract our desire.

Think about it. On autopilot, our mind recycles past memories by re-<u>imagining</u> them in the present moment, and energizes our unaware (mostly negative) manifestations, so that we end up with more of the same. However, if we use our conscious minds to place NEW thoughts into our imaginative machine, we will create new vibrations, which result in new possibilities for the future. We can either autopilot with our imagination to rehash the past, or **we can import new intentions into our imagination to create our future**.

Does it feel stupid to hang out in the imagination, dreaming up and vibrating out new possibilities? If your answer is yes, you are not alone. Visualization is a new concept for many. And it does feel unproductive at first. But if you can link the dreaming to your vibration and see it as productively building new pathways of feeling good, then you can see how incredibly effective it is.

Our imagination allows us to create and energetically try on new scenarios, which then get wired up as new thought synapse pathways in the brain. **The brain doesn't know the difference between an imagined memory from the past or a newly imagined visualization for the future**, but the body knows the difference vibrationally. The past can feel old and heavier, and the new imagined desire has fresh and exciting momentum that feels lighter. We have the choice to continue fortifying the brain synapses of the past, or to practice the new synapses through our imagination, which will create new body chemistry and hormones, new vibrations, and new manifestations for the future.

Remember, it is important to imagine the manifested state, the end goal, of your intention—not the *wanting* of the intention. If you focus on wanting, you will stay in the energetic state of wanting vibration. If you focus on imagining that you have it already, as if you are already experiencing the intention manifested, then you attract the intention.

Steps to Abundance: Ask, Allow, and Receive

The Universe is abundant. There is so much potential waiting for us. Our spiritual entourage, our peeps, are waiting for us to ask for what we want. Our Soul is waiting for our vibrational momentum to resonate with that which we want. The Universe is ready to serve. We just have to learn how to *ask* and *receive*.

When we ask for our intention and send it out into Source's hands, we are building the framework or matrix for our intention. It's like the vibrational outline of our desire. Source then fills that framework or matrix with all the energetic resources necessary for the intention to manifest. Once our matrix is filled, we just need to <u>allow</u> the physical reality to show up in our lives through our intuitive listening, aligned vibration, and purposeful action.

This works in the physical reality as well. One day, while teaching yoga, I was helping a student get up into handstand. She kept popping up and falling down, even though she had all the pieces to put it together. I told her to imagine the matrix of herself already in handstand, as if the scaffolding was built and all she needed to do was to pop her body up into the pre-formed matrix that was waiting for her. With a class of 30 students watching, she was able to do it immediately after building that vision.

Abraham-Hicks[1] presents these three steps to manifesting that which we want in life. Just three steps, and we are only responsible for two of them.

Us: ASK

Source: FULFILL DESIRE

Us: ALLOW and RECEIVE

---

[1] Please refer to the books by Esther Hicks, "Ask and it is Given" and "The Vortex" for details on these Abraham teachings.

STEP 1: Ask

The first step to manifesting is asking. If we want something in our lives, we need to ask for it. This seems obvious, but most of us don't do this! Instead:

- We look around our lives and complain that we don't have what we need or want, even though WE HAVEN'T EVEN ASKED FOR IT! We haven't even defined what we might like.

OR

- As soon as we put our intention out there and have that momentum around the desire to ask, we often go into a place of fear or doubt or negative thoughts about ourselves. Then we release our desire so we don't have to feel the fear and prove our (distorted) theory that the Universe doesn't have our back.

Either way, we're not even identifying what we want in life, or how we want life to look. And even if we *want* to identify what we desire in life, most of us don't know where to start.

I see this often. In fact, it wasn't until a friend came up to me after a retreat and said, *You know, we really need some help defining our intentions.* I'm like, *No you don't! You don't need help defining your intentions. I have desires creeping up every day of my life. You don't need help defining your desires.* And he said, *No really, we do. We need a workshop on defining our desires.* It didn't make sense to me. I hadn't remembered how stuck people can get at the thought of sitting down and defining what they want—or asking for it. All the fear, the doubt, the beliefs about ourselves creep right in and take our vibration over, and then we're paralyzed. Instead of releasing the doubt or the fear or the negative self-thought, instead of releasing the negative vibration around that which we want, we release our desire and rationalize it away: *I don't think I really need that anyway. I don't need to lose weight, I'm happy enough with myself. I don't need to manifest a man, my life is happy enough without my Soul mate.*

I always work with people to commit to what they want, *Wait! No, I clearly hear that you WANT to lose weight, let's set that desire, that's completely possible and easy to manifest.* Or, *You want to create a partner in your life, no problem, he's waiting for you to be*

61

ready! For some, it's an innovative concept to go for what our Heart desires. We have all this fear and doubt along with many limiting beliefs and assumptions.

- Some people believe they're not worthy of it.

- Some people believe it's just not possible for them to get what they want.

- Some people just don't trust the Universe, and think that if they ask and the Universe isn't there for them, it will just confirm their worst fears. They'd rather not prove their impotence.

It always comes down to one thing: We're afraid to ask for what we really want. In reality, we can ask for whatever we want, and the only thing keeping us from getting it is our vibrational alignment with our intention.

If we believe that the Universe is abundant, we are worthy of our intentions being fulfilled, and that it is completely possible (inevitable!) for us to manifest our Hearts' desires, we can easily manifest our desires. There are unlimited resources and potential for us ALL to have what we want in life.

Asking with Vibrational Momentum

The first step is asking. It's aligning with our desire, feeling the momentum of the desire. Now, here's what that doesn't look like:

Yeah, I'd like a million dollars and I'd like a fancy house and I'd like a beautiful partner and I'd like to have some kids.

Do you feel that? Do you feel any momentum or desire behind that list? There's no passion, there's no excitement, there's no eagerness behind many people's desires. There's just fear and negative emotions laying underneath the intention.

So, here's what asking for a million dollars might feel like to someone who really wants it:

I am asking for a million dollars. And with this million dollars, I will buy a house that sits on a cliff, overlooking the ocean. At this house, I will attract as many friends and good-natured people as possible. I see people coming and going and one of those people just happens to be the spouse I'm manifesting. There s/he is! This spouse totally aligns with my desires and when we get together, our love and alignment and clarity comes together. Whew! Our love creates a few children. Extraordinary! And we have this amazing life together and we're looking out over the ocean and we're just sitting in the abundance and the love and the crazy ability to attract whatever we want in our lives!

Do you feel the difference? We don't attract from disconnection from our desire. We attract with our connection and excitement and the momentum that we build with our desire. It's like that desire gets a life of its own. You didn't hear any fear there. It wasn't like: *And I need a partner, but I kind of have anxiety because I haven't really had a partner and I've never really had someone that I've gotten along with.*

Do you see the lack of fire and eagerness in the statement above? Often there's so much fear (of rejection), attachment (needing someone to validate that I'm lovable), and baggage (parents never showed they loved me), that it makes it hard to even have a desire. Let's not ignore all those negative vibrations underneath our intention, because we will attract from that negative vibration—even if we're trying not to think about it— and prove to ourselves that those fears and attachments are true.

Our fears set our <u>vibrational point of attraction</u>. Often our points of attraction are all those fears we have around attracting a mate. It will become a self-fulfilling prophecy, even though we thought we weren't thinking about the fears! So notice the reservation you may have around asking for what you want. Bring up the fears and give them some attention. Watch how the fears are holding you back from asking for what you desire. *Okay, there was some fear about being abandoned, okay, I see that. Let me feel that in my body. Yup, kinda makes me feel like I'm going to throw up. But I know I'm okay, so I will just sit with the vibration until it goes away. I'm going to release that and focus back on the excitement of attracting a mate into my life.*

This first step is the asking and believing it is possible. It's about presenting the desire with momentum and excitement and positive vibration, and building a solid intention framework matrix.

STEP 2: Source Fulfills Our Desire

The second step is not our step at all. Source energy, the Universe, fills our energy field, the intention matrix, with the desire, and all the potential of that desire gets put within our possible range—it's completely available to us. It's right there, folks. You put a desire with some energy out there, it gets fulfilled. Do you believe that? Well, what builds our belief is our ability to manifest. So just try it. The seeing brings so many of us to believing. Then we build our trust that:

- The Universe provides.

- The Universe is abundant.

- We can have whatever we desire.

- We can have our cake and eat it too—there is no *asking too much* if we are aligned.

- Our Soul puts in the best orders (not our egos).

It helps if we build trust in the Universe. Start small to begin building trust so that when your ego self-sabotages your intentions, you can interrupt the sabotage and remind yourself that the Universe abundant and generous.

STEP 3: Allow and RECEIVE

The third step is allowing and receiving the manifested intention. We do this by tuning into the vibration of the desire and allowing the fulfilled matrix to be received into our lives. We can lay the intention framework into the matrix and Source can fill in all the pieces, but if we don't come into the place of receiving, we won't be able to manifest it into creation.

As we practice the vibration of our desire, we're creating the vibrational environment and climate for the intention. You're setting it all up, you're making it exciting and vibrationally matched with what you desire. We get what we think about, we get what we feel, we get what we vibrate.

If we want an intention, we must vibrate like we already have it! To create the energetic environment, we use our creativity to stir up the vibration through our imagination. We must picture the already-manifested intention in our minds by thinking thoughts we would be thinking if it happened, and conjure up the feelings that we would have once it came true. When we do this, we begin to feel it so intensely as if it has already occurred—because vibrationally, it has.

If there's too much negativity built into our desire, if there's too much fear in our desire, if we have doubt in our desire, then it won't feel good no matter what we do. To work with this, we can simply practice feeling good in general. We take our attention away from the fear or doubt and go straight into feeling good.

We want to build feeling good as an *internal* state that's not dependent on other people, places and things. This helps us be less dependent on life situations to feel good. And then feeling good is something we can access at will, without any assistance from the world being the way we want it to be. When we are trying to get into a state of receiving, and want to access a positive vibration, sometimes starting our focus on external conditions (people, places and things in our life), such as gratitude for the people who support us, can help us feel good until we build it internally.

When we feel good, we're aligned with our Source, and when we're aligned with our Source, we are *allowing* the Universe to give us what we have asked for. Even if what you're focusing on is not your specific intention, you are releasing resistance when you feel good. You can watch for evidence of this feel good vibration around you, and see the magic and the synchronicity that starts to happen in your life.

Abundance Originates from the Heart— Giving and Receiving

Abundance is the constant flow of Love to and from your Heart, the flow of *receiving* from the Universe, and *giving* positive vibration back out to the Universe. Our ability to freely give <u>and</u> receive in harmony dictates whether we are in this harmonious flow. **Those who give too much tend to live a life of depletion, and those who receive too much tend to live a life of dependence.** Both are disempowering, and block our ability to freely give and receive through the Law of Attraction.

Receiving is an aspect of life where many people are blocked, and most don't realize that if they are blocked in receiving from others, then they are blocking themselves from receiving their intentions from the Universe. If I can't receive from others, how can I receive from Source? How can I receive from the Universe if I can't even receive help from a friend? If I'm stuck on being just the giver (because I feel unworthy, and giving makes me feel like a good person), or being just the receiver (because I feel unloved, and that's the only way I can feel love), then I'm not allowing alignment and flow.

When we look at how we're manifesting in life, we start to see our subconscious patterns everywhere, especially in our relationships. Do we suffer about our giving? Do we get angry because we haven't received? *Why am I the only one giving? Why am I giving it? What strings are attached? What am I receiving? Am I willing to receive?* How do you do birthdays or Christmas? Looking at the holidays is an interesting way to nail down how and what you're manifesting in your life.

My husband and I have been together for eighteen years, and when we first got together, we of course were not the most aligned forms of ourselves. Our pattern was one where he was the giver, the accommodator, the flexible one, and I was the angry, demanding, controlling one. I was the receiver and he was the giver. We had this pattern set up in our relationship from the start. I didn't give very much, and I felt entitled. It felt like he *should* be doing what I wanted him to do (so I could feel worthy, loved, and valuable). He was trying to feel safe, worthy, and successful, so he was willing to serve as long as it made him feel better about himself. We had an egoic exchange. He made me feel worthy, and I made him feel worthy. Our worthiness came from our ability to have the other person do what fulfilled our innermost deficiencies. Sound familiar?

You can make one person bad and one person good and say, *Oh the giver is the good person and the taker is the bad person*, but really, this is just a dynamic that gets set up around giving and receiving. It's all based on our fears about love, worthiness, and safety. It's all based on an idea we have about ourselves, which was built into the subconscious when we were children. Our process of giving and receiving is set at an early age, and we just play it out with everyone.

However, on the spiritual path, my husband and I were given the opportunity to look at how we exchanged. *How much am I giving? How much am I receiving? What are my expectations on giving and receiving? Is there a flow of giving and receiving in the relationship, or is there an imbalance?*

When there is an imbalance of giving and receiving, when there is not acknowledgement of the value being exchanged, the relationship is thrown out of alignment and feels bad. He never felt good about being an excessive giver and getting his worth or security from giving. I never felt good about being a constant taker and feeling like I was a little princess that everyone should be waiting on. Neither of us felt good about that dynamic, because it was coming from a place of non-alignment.

The way we give and receive in the world, and the reasons that we do it, are basically how we set up our whole paradigm around abundance. Our relationships show us these patterns. We don't need to judge it. We can just throw some Heart-based desire for change, *Hey Source! I'd like more alignment in my giving and receiving. I'd like to be less fearful. I'd like to feel my inner-worthiness.*

Through our breath and connection to our Heart, we'll start to feel our worthiness, value, and goodness as we further align with our Source energy. When we come back to ourselves, we feel worthy to receive. And then, abundance is ours.

Prayer Practice—Prayer of Bounty

Here is a prayer, written by Howard Wills, to help open your heart into the vibration of Abundance:

"Divine, please open my mind, Heart and being to your complete, limitless, bountiful prosperity and love. Please help all things that I think, say, and do be filled with your complete, limitless, bountiful prosperity and love. Please allow me to be blessed with the riches and bounty of your heavens and your earth always. Please lead me, guide me, and direct me into your life, into your light, into your love, and into your complete, limitless, bountiful prosperity and love. Celebrating life as the gift it is from you, Divine, now and forever. Thank you, thank you, thank you. Amen."

Allowing vs Resistance

To bring simplicity to this discussion of abundance in Law of Attraction, we can look at our lives from the perspective of whether we are in a state of <u>Resistance</u> or <u>Allowing</u>:

- If we are in the ego, we have all kinds of fear and judgement about what is happening, so we <u>resist</u> what the world is serving up. We don't see our participation in attracting our circumstances so we feel like a victim, and we resist against it and try to control.

- If we are receiving, we are in the Heart's vibration; we are flowing with and <u>allowing</u> what comes through life. We receive what comes without judgement and stay in a positive place despite what we have attracted (because we attract everything that comes our way!).

Fear, Resistance and Control

Since we are creating from our base thoughts and vibrations, and most of our thoughts and vibrations arise from our negative subconscious, we are often creating from fear and resistance. Resistance is what keeps us from feeling good. It keeps us from getting what we want out of life. It keeps us from our alignment with our Soul. The opposite of resistance is allowing, which is smooth. It feels good. It accepts the present moment and keeps us flowing.

Here is a story about how resistance creeps up and wreaks havoc in our lives:

The two weeks leading up to our trip to California, my husband kept talking about his briefcase: *I've got to pack my briefcase* and *What's going to get packed in my briefcase?* and *Do you need to put that in my briefcase?* There was a lot of talk and worry about the briefcase. Now, he has this thing about being prepared, which is backed up with lots of fear and resistance around traveling. He packed his briefcase and planned all the additional things that were going to go in the briefcase. One very important thing going in the briefcase was the kids' DVD player (i.e., his computer), because he wanted to make sure that the kids were occupied on the plane—the last thing he wanted was to have three unhappy children on a plane for six hours (*note the fear and resistance*). He wanted to make sure he was prepared with his briefcase. He wanted to make sure that the kids weren't going to cause issues and disturb people on the plane (*more fear for future resistance*). Clearly, he had a need for preparedness leading up to the trip to San Diego, which was based on fear (*resistance*) of things failing, and a lot of control (*resistance*) around things going well to mitigate things going wrong.

Within the first few minutes of being at the airport, the briefcase, which was balancing on top of another suitcase, falls to the ground. Bang! Crash! My husband looks at me in complete fear. I didn't think twice about it because I had forgotten about all the hoopla about the briefcase and the computer. When we got on the plane, he got the computer out of the briefcase. Of course, the computer screen was broken. Now the briefcase has failed, the computer has failed, and two of the three the children don't have a video to watch on the plane. (*All of his imagined fears came to fruition, creating lots more resistance.*) Needless to say, the plane ride was a little bumpy for him.

But for me and *my* computer, and for the kids I was in charge of, things were going smoothly, which gave me the opportunity to watch his experience and all that manifested. I was able to watch the thread of **fear** that got the manifestation rolling. It all started two weeks before that, when he first became concerned about the briefcase and what the kids would do on the plane. Then I saw the **control** around the briefcase, which attempted to cover up the fear. The control was palpable and screamed **resistance**, so much so that I didn't want to hear any more about the briefcase or the kids or the plane so early before our trip!

We're all doing this. We all have these underlying fears that set our vibration. Early on, when we start obsessing about the briefcase two weeks prior, we can notice the resistance and step back with mindfulness to say: *Oh wow, look at me. I'm talking about this briefcase a lot. What's going on here? There's some nervous energy about the briefcase. What's going on with me and the briefcase? What's the underlying fear?* As we breathe in and we feel, we see, *Oh, I'm a little afraid. What am I afraid of? Oh, I'm afraid I'm not going to be able to fit everything with my computer. Okay. Then thinking about the kids on the plane, I'm pretty afraid of the kids not behaving themselves. What's that all about?*

Remember, we are always manifesting, whether we are doing it mindfully or not. This mindful, introspective line of thinking is what helps us unravel unintended negative manifestations. We can only access that if we come into the present moment and consciously breathe into it. Once we reconnect to our breath in the present moment, we can jump off the hamster wheel of the subconscious to investigate the way we're vibrating. That's how we bring these autopilot subconscious patterns and belief systems up into a place of consciousness.

When we start asking those questions and bringing that to consciousness, the fears begin to dissolve. Our fears have less influence over our vibration because we are mindfully handing the steering wheel from the ego to the Heart.

By allowing and accepting the presence of the negative vibrations, we automatically begin to release the resistance. The allowing of the NOW is the opposite vibration of resistance. **As soon as we bring awareness to the resistance, we change course into accepting and allowing.**

When I mentor people on their intentions, I hear their intentions, as well as the fear that is creating resistance and preventing them from attaining their intention. When we examine the subconscious fear with our conscious adult mind, we can unlock the fear that's keeping that intention in place and preventing us from attaining our intentions. The fear is loosened, and that intention becomes less restricted by the ego and more aligned with what the Heart is yearning for underneath that intention.

When we are first working with Law of Attraction, our intentions usually arise out of a sense of fear. For example, *I want to manifest a soulmate* may come from a fear of *I'm not worthy of love*. From the start, the intention has fear and resistance attached to it. For us to even have the urge to develop an intention, often there is something underneath that we're afraid of, something that has caused resistance for ourselves. When there's fear holding the intention in place, we will just keep manifesting from the negative vibration. We will get more of what we don't want. But the conscious observation of the fear behind the intention allows us to dissolve the negative vibration of fear, so that we can go forward with our intentions with an improved vibration, with a little less resistance for our intentions.

The Other Side of Resistance

As we cleanse our base vibration, learn to see our responsibility in everything, and find some consistent stillness in our lives, we start to watch how others' vibrational resistance begin to affect us. We start to see how their negative vibrations literally draw resistance out of us ... even if we started in a generally peaceful state!

Let me tell you a personal story. There is someone in my life who I care about very much, and I was feeling like I *should* feel more connected to that person, but I was feeling kind of repelled by them. I was feeling resistance, and I couldn't understand why, because intellectually we *should* have been getting along, and everything *should* have been great. I *should* have been able to feel tons of love and support toward this person. But I kept feeling repelled by them. After questioning it in my meditation, I had an interaction with the person where the person revealed to me how angry they were with me, how resentful they were, how my happiness triggered their misery, and how jealous they were. It was very honest and authentic of the person to share it with me. They said that there was nothing specific that I was doing toward them, nothing in our relationship that I could've changed. Me being me was triggering a lot of resistance and anger in them.

What I realized afterward was that my chest, my Heart, my vibration was picking up their resistance. When I felt repelled by them, I was feeling their resistance toward me. It didn't make sense to me (because not much does as an energetically sensitive person), but I feel others' vibrations, and I often cannot make sense of why it's happening or what the reason is. I don't get an intellectual description of it, but I am learning to trust the vibrations without overriding with my intellectual *shoulds*.

[Be careful in reading this ... because our ego's projections will want to blame others for our vibrations, and this is not what I'm describing here. In this example, I worked hard to take responsibility for MY resistance toward another person, but I could not find a seed of it being mine (and really, I searched). It is always tough to determine whose stuff is whose, but in some cases, we are picking up on others' resistance and making up a story based on our fears and projections.]

In that case, my mind thought I should work to create the ideal vision of the relationship, but my Heart was picking up their resistance. My Heart told me to back off for a while, to let the relationship air out. Even though it didn't make sense, I listened to what felt good, instead of what made the most sense. And later, I was given the explanation—because I had asked for the *reason* in my meditation. In this particular situation, because I asked, I was given the explanation and it allowed me to evaluate my experience. I had all of the shoulds for myself—*I should feel closer to this person. I should be pouring love on this person. I should*—but this person was in a place of resistance and anger and pushing away.

What a lesson for when I'm resisting! **If we want love but we're in a place of anger and resentment, we're literally energetically pushing people, opportunities and situations away.**

In that scenario, I could feel myself being pushed away, like a repelled magnet. No matter how much I wanted to go toward the person to give them love, there was a repelling energy, and I just couldn't breakthrough the barrier.

Here's another example: I was taking applications for a yoga teacher training that I was offering. An application came in via email from someone I hadn't known. As I looked at it, it looked good but I felt resistance. I set it aside for a while because I didn't know what to do with that feeling. The person followed up and seemed to be a fit so I told her that I'm happy to accept her into the program, but she needed to take three classes with me to make sure we were compatible (i.e., my voice didn't drive her crazy!) before finalizing. At this suggestion, she went straight to fear, inadequacy, and accusation of my not thinking she was good enough. *What?!?* I hadn't felt any of that! But SHE felt fear about applying, resistance in her application, and self-doubt in her yoga, and projected it all over me. (I didn't care what her yoga practice looked like.) This was such a great lesson to me about why it's important to have a solid vibration before you submit your resume, your match.com profile, or your application for anything! If there is resistance in your vibration, you can count on it having a negative effect on what you attract!

That's how it works. When we're in a place of negative emotion and resistance, we're pushing away all the things that we're longing for. Our vibration of negativity isn't allowing in any of the positivity we think we want. That's the Law of Attraction. By coming back to the breath in the Heart, we can witness our resistance, allow it ... and most often, it will dissipate. But if it doesn't dissipate, we can examine it and dig underneath to see where we're confused and misaligned.

If we can witness the resistance, we can move through it, but if we judge, deny, and resist our resistance, we fortify it.

Allowing

Remember that there are three steps: first we ask for what we desire, then Source organizes it and gets everything in place, and then **we allow it to happen by our connection to the Heart.**

Being in a state of **allowing** is our ideal state, and the default state of our Soul. It creates a ripe environment for manifesting our Soul's desires.

I happened to be in a nice place of allowing on that flight to San Diego. I was just watching the movie of my husband's resistance. I watched his behavior and felt his resistance pushing against the Now. I was in a place of allowing when my friend was repelling me through her resistance. That was how I could identify it as hers and allow her to move through it in the Light. I was in a place of allowance when the student submitted her application that was drenched in fear. That was how I could feel that something was out of alignment.

When we live from the Heart, we give others permission to do so as well. Residing in our Hearts sets the resonance of the relationship. If we are present and loving to ourselves as we struggle through our life, then we help provide the vibration for others to live that way as well. This allows their resistance to come up to be released.

In a state of allowing there is **no judgment**; good or bad, right or wrong, acceptable or unacceptable—everything just IS. It is what it is. And whatever it is ... is okay. We allow it. We examine it curiously. We breathe into it. We allow it to move through us, and are not scared or threatened ... because we are in the FLOW.

Flow

Working on developing a state of allowing, of ease, of being okay with how things are, will bring us into the flow. The flow is a place where synergies and pure God-cidences happen. When we're in the flow, we're allowing the Law of Attraction to work for us. We're filtering the world for how it's going to work out for us. We're seeing all the synchronicity that allows us to achieve absolutely everything we had intended, moment-to-moment.

If you've experienced this flow, you know that it's an extraordinary state. I've had the opportunity now to watch many people experiencing the flow. They set Heart-based intentions (that they're not attached to), and envision and feel them until they're vibrating with the intentions. Then there's the delightful surprise when that intention is delivered on a silver platter. It's like a little kid on Christmas: *Look at the gift I received!* Because they weren't trying to control or NEED it. They were delighted by the surprise of it. My teacher calls this "green Light city." It's when things start to flow your way and you enter into such ease and grace.

When we get into the flow, things align because we are aligned, and when we're aligned with our Heart we can see all the gifts the Universe is delivering to us based on our desires and what we've asked for. We ALLOW more to FLOW toward us!

Negative emotions will show us where we are resisting. Whenever we have a negative emotion, it means we're resisting the flow in that area, and need to shift back into the Heart for good things to happen.

The HOW Is Not Our Business

Often, when we are clarifying our desires, we will get stuck on the HOW. *But what position would include my passion AND my salary requirements? Where am I going to meet this amazing partner if I work sixty hours a week?* We may believe our intention is possible, but are unable to see how it will come to fruition. We paralyze ourselves in the intention-setting phase when we can't see the linear path. I have witnessed most of the people I mentor getting stuck in the HOW. In day-to-day life, if we set a goal, we need to chart the steps (HOW) to get there. That's not exactly how the Law of Attraction works. With Law of Attraction, we are acknowledging a higher Source, with many more resources and a much broader perspective, to help us along the way. This is where we must trust the *General Manager*.

General Manager

Let's say we have a General Manager that we have appointed and paid a $500,000/year salary to help us implement our desires. But if we're worrying about every little thing the manager does, and how they might be doing it, we're not using them to their full potential. In fact, we're trying to do their job for them. That's a bit of a waste, no? We're missing the opportunity to take advantage of this high-paid General Manager in our lives.

The Law of Attraction is the spiritual General Manager in life. When we have the thoughts, energetic momentum, and the positive vibration together, we put our order in for our General Manager to make it happen. We don't need to control *how* it happens. We don't need to know the mechanics of it. Our General Manager has so many networks and contacts and possibilities for how to execute our desires that we need not worry about it. **In fact, our General Manager can come up with scenarios that we never even dreamed of.**

Four years ago, I had a list (because I always have an ongoing list of things that I want to manifest in my life!): I wanted to *spiritually awaken as many people as possible in as little time as possible, with the most profound impact possible*. I also wanted to be *lean, strong and healthy*, because I'd had three babies and wanted my body to feel strong and vibrant.

As time went on, I felt myself being drawn to yoga teacher training. Now mind you, I had practiced yoga for about eight years, but only once a week, and I was a bit lazy. When I felt the draw to go to yoga teacher training, I was like, *I think I'm a little lazy for this, dear Universe! Are you sure?* But I kept feeling the draw. It felt like a magnetic pull in my chest, and because I knew this pull all too well, I signed up.

I went into the place of allowing (instead of resisting) this yoga teacher training, even though it wasn't the *how* that I anticipated. When I wrote the intentions, I pictured myself sitting in a room counseling clients. I didn't picture myself expending a lot of energy at the front of a yoga room and exercising five times a week! Even though it wasn't exactly the *how* that I was imagining, I allowed it and said yes, *Yes!* And I will tell you, yoga teacher training was very challenging for me. It was not what I expected when I asked the General Manager, *Can I please have a nice, positive impact on people?* I hadn't anticipated that would mean getting my butt kicked in yoga teacher training!

However, anyone who watched the following few years of my life would testify to the fact that becoming a yoga teacher was the most perfect expression of my desire. Even though it was a pretty obvious choice looking at it now, I never could have seen myself teaching yoga. What I wanted was to become a spiritual teacher to awaken people, and yoga happens to be a very mainstream spiritual practice, an ancient, effective, and well-studied mainstream spiritual practice. The way I teach yoga is a very physically rigorous practice, and so yes, it did allow me to have many people in the room so I could have the most impact possible through mind, body, and spirit … while keeping myself balanced, strong, and fit at the same time.

And almost two years after originally writing this book, after four years of being a yoga teacher, I can tell you that NOW I am doing spiritual counseling. Teaching yoga was the *how* that gave me a platform to build both this book, and the ability to find my voice as a spiritual counselor. It's phenomenal when we can see the path in hindsight, but it feels like we are groping around in the dark when we are in the microcosm of it all!

Brilliant, absolutely brilliant. Our Divine Source General Manager is brilliant. We don't need to control the *how*. We just need to allow and say *Yes!* when the opportunity knocks on our door. If we're connected enough, we can go into our vibration and say, *Is this really it? Is this what I asked for?* And if it feels good, then we say yes, and we allow, and we ask for whatever we need to move forward with what our General Manager has served up. Sometimes we must create a sub-intention to request guidance, strength, and support to follow through on our General Manager's delivery of opportunities—but it's always worth it!

When we ask our General Manager to manifest our intention, we don't know exactly what it will look like or how it will be brought about. What we *do* know is that what we've asked for will, without doubt, be brought about—so long as we continue to align our vibration to the desire. That can't be stated enough.

Trust the General Manager

We need to be careful not to micromanage our General Manager or the *how* of our desire. That micromanagement comes from a place of fear and low vibration. If we find ourselves attaching or needing or really wanting that desire, then we are not in the vibration of *allowing* the desire. *Needing* our intention suggests we are resisting the present moment. If we feel desperate, and in a place of lack and scarcity, we will stay in the vibration of lack and scarcity. If we feel like we really *need* this desire, and that we won't be okay without the desire, we will stay in the vibration of *need*.

We must keep our focus on the fulfilled vibration of the manifested desire while still being 100% perfectly happy and content in the present state. We need to keep our vibration high, content, happy, and in the place of love while we are anxiously awaiting our desire to manifest.

We must be maintaining the vibration of the manifested state, while being content <u>without</u> the intention being manifested. *Kinda tricky, eh?* Many Eastern traditions would see this as a practice of non-attachment or detachment—being happy in the present moment and not needing anything to change. As long as we maintain the vibration of the fear of not having something, we will continue <u>not</u> to have it. We are working toward mastering present moment contentment while still working our vibration toward a future state.

When we submit our desires vibrationally to the Universe, we're putting our order in with the General Manager, who is anxious to give us the actualized desires. The Universe is waiting to deliver to us. We just need to align. That's it. That's our only job.

In Summary...

It is our birthright to create and manifest our desires. We were born to expand, and the Universe is here to work *with* us. Our imagination facilitates this expansion because it moves us past the current conditions, and breaks our thoughts and vibrations into new territory. It allows us to attract new situations by building new thought and vibration matrices filled with possibility and potential.

With new thoughts and vibrations, our job is to work through resistance toward a place of allowing and receiving. Working ourselves into the vibration of the flow creates a ripe environment for our desires. When we are in the flow, we can hand the *how* over to the General Manger, and trust that the Universe can develop scenarios we can't even imagine!

Recorded Meditation Practice: Allowing

You can access a guided meditation to help you get to a place of allowing at: www.enLIGHTenWithKim.com. Click on **Community Resources** and **Book Meditations**, log in for free, and find the meditation called #**3 Allowing Meditation.**

Personal Meditation Practice: Law of Attraction Resistance

Throughout your day, you can bring up thoughts and visualizations around your intention. Simply daydream about your intention. Think like you would if you ALREADY had your intention in your life. Feel the emotions you would feel if the intention had ALREADY come to fruition. Dive into your thoughts, feelings, and energies of what it's like to have this intention in your present-day life. **You are trying it on as if it already exists, like you are importing the future manifestation, creating the vibration now, and then releasing it back to the future**. And in the process of creating the manifested vibration, you have attracted it to yourself.

Build onto your meditation from Chapter 1, by adding the connection to your Heart, breaking down your fear and resistance, and finding your flow.

1. Breathe into your Heart and connect to yourself. Now, imagine your intention having just occurred. (For example, you found the love of your life, OR you landed the perfect job, OR you found true joy within.) Play out the scenario visually. Watch what happens. Have the thoughts. Feel the positive emotions associated with it having happened. Let the movie roll. Allow yourself to feel like it occurred and sit in those vibrations for as long as you can.

2. Identify where your fear and resistance is around your intention. Where do you get stuck? In the possibility? In the control of the <u>how</u>? In your unworthiness? In staying focused? Simply sit with your resistance until it begins to dissolve. I assure you, it will!

3. After you have explored the resistance, see if your intention feels better. Work yourself back into the vibration of the desire. (If your resistance remains, set an intention for the resistance to release, and let it go for now.)

4. Give gratitude and bask in that high vibration.

Navigate the Negative Waves

In a dark time, the eye begins to see.
-Theodore Roethke

Let's face it. Life doesn't always feel good. You may get thrown a curveball, or the people around you start causing chaos. You want to stay in a positive vibration, focused on your intention, but sometimes it feels impossible.

Often, books and guidance on Law of Attraction will urge you to simply stay in the positive vibration no matter what. But I find that forcing yourself to stay positive when you can't get yourself out of negativity just creates more resistance to reality. In my experience, there is another way ... a way that honors where you are at, and helps you find an easier path toward feeling good.

- If we change the way we view life's curveballs, then we can lessen our resistance to them.

- If we learn to work with the negative vibrations, then we can transform them to feed positive desire.

- If we take full responsibility for our negative feelings, then we can change our outer circumstances.

Contrast and Desires

Have you ever noticed how life is just a series of challenges that we're continuously working through or overcoming? That every time we turn around, there's something else presenting us with an opportunity for challenge? Well, what if we started looking at these challenges differently?

The Universe throws us challenges that seem to be in contrast to what we want or expected in order to be happy. But the term *challenges* has *resistance* built into it. It sounds like it's hard work or difficult for us to have to endure. *Struggle* is inherent. **Instead, we can view these life challenges as CONMTRAST**[2]. If we consider it contrast, it feels less burdensome, less resistant. We are getting contrast to what we thought was going to happen or what we wanted. We just see the contrast as that: contrast to what feels good.

The contrast comes into our lives at various points, to teach us something. The lessons vary, but **the wisdom in the contrast is to provide us with the opportunity to see that which we DON'T want in our lives**. We get contrast along with a corresponding negative emotion, which serves as an indicator that we need to pay attention. Then we have the opportunity to focus on the contrast situation and figure out why we're having a negative emotion. Perhaps the lesson of the contrast is:

- To show us how we are vibrating and what we are attracting;
- To help us learn a lesson because we haven't been paying attention to a pattern in our lives;
- To bring more acceptance to a reality that we have been resisting;
- To help us clear negativity that we've been carrying.

Contrast shows up to help us focus inward and gain clarity. It appears so we can achieve better alignment with our Heart.

The problem is that we get stuck focusing on the contrast, and the people or situations involved. **We resist against the contrast and lose focus on the intention**, the inward lesson, and the future manifestation.

Most of us have spent lifetimes focused on contrast that we don't want. We look at it, we write emails about it, we have

---

[2] Gratitude to Abraham and Esther Hicks for this profound perspective on Contrast and Desires!

tea and coffee with our friends, and belabor over that which we don't want. Right? We're all doing it! It's human nature to focus on the things that are showing up in our lives, and suffer over them or complain about them. The problem is that we get focused on that which we *don't* want. We spend a lot of time and a lot of energy with our minds circling around that which we *don't* want. So, what do we create as a result of focusing on the contrast? That's right, more of what we *don't* want.

If we focus on the contrast, and the external circumstances involved in the contrast, then we miss the opportunity to align with our Heart. We lose our potency.

Contrast Brings Clarity of Desire

The purpose of the contrast in our lives is to give us clarity on what we *don't* want, so that we can shift our attention, and therefore our intentions, toward that which we *do* want. With the clarity comes the drive, fire, and desire to build what we do want. That desire catapults energy—as Abraham-Hicks calls it, **rockets of desire**—toward the intention of what we want. The contrast gives us clarity, drive, and momentum toward what we want in life. The contrast gives us some excitement and fire toward our intention.

Now, many people will spend decades railing against the contrast, and vibrating lower and lower until they're creating more and more contrast in their lives. We don't have to beat ourselves down with the contrast. We just have to see it for what it is, and instead of continuing to focus on it, be grateful for it, and use the momentum to provide clarity of what we desire.

We need to shift our focus AWAY from the contrast and toward the desire born out of the contrast. If we stay in the energy of the contrast, then we have fear and suffering and negativity and we stay in that low vibration, and get more of it from the Universe!

Once we get clarity and define our desire, our energy shifts into anticipating desire. This is *not* an attached expectation. The Heart-based momentum of desire has a positive high vibration, with excitement and anticipation. The energy of the desire does *not* contain fear, attachment, or need—those are all low vibrations connected to expectations. The energy of the desire is pure, Light, and high vibrational, because we live in the present moment and realize that life is perfect with *or without* the desire (allowing!).

Vortex of Desire

Once we can ride that high vibration of desire, we are thrown back into the flow, or as Abraham-Hicks calls it, the Vortex of Desire. Here, the energy shifts from negative focus on contrast to excited energy toward our desire. The alignment of our energy with our desire brings us into a higher vibration. With that momentum, we can reach for a thought that vibrates more positively than the thought we had a moment ago. We can reach for the next level of vibration so that we can work our way up the vibrational ladder. We work the ladder of vibration to the highest rung possible so we can vibrate at the level of our desire.

Now, imagine a vortex of possibility around us. Everything that we desire has the potential to be fulfilled in our vortex, *from* our vortex. As Abraham-Hicks says, **we would not be able to come up with the concept of the desire if we didn't have the potential for the desire to be fulfilled by our energy vortex.** We cannot come up with a desire that cannot be fulfilled, whose potential doesn't exist within us. Isn't that amazing? Our Higher Consciousness has complete access and ability to create anything we can dream up. Our job is to develop our desires and clean up the fear and low vibration that keeps us from manifesting.

The key is to take the focus off the contrast, off the challenges, out of the negative vibration, and shift it into the desire. **Transmute all that contrast momentum into the vibration of the desire**. We can trust that the potential of fulfilling that desire is completely at our fingertips. The only thing we are missing is the vibration that matches our desire.

If we are starting from the vibration of the contrast, we might not be able to immediately shift into the vibration of love and manifestation. However, if aligning our vibration to our desires *becomes* our desire, we can ratchet up our vibration within 24 hours!

Shift from Contrast Vibration to Desire Vibration

Bringing our intention to conscious awareness makes that shift possible. This can be a very quick process if we apply the following steps with conscious awareness.

1. First, we need to **believe that our desire is POSSIBLE**. If we don't believe it's possible, we shut ourselves off from the vibration of our desire.

2. Second, we need to **release focus from the contrast** so we can release the negative vibration of the contrast.

3. Third, we need to **re-focus our thoughts on the positive direction of the desire** so we can vibrationally adjust to how the desire feels. Even though it's still in the state of potential and we haven't fulfilled the desire, we should be able to imagine that it will feel good when we do. (If it doesn't feel good, there is either a fear underneath, OR the desire is not aligned with our Heart.)

Let's play with how this looks in real life, because it takes mindful awareness to implement. Here's an example that happened to me:

Someone told me I did a bad job on a meditation recording. This felt like contrast because I had assumed that I was doing well with what I was doing. I've got a deep confusion about myself based in my subconscious—a fear that I'm not a good person (we will explore these deep confusions later)—so the feedback immediately triggered my subconscious recurring fear. As this person brought this contrast up to me, I saw myself first going to the vibration of *I'm a bad person, I've done something wrong*.

Through my daily reflection, I breathed, checked in with my vibration, felt the negative emotion, and then looked further into what was going on. *Okay, this is just contrast. Let's hear what this person is saying. Let's see what the Universe is presenting to me so that I can take this contrast as a lesson and a seed for a new desire.*

If I was in a place of *resistance*, I wouldn't have been able to evaluate my behavior or the situation. I would've gone straight to judgment and negative vibration, and stayed in the subconscious pattern of my hamster wheel. But I was in a place of *allowing*, and open to the Universe showing me a lesson, so I was willing to evaluate.

First, the person was showing me where I wasn't aligned, because I had a negative emotional reaction and reacted with my *I'm a bad person* issues. That gave me an opportunity to see those deep fears from a new perspective. I sat with them and examined them with my conscious adult mind. From the present moment, I could see that *I was a good person, I was safe, the feedback was not invalidating who I was*. I felt the vibration of that reality and let that positive vibration sink deeply into my body, to remove another layer of that subconscious onion. Once I examined the feedback with my present moment adult brain, I let the contrast help me develop desires for feeling good and whole, for releasing those old subconscious fears about being a bad person, for feeling my inherent goodness forever. I moved even deeper into these positive vibrations of my *good*ness.

Second, this contrast required me to evaluate for myself whether it was a valuable recording. As I evaluated my work, I acknowledged her opinion, however I felt that the recording was in alignment. That person brought up the question to encourage me to feel even more secure in my alignment with my work. The contrast gave me the opportunity to feel good about my work, while still honoring her opinion from a different perspective.

Third, I used her feedback to inform my future recordings to make sure they met the wide range of needs of all listeners, including her opinions. While I didn't agree with her judgement of my performance, I was still able to hear her needs.

From each perspective, the contrast brought me into better alignment with myself and my work.

Because I was in an open place of allowing, I was able to acknowledge the contrast bringing up the *I'm a bad person* thing, so I was able to look at it and set a desire to further release my fears. It brought up the areas where I was in alignment and doing good work. I wanted to do more of that good work, and so it allowed me to go further into the desire of doing more good work. The contrast brought me back into my truth, and it shifted my desires into further alignment for my vibrational potential.

I could get these lessons as long as I wasn't resisting or judging. If I was resisting, I would've flung the contrast back at the person, because that's what we do. If we're judgmental of ourselves or of other people, when someone brings contrast to us, we'll just whack it right back at them—we won't actually look at it. If this situation arose ten years ago, my ego would've had a ball resisting the contrast, making up all kinds of garbage: *How could she say that? What is she thinking? What's wrong with her? How dare she question me! Where does she even come off doing that? You know, I don't even think anyone respects what she's doing* ... and so the negative spiral goes.

Had I gone into the judgment, had I gone deep into the contrast and the negative vibration of the contrast, I could've just sank in there with weeks of obsession and conversation about this person and how wrong they were. I could've made a career out of it. I could've sucked up so much of my energy to make her wrong and bad and completely invalidated. I would've had to make up a lot from my ego to be able to do that.

However, the contrast is coming into our lives so we can learn something about ourselves, get clarity about what we don't want, and then get clarity about what we *do* want. That is what we have control over. We cannot control what people say and what type of contrast comes into our lives. We can control how much we focus on that negative vibration versus our positive Heart-based desire vibration. Another example from the perspective of children is this:

When my daughters were ages 6, 8, and 10, they enjoyed playing with our 5-year-old neighbor, Michael. All three girls loved to play with Michael, and my husband and I got along well with his parents. They would wake up each weekend morning and head straight over to play for hours. One day, a new family moved in across the street with their 5-year-old son, Johnny. We welcomed the new family and all three families got together for dinner. A week after the new neighbors moved in, the girls went over to play with their good friend Michael, but he was off playing with the new boy, Johnny. Michael was not so interested in playing with the older girls with a new 5-year-old boy across the street. The girls were crushed (*contrast*), and their negative reactions varied with ego stories ranging from blaming me for not doing something, to blaming the new boy for "stealing" their friend, to worry that they'd "lost" their friend. Their emotions ran the gamut, but focused mainly in judgment and blame, which was covering up their sadness.

So we examined their negative emotion of sadness (*underneath their anger and ego's blame*), and they sat and felt it for an hour, without a plan to change their contrast externally. They sat with the sadness around the fact that they didn't have their friend all to themselves anymore, and that he may prefer to play with someone else. Once they truly *felt* their sadness, it dissipated. They then played for an hour with each other (*shifting the negative emotion of the contrast to positive playfulness*). And later, they were able to focus on the appreciation of their sisterhood (*the lesson from the contrast*). They found themselves with acceptance of the new boy, a new-found appreciation for when they get a chance to play with their old friend Michael, and a recognition that in a family of three sisters, there is always someone to play with.

The critical step for my daughters was to authentically feel their negative emotion, their sadness in the presence of the contrast. Feeling the sadness allowed it to air out. Once it aired out, they could focus on playing together, which shifted the momentum into feeling good. (Kids do this so easily because they don't get stuck on the contrast as adults do!) Then they processed their lesson and moved on. Amazing, really.

Contrast Creates Expansion

Many of us spend a lot of time wishing that we didn't have contrast in our lives. We want things to go smoothly and perfectly all the time, but that's not how life works. We are part of an expanding Universe, and are meant to continue expanding. The way that we continue to expand is by experiencing variety and contrast in our lives. That is what gives us passionate desire for things to be different. It is how we become creative manifestors of our own desire. The contrast is our tool for getting clarity for desire so we can re-shift our focus into our desire. It is a gift from the Universe to help us uniquely align with our Soul. The feedback about my work gave me the chance to see the *I'm not a good person* belief living inside of me. The new neighbor gave my daughters a chance to deeply appreciate their sisterhood of built-in friendship.

Imagine for a moment a life without contrast, without variety. Everyone would just be doing the same thing every day, everything being easy, predictable, and comfortable. But there's not a lot of growth in that. There's not a lot of expansion. The contrast gives us variety and expansion.

What if we simply saw contrast as the mechanism to fuel desire? As the means through which we gain clarity and growth? We don't need to suffer about it. We don't need to get our vibrations caught up in it. We don't need to spend a lot of time and energy there. We just need to use it to feel where our vibration is at that moment, and then define and fuel our desires. Contrast gives us clarity, which gives us focus for our desire.

Contrast and Desires in Relationships

The concepts of contrast and desire seem straight-forward—my car starts to break down (*contrast*) so I set forward the intention for a new car (*desire*)! But applying it to relationships can present some complexity. In relationships, we are dealing with someone outside of ourselves, and their intentions, ego, and free will. If I have contrast in a relationship, creating a desire for change requires the ability to attract something new from the relationship.

If something is not working for me in my marriage, I can spend a lot of time focusing on the thing that's not working—*how my husband is not doing what I want him to do*, and *this will never align* and *I will never get what I want out of my marriage*—which would create lots of negative vibration momentum around the contrast. Typically, we focus on the contrast so much that we don't even turn our heads toward the other side of desire. We try to control the person and make them different, and we put all this energy on the contrast, when in reality, all we have to do is shift the perspective over to the desire.

We must clearly define the desire for our relationships without fear, without worry that it's not going to happen. We must believe it's *possible*. All we need to do is align a positive vibration to our desire. How does that look in a relationship?

1. I **develop awareness** that I'm focusing on the contrast and feeling negative emotion. That brings me into a state of awareness.

2. I **feel the negative vibration** around the contrast—sadness or disappointment covered up by anger and resentment. Feeling it deeply begins to release the resistance.

3. I **identify my desire** to be more connected with positive interactions and lots of love.

4. I work myself into recognizing that **my desire is** *possible*, because it may feel impossible from my current vibration.

5. I completely **accept the present moment and circumstances** and release the need and expectations for things to be different. Release more resistance.

6. I **visualize and vibrate the manifested state of that desire** without attachment. I watch it play out and begin to feel the positivity I could feel with my husband. Feeling the manifested state of the desire allows me to hold that vibration, which puts me into a state of allowing, which attracts the situation to me by bringing out those qualities in the people around me.

7. I **observe what the Universe vibrates back** and let myself feel through until I'm in a place of allowing again. Maybe I get lessons about my responsibility for the issue in the relationship. Maybe I let the relationship air out until the negative momentum peters out.

In this example, it's possible that the other person isn't able to vibrate with me because they are in their own resistance. I can hold space and stay in my Heart to allow the person more time to vibrate at the place of love. Or maybe I notice that new friendships are beginning in my life which can vibrate in this new place of love. Or maybe, I attract a new situation. Either way, because I'm in my positive vortex, what happens is less relevant because I'm holding the feeling of love so the external circumstances become less critical. When this happens, choosing what to do with the relationship feels more like choosing between *chocolate* and *vanilla*, whereas before, the relationship changing felt like *life* or *death*.

Once we start vibrating in alignment with our Heart, we raise the vibration of our relationships. Once we set our vibration to our desire, and ratchet up our vibration, **our relationships have no choice but to shift**. The people around us begin to shift, our situations begin to shift. With a higher vibration, our relationships cannot operate the way they did in the lower vibration. It's impossible, because we're not vibrating the way we were before.

That's not to say that our partner will become a different person; it's just that we will be attracting a vibration closer to the vibration we are feeling. We will be vibrating at a higher level, and when we vibrate more positively and have a more positive outlook and start setting up some nice, positive desires, it becomes less likely for us to continue to have the same issues and the same negativity around us.

When I'm finding contrast in my marriage and I'm seeing behaviors that I don't like, I realize that I must be vibrating in a way that attracts those qualities. If I can stop focusing on the negative qualities and stop vibrating with those negative attributes, and shift my focus to the desire, which is to have a better Heart connection, feel more connected, feel more joyful, and share more positive values together … it is impossible for me to stay in the negative contrast. I am attracting positivity, love, and higher vibration to myself.

My husband and I used to have unconscious suffering competitions when we first had kids. I would feel depleted and *taken advantage of* like I was *giving too much*. And he would feel the same from his perspective. Knowing about abundance, Law of Attraction and how I was feeding this negative pattern, one day I started to shift my desires, thoughts and feelings around my suffering. I built some gratitude that I had children, chose to mindfully relax and sit on the couch when I needed it, celebrated when I had enough energy to clean up, and shifted my overall vibration about my responsibilities. I slowly started to feel less suffer-y. Then, when my husband would suffer, because I wasn't vibrating in suffering, I would offer to help him or suggest that he go out with friends and take a night off. He started to see the difference in our vibrations, and couldn't help but notice all his suffering. Without the suffering competition, he could hear the weight of his suffering, and soon he began to vibrate to the tune of abundance and self-care too! My vibrational awareness eventually shifted our dynamic.

Interestingly, my shift out of suffering wasn't intended to get him to change. I was just looking for a more joyful experience of life. But the perk was that, instead of focusing on *changing him* and his suffering so he didn't annoy me, I let the contrast of his reflection inspire my desire to shift out of suffering, which eventually changed the dynamic of our relationship.

We Are All Just Playing Parts for Each Other

When we see contrast playing out in our relationships, we tend to go into separation from the other person and lose sight of the lessons we can be receiving about ourselves and the deeper purpose of our relationships.

Neil Donald Walsh wrote a children's book called *The Little Soul and the Sun*. In this book, he tells a story about little Souls up in heaven, and how deLightful it was there, but that there was no dark, and no contrast to all of the Light. So a Little Soul was burning with desire to go down to Earth to take a body, so it could learn the lesson of *forgiveness* in this next lifetime.

God granted the Little Soul the opportunity to go down to Earth. The Little Soul asked who was going to help him in this process of learning forgiveness, and God told him to take a look around at all of the other Souls and ask who was willing to go play the role of the person the Little Soul could forgive. Out came another Soul to assist, and it was actually a friend who had been with the Little Soul for many, many lifetimes on Earth.

The little Soul said warmly to the other Soul, *You'd do that for me? You would lower your vibration so much that you would come down to Earth and be so dark for me?* The other Soul said, *Yes, of course I'd do that for you, but you just have to promise me one thing. When I'm dark and my vibration is really, really low, you have to promise me that you won't forget who I am. You won't forget that I'm this Soul up here with you.* The little Soul said, *Of course I wouldn't forget you. How could I forget you? You're so bright and you're so lovely.* The other Soul said, *When we get into the thick of it and things get really low vibrational, you may even forget who YOU are.* The little Soul said, *No way. I could never forget who I am.* God intervened and talked about how when we lower our vibrations and come to Earth, and start to experience the contrast of Light and dark, some people get lost and forget who they really are.

What if all the people who deliver your contrast are your allies, trying to help you find your way? What if the "pain-in-the-ass" was just there to help you find your Soul? **The people who are providing the most contrast in our lives are in fact our biggest allies in our quest to find out who we really are.**

Our enemies are our Master Teachers. If we didn't have the contrast that our nemesis provides for us, we wouldn't feel the negative emotions that give us momentum to launch those rockets of desire. We wouldn't desire so much and so deeply for something to be different. We wouldn't have the ability to fully expand. These Master Teachers, these people in our lives who bring us the most contrast, are just helping us clarify for ourselves who we are and who we want to be, or better yet, where we want our *vibration* to be.

Personally, I grew up with a very dysfunctional family, and the way I was brought up didn't set me up to be successful in society. The way we thought about things was not aligned with the Heart, so just about everything included in my upbringing felt really bad. For many years, I felt like a victim of that dysfunctional childhood, and was jealous of those with *good* childhoods because I thought that they had everything put together for them on a platter, and that they felt good. (Later, I discovered that wasn't true at all since they have their own set of subconscious programs.)

In the last ten years, however, I started to see the golden nugget in my childhood. I began to see that every single thing I was taught had to be reevaluated through the practice of mindfulness. Everything that brought a negative emotion up for me showed me an area that needed to be reevaluated to attain alignment and happiness. If I was bumping my head up against the wall in a certain aspect of my relationships, I had to define who I was and how I wanted my relationships to be, and create that vibration. Since I started living on my own at the age of 16,

I've had to put life together in a way that felt good, because not much from childhood did. Really, I had nothing to lose because life was pretty uncomfortable where I started out.

For my path and my Soul's purpose on this earth, that was the perfect childhood for me. Those were the perfect parents for me. All of the contrast that I experienced allowed me to define how I wanted life.

Those heavier or lower vibrational relationships are in fact our gifts. They help us define and clarify our desires for how we want our relationships to be, and how we want our life to work. **Our contrast is our gift.**

Allowing the Wisdom of Negative Vibrations

I love doing Law of Attraction work with people because I get to watch the process of them coming alive, coming into themselves, awakening into their potency. That said, this path is not about feeling *only* the positive. Sometimes on our path, we have to feel through the darker, deeper, lower vibrations that exist in our body to clear them away and feel the highest part of our being. When we start to see challenges in our lives simply as contrast, that helps us to define clarity of desires, and then the contrast doesn't have as much potency. We just see it for what it is. It's not personal. It's just contrast. *Contrast is here to show me what I want. What do I want? Let me go after that.*

For some of us, negativity is a well-worn pathway. Vibrationally, it's familiar, so it feels good, or at least normal. Chances are, we programed that stuff in when we were 5 years old, and we've deepened the grooves of that pathway for many years. But the truest part of ourselves knows that while the external focus and negative grooves may be familiar to us, they're not truly comfortable and in alignment with our Heart. It doesn't feel good to stay in the negativity, though that's where we've been from a very young age. It does feel good to align with the Heart and follow what our Soul desires.

But how do we even know what our Soul desires? How do we even know the way to feeling better? Most of us are so stuck in negative vibrations that we don't know which path will take us toward the Light. We can't see that little gleaming Light pinging through the bottom of the door. We don't know where it is. The good news is that our **emotional guidance system** has been installed in each of our bodies to guide us toward that Light. Our emotions are our indicators for whether we are aligned with our Heart and Soul. Positive emotions mean we are in alignment, while negative emotions mean that we are not. *Pretty simple, right?* For the longest time, it's been a hindrance, having to feel all these negative emotions. *Oh, I don't know what that bad feeling is about. Just push it down and ignore it. Let's just have a bowl of cereal and not focus on that vibration. That doesn't feel very good. Maybe we'll go for a couple glasses of wine because we've got a vibration going and don't like it very much. Maybe a little anger and yelling will feel better.*

We've been ignoring the underlying negative emotions and vibrations, stuffing them down, pushing them away, because we haven't known what to do with them. We begin to grow numb to our emotions because we've gotten so far away from ourselves that we don't even know how to get back. In most cases, we have journeyed straight up into the head and cut ourselves off from <u>all</u> feeling because much of life feels bad, and we don't know why. We stay in our head and let our ego make up all kinds of stories about how the bad feeling was caused by something or someone else. Life is triggering all the subconscious programming and vibrations from when we were 5 years old, and then our ego puts a big fat story around the negative vibration and emotions. **The ego says the external triggers are to blame for the bad feeling in our bodies.** Our mother is to blame. The boss. The kids. The messy house. The uncooperative spouse. The subconscious mind wants to project negativity on those around us. Our negative vibrations don't feel good, so we automatically make it about *anyone but us*! But it's always about us, our own vibrations, and what we've attracted. Always.

Our Soul is screaming at us through our emotions! We've been ignoring the red flags that are waving through our bodies because we didn't know that the negative emotions were warning us that we'd veered from the truest part of who we are! We have veered from our joy.

Oh my gosh, I'm trapped the ego's hamster wheel! How do I get off? I'll tell you, the very simple way to start aligning is to **do what feels good**. This internal emotional guidance system that you've been railing up against your whole life has just been screaming to tell you, *Do what feels good! Do what feels right! Do what nourishes you!* But that goes against absolutely everything we've learned growing up. *Taking the path of least resistance is the <u>lazy</u> way. It's the <u>irresponsible</u> way. Going with what feels good means that we'd just be eating and having sex and drinking all day. That can't be right!* The path of least resistance is different for everyone, but it's the way back to learning what your Soul yearns for. If we listen to ourselves, and do what feels good in every moment, we will find ourselves in a very joyful place.

Many of us fear that feeling good and following the path of least resistance will just take us into an even worse scenario. This is because we have been driven by the ego. **What feels good to the ego is artificially covering up the bad feelings and numbing the body—anger, eating unhealthy, alcohol, overindulgence, unhealthy relationships, working too much— behaviors that create temporary good feelings, to override the underlying bad feelings.** The ego works on making the self feel good by dealing with the effect. *I had a bad day, so I will numb it out with food. My marriage is falling apart, so I will have an affair. I feel powerless when my kids don't listen to me, so I will punish them to feel better.* Feeling good from the place of the ego creates more problems: *too much food=excess weight gain, affair=relationship problems, extra punishing for kids=damaging trust.* The ego's desire to cover up the issue always results in more issues.

Our society has told us we need to be a *good* person, stay productive, be of value to others, and show results for who we are and what we're doing. We need to be focused on what we've committed to do. Doing, producing results, and looking good are the most important things in our society, but that isn't always aligned with what the Soul is yearning for, and therefore it may not feel good.

Society says:	Soul says:
Work hard to prove your value. As long as you prove you are busy and producing results, you are valuable. (Suffering)	You are valuable. Trust that and find stillness. You don't have to prove your value. Your pure life is valuable.
Put others before yourself. Sacrifice yourself for your relationships/family. (Depletion)	You have permission to take care of yourself. Once you are nourished, you can give from the overflow.
Doing/working overrides personal needs. (Self is not important)	You don't HAVE TO do anything! Everything is okay exactly how it is. Just breathe and take good care of yourself! Work comes after.
If you look like what society says is beautiful, then you are worthy. (Beauty and worth is external)	You are beautiful and perfectly imperfect. Your worth is inherent.
If you are a good [insert role: parent/employee/spouse], then you are a good person.	Your goodness is inherent. You are already a "good person." You are pure light and love and goodness. Your goodness has nothing to do with what you do.

Do you see how society's expectations are steering us away from the truth of who we are? Society puts our value outside of ourselves, which feels terrible.

Going with what feels good is how we go toward what would nourish us, and is the most responsible thing when it comes to aligning with ourselves. Feeling good exists in our body, not our ego's override of what's going on inside of us.

But we haven't been taught how to stay connected with ourselves. Our society's view of "the right way to be" never factored in listening to ourselves, listening to our vibrations, listening to our bodies, and acting on that natural instinct. We lost our natural instinct to listen from within. And we've gauged ourselves on a set of external *shoulds*. We need to reconnect with how we feel, and remember how to follow inner wisdom toward feeling better. The ego is just trying to make things logical, but in doing so, we've lost connection to what FEELS GOOD and TRUE within. This leads us to a life drenched in negative vibration.

Feeling Our Way THROUGH the Negative Vibration

The most common thing I hear from people is: *I'm in a negative vibration and I'm really unhappy about it and I feel stuck. What is the quickest way OUT!?!*

We resist our negative vibrations. Why resist? The vibrations are just trying to tell us something. What if we just listen to them? What are they trying to tell us? It's like the Universe is trying to speak to us. It threw a little roadblock in front of us because there's something we need to pay attention to. Once we pay attention to it, it releases, and then the negative vibration and contrast have less power over us.

There's a lesson from the Universe underneath the negative vibration. We must allow the negative vibration and listen to the lesson so the contrast doesn't get louder or harder. If we hear the whispers, we won't need to get slapped upside the head! The Universe is talking to us through the contrast, but most of us feel so uncomfortable when we're in the negative vibration that we never get the opportunity to hear the lesson. It's good that we're wired to want to feel better, but if we find ourselves in the negative vibration, we might as well listen!

I find that most people I mentor need *permission* to dip into those lower negative vibrations. We have developed such a pattern in our society to feel a low vibration or a negative emotion and immediately resist it, judge it, judge ourselves, and think it's ridiculous that we're in this low vibration because *we should be elsewhere*. But when we allow it and say, *Oh, this is here for a reason—what's the reason?* and we question it, we can go into a vibration of allowing. With time, it feels better when you just allow that negative vibration to exist so you can listen to it.

Listen to the negative vibration and ask: *Can I accept the fact that I'm in the negative vibration? Let me feel what this feels like. What's underneath here? What's going on, self? What doesn't feel good, dear? Tell me. Oh, okay, I hear you. Let me feel that pain.*

It may sound corny, but if we have a negative vibration and we're railing up against a lot of contrast, all we need to do is come back to ourselves, listen, breathe, hear the lesson, listen for the truth, and move on into the higher vibration. But, most of the time, we're plugging our ears, screaming, *La la la la la, I don't like the way this feels. Take it away. Get it away from me. I don't want it here. La la la la la.* Fifteen years later, it's still *la la la la la la la! I don't want to hear it.* Right? How are we moving forward if that's what we're doing?

Just sit in the negative vibration for ten minutes. It'll go away. The negative vibration is just there to teach you something. How are you not aligned with your Soul? What's the lesson? And once the negative vibration wanes, what rocket of desire can you shoot off, focus on, and feel good about because of the lesson that's coming in right now? I'm going to give you a very practical example of how this looks for me:

During a meditation series I was holding for students, I was doing something that I'd never done before. I didn't have a live audience and I was sending out recordings. This was new for me. As I stepped back after the first few recordings, I thought, *Hmm, the recordings aren't as exciting and inspiring as I thought they were going to be, and it's actually kind of bleh.* I was bummed about it not being what I had imagined it to be. Then I talked to a friend who was doing my program. She said, *Yeah, it's really not as inspiring as your live meditation programs.* I thought, *Ugh, damn, there it is. It's confirmed.* Here I was pouring myself into something that I cared so deeply about and I wasn't getting the results I wanted. Contrast. Confirmed contrast.

The first vibration I went into was feeling sorry for myself. *Oh, woe is me. I committed to this and I'm not doing as well as I wanted to. Wah, wah, wah.* Negative emotion, negative vibration. This was my ego's attempt to comfort me through the suffering. It was an override that temporarily felt good, because the suffering was an old pattern of self-comforting. I sat in that vibration for a while until it didn't feel good anymore.

When the suffering stopped feeling good, I went for the next higher vibration provided from my ego—justification. *Well, I'm doing mentoring this time and the mentoring is going really well, and so even though the recordings aren't as exciting as I wanted them to be, the mentoring is going well. It's not like people aren't getting their money's worth, because they're really paying for the mentoring. So it's okay that the recordings suck.* I went to this big story and I tied a nice red bow around it. It sounded good, and it felt good for about five minutes. I mean it sounded like I could buy it and I could accept. But I didn't.

Next stop on the vibrational train was self-acceptance. That felt better than ego suffering and justification. It was a step up on the ladder toward compassion, so it was more Heart-based, *Okay, it's not as great as I thought it was going to be, but it's good and that's good and I accept myself. I'm doing the best I can, and that's good.* Now I was able to glean some insight about why they weren't as good: *Actually, I'm feeling pulled in many directions. I need a little bit more self-care and I need a little bit more childcare to do things with more passion and inspiration.* So, some desire (more childcare and time in nature) came from the Heart-based compassionate vibration.

For some people, it would be an improvement to just hang in self-compassion, because they could get a sense of self-acceptance and that would feel good. But based on where I was in my path, that didn't feel good.

That was when I felt a natural rocket of desire start to fill in me. It was like my Soul was firing up, and I heard, *No, Kim. Your job is to awaken humanity. Your job is to send this Divine Light out into the world so strong and so fierce and so profoundly,* and it was then that I felt, *Yes, yes! I need to rock people's world into enLightenment!* The desire started to gain momentum, and then I started to picture lots of high vibration going into these recordings, and I started to picture tons of high vibration going into the book I was writing, and I started to picture people sitting on their couch waking up and being enLightened by touching the book, starting the program, and going into their first positive vibration momentum. I could imagine so much vibration coming out of my work, *All that people need to do is physically touch the work I am doing for them to awaken and enlighten!*

There was my shift. It wasn't for self-acceptance, because I had a good amount of self-acceptance. It was to shoot this rocket of desire so high that I could see everyone waking up at just hearing or reading my words, because my mission and purpose was to bring Light and vibrancy and love and purpose to everyone, and to give them alignment on a silver platter, so they don't have to go read every spiritual book.

What a blessing it was for me to have some contrast, to feel like I was failing with this meditation program, and get the beautiful contrast of confirmation from a friend that sent me lower into that negative vibration. What a blessing that I allowed myself that negative vibration, and sat in it. I asked, *What has this negative vibration come to tell me?* I tried to tie a little (ego) bow around it, but that didn't feel good. What felt good was to go deeper into alignment. The contrast pushed me straight into the alignment that I had been waiting for, for a week. I needed the contrast. I could have gone status quo and just been like, *Well, it's good enough,* but no, that didn't feel good.

We must honor those negative vibrations. They're teaching us something. Feel it, surrender to it. Sit in it for a week. Don't push it away, and don't wish it gone. Go into it, feel it, listen to it! There's wisdom in the negative vibration!

After the holidays a few years ago, I had one of the lowest weeks possible—with good reason. I had dysfunctional extended family stuff stirred up, I had all kinds of health stuff going on, and I was low. People kept trying to cheer me up and remind me, *Get into that positive vibration.* I very clearly knew that I needed to stay in the negative vibration and just listen for a little while and surrender to it, because I know I don't usually live in such negativity. If my journey wants to take a little dip into the negative vibration world because I've got some big, fat lessons that are coming to provide me clarity, I'm going there. I'm going deep into the negative vibration, and I'll stay there for as long as it takes until I can learn the lesson. I trust that the Universe is just trying to communicate with me, and that sometimes I need to get some contrast thrown into my life in order to hear it.

Even though the negative vibrations don't feel good, they lead us to the thing that does, and that's how we can feel our way out of the negative vibration. Once we have gained the wisdom we need from the negative vibrations, their vibration momentum slows. We can more objectively look at the contrast and see the clarity it's presenting. The clarity helps us shift the focus, and the natural momentum of the desire begins to build. We can use the energetic momentum and feed this fire until we feel the positive desire vibration in every cell of our body.

In my example above, I fully acknowledged and felt the negative vibrations from the contrast, and the wisdom and lessons were evident. Once I gained the lessons, the clarity of desire and the momentum for change arose naturally. I just had to ride the wave of positivity and feed it. And in fact, it shifted the trajectory of the rest of the program. The program went from mediocre to amazing from the next recording on.

When Relationships Create Negative Vibrations

What I hear often is, *I was feeling good and I had really good momentum, and then I was around my spouse and he has a really low and negative vibration, and it just doesn't feel good to be around him. So I was feeling good but then I stopped feeling good because I was around someone who doesn't feel good.* This is how most of us feel. We get into a situation where there are external conditions and we lose our alignment because we let the external condition set our resonance.

If we're focused on the external conditions of the other person, and their negative vibration, we have no power in the situation, but if we can shift from the contrast to Heart-based desire, we get our power back. Shifting vibration is an internal process that affects your external conditions, but it can't come from a place of *wanting* to affect *them*. Resolving negative vibrations related to our relationships is our inner work to realign back into the Heart and find some Heart-based desires. We shouldn't come to any major conclusions about our marriage/job/health while we're in the lower vibration, because **we don't have any solutions when we are in our negative vibration**. Our job is to get back into alignment. What happens in our relationships once we become aligned is one of two things:

- Either the relationship or the other person cannot jump to that level of vibration with us, and the relationship starts to break down,

OR

- That person begins to shoot off their rockets of desire to up-level their vibration to match ours.

Either way, because we're aligned, we're okay with whatever happens. *Could you imagine?* We're okay that the person is choosing what works and feels best for them, because we honor our choosing of what feels best for *us*.

Now, what happens here is people's fear of relationship breakdown (divorce, job loss) starts to creep in, but what I can tell you is that the more aligned we are with our Heart and Source, the more love, beauty, joy, freedom and fun happens in our lives. If it is a Soul-based contract of love, care and compassion, and that's what the relationship was built upon, then in my experience, the relationship will rise to the occasion, because one of us was willing, was bold enough, to shoot off the rockets of desire for better, for more.

The desire doesn't need to be a new partner with a whole set of vibrations, or a new job with a new set of characters. We don't need to picture the Universe fixing our external circumstances so they can meet our vibration. **We don't need to set desires and expectations for our <u>external</u> conditions to change.** As long as we are looking for anything outside of ourselves to change, then we're in a vibrational prison. We will never be happy or enjoy life for more than a moment.

It's exhausting when we're trying to control everything outside of ourselves so that our vibration can feel good. *If you could just be this way. Now, STAY that way. And hey you, you be THIS way. My kid, you have to listen to me. Listen to everything I say so I can feel good vibrationally. Husband, you need to vibrate really high so I can feel good vibrationally. Work, nothing can go wrong. There should be no contrast so I can feel good vibrationally.* But of course, that's not how it works.

We can be working the root *causes* or the outer *effects* in our lives. Our Soul works the *cause* of the situation: our baseline vibration. Our base vibration is what attracted the contrast in the first place. So if we shift our base vibration, we will attract something different. Our egos work the *effects* in our lives: We start with a negative vibration. Life throws us contrast that coincides with our base vibration. We blame and control the contrast, and avoid working the cause, which was our original baseline vibration. We end up attracting all kinds of new negativity to ourselves. And so the hamster wheel continues.

Once we work our base vibration, we take 100% responsibility for ourselves, for what we've attracted, for the

lives that we've manifested. We then jump off the ego hamster wheel and allow the Soul to take the steering wheel, consistently adjusting our thoughts, vibrations, and emotions to attract more of what we want in our lives. And the journey of alignment begins.

Spiritual Bypassing

Those of us on the spiritual path often get stuck in what we think is the "spiritual thing to do" (and I put quotes around that because there isn't a prescribed spiritual thing to do other than to get into alignment with the Heart). In spiritual community, there is often a temptation to go with the *spiritual thing to do/say* even though there is resistance underneath the surface. Avoiding authenticity, ignoring the deep resistance and pretending that everything is all super spiritual when it doesn't feel good is called Spiritual Bypassing. This is very common especially now that yoga and meditation have become more mainstream. People know *the spiritual way to act*, and will cut themselves off from their true vibrations to convince themselves, or others, that they have evolved past a certain level of consciousness. But of course, this doesn't work because we are always attracting from these deeper vibrations.

Everything is based on what feels good for us, what feels aligned with our truth. For one person, indulging anger may be a very bad thing, because that's just their well-worn pathway or bad habit, but for another person, accessing anger may feel better than that slump of depression that they've been in for twenty years. We can't put a blanket judgment on anything that we're seeing or feeling, because we're all just working to raise our vibrations, to sift through our life lessons and our life struggles.

We are all just doing the best we can in every moment. Really, we are.

Only our inner feelings can tell us whether we need to stay in a vibration and get a lesson or whether it's time for us to move on to our rockets of desire. Many of us get stuck because we have thoughts about how we *should* think and act in certain situations, and our vibrations are leading us in a different direction. The lesson isn't always evident, so if we don't feel into the wisdom, we can't get the lesson. Here's an example:

My husband and I were in California and he had worked to become present in enjoying California, to stay in the moment. Now that we were leaving in just two short weeks, I'd started to suffer a little bit. I heard everybody say, *Just stay in the present*, and I was like, *No, I don't want to stay in the present.* Normally I would have judged my suffering and said, *He was acting appropriately because he's staying in the present, and I'm wrong because I'm struggling with leaving.* But no, not this time. This time, I allowed myself to feel negatively about leaving. Instead of judging it and telling myself I shouldn't feel that way because it's not the *spiritual thing to do*, I allowed myself to struggle with leaving. I recognized and listened to that struggle. *You know what, Kim? You want to be in California more.* That was the desire coming out of me. *No, I don't want to leave. I want more California!* It was okay that I was feeling the negativity of leaving, because it was informing me of my desire for *more California*. I didn't have to judge the fact that I was resisting. I could look at my resistance and say, *Oh, there's a desire underneath there. Beautiful.* I could've been all spiritual and acted like I was fine with leaving but then I would have abandoned my desire to make sure we came back to California the next year!

If you can't get to a place of acceptance about something you feel you <u>should</u> accept, stop to feel and receive the lesson or message.

If you have a parent who is dying, and you know that at 80 years old they lived a long life, and you think you *should* be accepting of their death because you believe that they are *moving on past their pain*, and *it's the circle of life*, and *it's their karma*, but emotionally you still feel resistance … then allow yourself to feel the *I don't want my mom to die! No, no, no!* feeling until it releases. If you let it live, allow it and feel it, you can move through it. If you resist it with your mental stories about how you *should* be accepting it, then it takes longer to move through it and you find the pain is just as strong twenty years later because the negative emotions were never fully felt.

If you're in a marriage that doesn't seem to be working, and you're hitting the wall, you may feel that it would be nice to be able to be compassionate and accept, but if that's not where you're at, you have to FEEL and HONOR where you are. *I'm not accepting right now and I'm not allowing and in fact I'm really resisting the situation.* Okay, well why? *Well, because I don't want to be unhappy and I don't want to live with someone who is angry, and I don't want to have a numb marriage, I just don't want that.* Okay, well feel that. Feel the <u>not wanting</u> of the way life is right now. Allow yourself to go into it and feel it, instead of resisting it because you *know better.* **Allow the resistance.** Allow the negative contrast, just allow yourself to feel it. And when you're ready, when you've felt it fully, watch the momentum of your desire. Because as soon as you feel what you don't want, and you feel it strongly, it launches you into desire. *I don't like the way my marriage is, I want ... I want to wake up to someone who is warm and loving and kind, and I want to feel good in my marriage, and I want my spouse to love me back, and I want my spouse to vibrate higher, and I want to wake up to someone who wants to hear about me and how I'm feeling, and I want to go to bed next to someone who is warm and okay with who they are, and they're okay with who I am. I want to feel love for someone and feel loved back!*

When we start shooting that out into the world, even though it's a bit of a temper tantrum, at least it's a desire and it's honoring what you're desiring instead of covering it up and going with, *Oh I <u>shouldn't</u> have those desires, I <u>should</u> be more compassionate, I <u>should</u> be more patient, blah, blah, blah, blah. Should, should, should, should.* **Should-ing all over ourselves.** Allow the negative vibration. Allow yourself to very honestly and authentically admit what you want. Why not? It's going on underneath the surface anyway. Just let it rip. By feeling the dissatisfaction in the relationship—in the job, the friendship, the parenting—by feeling the disappointment and the sadness, we can then shift to what we're yearning for.

Even if it feels like you're resisting against the present moment, let it come out of your mouth. Voice your desires. Allow them to live. They're already giving you the negative vibration. You don't need to do much to turn it around to the positive, and start asking the Universe for something different.

This doesn't mean it'll all be smooth sailing. You may start your spiritual journey and all of a sudden have your life turn upside down. Suddenly you're having all these negative vibrations, and it becomes challenging to stay in a place of allowing in the midst of the storm. When we are getting pummeled by the contrast, we forget to focus on the desire.

That's our work. Remember, when we're in the negative, we cannot solve the negative. We can only feel through it. We are pretty much powerless as soon as we go into a negative vibration. The only thing we can do is feel it and shift our focus over to something positive, more pleasurable, so we can feel good until the momentum of the negative energy peters out.

Recorded Meditation Practice: Contrast and Negative Emotions Meditation

You can access a guided meditation to help you work with Contrast at: www.enLIGHTenWithKim.com. Click on **Community Resources** and **Book Meditations**, log in for free, and find the meditation called **#4 Contrast Meditation.**

Energetically Sensitive Empath

Have you gone through your life with people telling you you're too sensitive, you feel too deeply or you're too dramatic? Many of us spiritual folks have a lot of sensitivity, and we've seen it as a disadvantage in life, a dysfunction. We feel more deeply and intensely than other people, so we've learned to cope with it in different ways. Many spiritual people are very energetically sensitive, and don't spend much time in big groups of people because it just doesn't feel good. For example, if I go to a party I feel people's egos and judgement, I feel my own ego and judgements projected on others, and the whole experience feels so jarring because I can't figure out whose vibration is whose. There are people talking about other people—that doesn't feel good. There's someone acting happy but feeling miserable—that doesn't feel good. Another person feels super angry—that doesn't feel good. A group is bringing up negative politics—that doesn't feel good. Really, I just want to go home and hide from all the negative vibrations accosting me. It takes me two days to recover from all the negative vibrations at a party. And I begin to think I'm crazy!

We have seen this extra-sensitivity as a disadvantage most of our lives, because we just can't escape how we feel—our feelings scream at us! *But what if that is our biggest gift?* **Our extra-sensitivity to how we feel provides a more precise tool for inner listening.** Most of us energetically sensitive folks just haven't learned to understand how gifted we are with all the feeling. It is such a gift to feel so intensely. Yes, when things are out of alignment, we feel it and it feels so intense that we cannot deny it. BUT, we get early warning signs; we get the negative feeling loud and clear, so we can work ourselves into alignment quickly.

When we feel low vibration, and we are around other people, they reflect back where we're not aligned. We feel bad, then we're around someone and we feel worse. *Is it them or me?* That question can drive you deeper into the negative vibration to gain clarity about your own vibration. The energetic sensitivity can trigger your deeper alignment.

The goal is to go back and regain our alignment and focus on feeling good, so that we can feel aligned *before* we go to the party. Instead of blaming it on the party or on the fact that we're dysfunctional, we know, *This is just reflecting back that I don't have my alignment today. Let me get back into my happy place and feel those positive vibrations.*

For those who are disconnected from their bodies and don't have a high level of sensitivity—who may not even know that they're feeling bad (even after they ate a gallon of ice cream for comfort)—they must practice sensing the body. That daily connection of, *How am I feeling? Let me go into my breath and see what's going on in there. Any red flags? Any negative emotions?* It maybe buried a few layers deep, so they'll need to work on bringing it up.

For those who are energetically sensitive, we feel everything that's going on because our negative vibrations are at the surface. We just need to feel the negative vibrations, allow them, and listen to what they're telling us ... instead of doing what we do to cope and comfort ourselves around the negative vibrations.

On top of energetic sensitivity, you may also be an **empath**. This means you deeply feel, and possibly take on, the energies around you—you feel others' vibrations as if they are your own. Again, you can ask, *Is this MY vibration, or am I tuning into someone/thing else's vibration?* Either way, the Violet Flame exercise at the end of this chapter is incredibly useful to clear your energy field including all layers of your body: spiritual, mental, energetic, physical.

Setting Resonance

When we arrive at a party, and nothing feels good, we are shown that we are out of alignment. When we are out of alignment, we let *others* set *our* vibration. We RESONATE with *their* negative vibration, because we weren't able to stay in our vortex. When we have well-practiced alignment, we set the positive vibration for others. If we are not practiced in our vibrations, though, and we wobble from positive to negative (like most of us do), we become susceptible to the strongest vibration in the room, which is usually the most negative.

Have you noticed how someone with a well-practiced negative vibration can bring down the energy of the room? You know these people—they seem to have a dark cloud over their heads. They walk in the room and can immediately take down the vibration of everyone around them. Their low vibration is so well practiced, so dense and consistent, that those who fluctuate emotionally will automatically resonate with the strong negative emotion.

If we are practiced in our positive vibration, we can bring the vibration back *up*! I find that 90% of my work is setting a high vibration for my clients to ratchet up to. If I can stay in my vortex, find out where they're at vibrationally, and work them into my higher vibration, then they will often leave me riding the wave of possibility and potential for change, or be in gratitude for all they have or have created. I build that vibration with them for about 20 minutes, so they can leave class/counseling with a new vibration. Then their job is to keep their vibration high and avoid resonating with the next negative person that comes their way, or crashing with the first contrast they encounter.

We can keep our vibration high even when we are not feeling well. We don't have to create resonance with the symptoms of our illness. I had bronchitis when I wrote part of this book, so I had to work my vibration high, change my mind about the coughing (*It's my body cleansing!*) and connect with my Heart *instead* of the vibration of the relentless coughing. It took mindfulness but I did it. And that experience helped me learn to override my PMS! I witnessed the vibration of my Heart in contrast to the vibration of my hormones, and consciously chose to resonate with my Heart. It takes our: mindful awareness of what is happening in our body, a witnessing state to realize that we are not our illness, allowance to move through the low vibration (instead of resisting it), and the ability to choose where we resonate vibrationally.

Energy Field Protection and Cleansing

We have established that we are made of energy and vibration, and sometimes we can get stuck in some pretty negative vibration. There are always lessons and desires in the negative vibrations so we don't need to bat away all negative and pretend it doesn't exist. By now, we're on the same page on this, right? Great, because I want to share some energetic tools to clear some of the energetic interference that we pick up throughout our day. Here are three practices for you to try:

1. Draw colored Light into the Chakras—A general way to cleanse your vibration is to bring in the colors of light associated with each chakra. (See Chakra Resistance Clearing Meditation at end of Chapter 7).

2. Chanting Mantras—As discussed in Chapter 3, **Sanskrit mantra** can be useful in releasing denser energies. Start with *Om Gum Ganapatayei Namaha* 108 times for forty days. (Check YouTube for pronunciation.)

3. Violet Consuming Flame—In my experience, the **Violet Flame** is the MOST effective way to feel better, get the lessons, and clear your energy field so that you don't spend too much time stuck resisting resistance. I have witnessed the Violet Flame meditation practice shift the lives of SO many people—Marriages that were about to end had a quick turnaround; panic attacks were held at bay; suffering and scarcity turned into presence and joy; lack of clarity turned to laser beam vision; Lymes disease transitioned into better wellness; anxiety cleared up. It has become undeniable in my experience. Try it for a few weeks, and I trust your life will start to transform toward your intentions in ways you never anticipated.

There are many books on using the Violet Flame with the theory and concept behind the flame. What I can share here is that it is a gift of St. Germain and can be used to consume anything that is not of the Light. Anything that does not feel good suggests that it is not in alignment with the Light, so the Violet Consuming Flame can work on everything. It accesses the love, power, and wisdom of your Heart and reignites that energy within your body so it will bring a soft, powerful presence.

Meditation: Violet Consuming Flame

This energy clearing practice can be a 15-minute practice to use daily.

Step 1—Invocation

You can invite in whomever you speak to on the other side of the veil: "I invite in St. Germain, the Ascended Masters, the Archangels, and the Divine Light (God)."

Step 2—Protection

Whenever you invite in Light, it's important to <u>always</u> invoke protection: "Please put a white tube of light around me for protection."

Step 3—Intention

You can state your specific intention for clearing or manifestation, for example: "Please remove fear and panic."

Step 4—Decree

Repeat one of these statements with lots of energy, emotion and willpower while envisioning a Violet Flame around you. Repeat 15 minutes a day, or a minimum of 9 repetitions several times a day.

"I AM a being of Violet Fire, I AM the purity God desires." OR if *God* doesn't resonate with you, use the following: "I AM the Violet Consuming Flame in Action."

Step 5—Closing:

End by saying, "And so it is. It is finished. Amen."

In Summary...

Learning to navigate through the negative emotions and vibrations can be tricky, but we can change our perspective and begin to see that life is throwing us contrast to inform our desires. As we release our resistance toward the contrast, we can shift our attention from contrast negativity to our desire's positive momentum.

The people who provide us with our contrast situations are helping us get our lessons in life. They are our partners in the process of aligning with the Heart. The more we resist them, the more negative life gets. Relationships are our playground to learn more about ourselves and how we do the world, so that we can push through the discomfort and make changes toward vibrations of peace and joy. Once we master our own vibration, we can begin to set the positive resonance for others.

The contrast and negative vibrations are here to serve us in this life journey. If we ignore them or cope by numbing, we miss the wisdom they can bring. If we feel our way into the negative vibrations, we gain the wisdom they bring us in our movement toward our desires. Manifesting a desire may require for old situations to break down before they improve.

Many of us on this spiritual path are super sensitive. While this feels like a disadvantage at times, we can use this to our advantage to get the signals and wisdom when they are whispers (versus feeling slammed out of nowhere). We mustn't fake our way through the contrast with spiritual bypassing. We must feel *through* the negative vibrations, like walking through the fire of purification. To help with our sensitivity, it is important to cleanse and protect our energy fields regularly. Just as we take a shower every day, our energy field requires regular upkeep and cleansing. Incorporating mantra and the Violet Flame can be incredibly helpful in releasing negativity on our journey toward our desires.

Unlock Your Deep Confusions and Life Purpose

Begin today. No matter how feeble the Light, let it
shine as best it may. The world may need just that
quality of Light which you have.
-Henry C. Blinn

Our early life experiences have a deep impact on how we interact with this world. These experiences often leave imprints of low vibration until we raise the underlying belief systems and emotions up to the present moment in the conscious mind to get the lessons for our Soul's evolution. Sometimes it's important to unravel where these limiting belief systems originated so we can begin to call them out as erroneous and non-reality based. This level of awareness dissolves the confusions and allows us to get the lessons to help expand our experience of truth.

Separation and Confusions

The impact of early life contrast helps to form our life lessons as we move forward in our purpose in this lifetime. The impact we can have in this world is built upon these early experiences that helped form us. Even the negative or darker experiences can be alchemized, or transformed, into positive and Lighter contributions in our lives.

My Inner Child "Rescue"

Earlier in the book, I told you about how I manifested my husband. He was on that first list that I created back in 1997. The next extraordinary manifestation happened seven years later in 2004.

Early in our marriage, my husband and I were planning a trip to Sedona, Arizona. I had never been there. I didn't even know what the landscape looked like, but before I went, I started a huge oil painting of these big orange mountains with Light shining on them. I completed the large painting in two days (and they just happened to look exactly like the Sedona mountains). As I stepped back, I was just in awe of the creativity that flew through my hand onto the canvas. I was truly in the flow and in alignment with myself ... before I even knew what the flow was!

We boarded the plane to Sedona, and up comes this conversation about having children. Now my husband married me under the agreement that we probably would *not* have children because I had such a dysfunctional childhood and didn't think that I could raise children in a healthy way. But here we were, three years after our marriage, seven years after meeting, broaching the subject of having children. Now, I had been doing a lot of personal growth work over the year leading up to this trip, releasing fears and aligning more closely with my true self. I looked at him and said, *Maybe we could have kids. Maybe I could do it and not screw it up.* (Not a lot of momentum, but I definitely opened to the POSSIBILITY!) We left the conversation there.

Two days later, while roaming around Sedona which is full of new age spiritual stuff, I decided to do something *weird* and go to a psychic. At my appointment, the psychic looked me in the eye and said, *So there's something about children.* I'm like, *Nope.* He said, *Do you work with children?* I said, *Nope.* I didn't give him much information. He said, *I'm going to use this sage and I'm going to smudge your body.* I had no idea what that meant. I put my arms out and he's smudging me, putting burning dried sage around my body and clearing my field. Again, I was just like, *Well, okay. When in Rome...*

I sat down and he said, *I sense we need to do an inner child rescue.* In my head, I was rolling my eyes like, *Oh dude, you've got to be kidding me*, but I agreed. As we sat down, he started what I now know was a guided meditation. He said, *Now imagine yourself going to save little Kim. You're with an eagle and the eagle takes you over the mountain and you can see little Kim. Do you see little Kim?* I'm like, *Um yeah, I see little Kim.* Now in my mind, I was totally judging this experience, but I was trying to go with it. He said, *Call out to little Kim*, and I was like, *Oh man.* I called out to little Kim and he told me to follow the eagle, and then he started talking like the eagle (in a squeaky voice), saying, *Come on, Kim. Let's go find little Kim.* I was dying laughing inside, but just still going with it. I said, *Yes, okay, we're going to find little Kim.* We went over the mountain and there was little Kim. He told me to take her by the hand. I imagined taking her by the hand, and he said, *Talk to her.* So I was like, *Okay, little Kim. Here we go. We're going together now.*

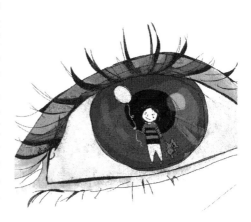

Well, as soon as I held hands with my "little Kim," my body started to release and I started to cry my eyes out. My whole face was purging. My nose was running, my eyes were pouring tears. It was like I had experienced the most significant release of my life. I had no idea what was happening! I just sat there sobbing … in confusion.

I walked out of this session and went straight down to the river. I had no words. I was in this state of peaceful spaciness.

We decided to go to an energy vortex nearby, the Airplane Energy Vortex. It was a place where there was supposedly a ton of energy coming out of the ground. You could see it in the twisting trees. I felt like I was on a different planet— so spaced out. Then we went to dinner, and afterward I looked my husband straight in the eye and said, *We need to make a baby.* He was like, *Huh? Um. Okay.*

On the plane ride home, we told each other, *Wow, that was kind of crazy.* And of course, two weeks later, in my Heart and Soul, I knew that I was carrying a baby. One try, one inspiration out of the Soul right after I had saved "little Kim," and my daughter arrived nine months later—with red hair the color of the Sedona mountains!

My first child was birthed out of an *inner child rescue.* I still can't mention it without feeling like it was ridiculous, but there was no doubt that reconnecting with my inner child was momentous. I had separated from that inner child self early in my life. The experience that I had in Sedona helped me transcend time, make peace, and reconnect with that part of myself, almost reclaiming and bringing me back into ME.

Separation from Self

It wasn't until ten years later, when I became immersed in the whole New Age spirituality thing, that I came to understand that at some point in our childhood, we begin the separation from ourselves, from that deepest part of ourselves. We separate from our inner wisdom, our inner voice, our inner connection to our Soul. And through time, we just get further from ourselves.

Initially, we come into our human bodies from the vibration of love and worth, in a place of oneness and unity with all. We feel our interconnectedness. We don't even know that anything is separate from us. We come in Heart-centered, feeling-based, and very intuitive. As we begin to incarnate more deeply into our bodies, though, we become more externally focused. We go into our mind and our ego is developed. We start to see ourselves as separate from others. Life takes on a sense of duality and separateness. We see things as good or bad, right or wrong, okay or not. Everything starts to become categorized in our mind.

To view life from this dualistic perspective, we have to disconnect from our intuition and place of oneness. We must separate ourselves from others to operate from this black and white place of judgment—right or wrong, good or bad. As we shift into the place of judgment and separation, we begin to feel the vibration of fear. **Fear indicates the vibration of separateness** for us. Separateness builds the confusions of *unsafe*, *unworthy* and *unloved*. We lose our alignment as we shift into the ego and the mind, because separateness and judgment is not who we really are. As we spend more time in our mind, the separation, judgment and fear begin to take over.

During the early years, our childhood contrast impacts us deeply, our recurring thoughts form our belief systems, and deep confusions get programmed in vibrationally. Our egos try to make sense of this by creating stories about everything, and we then spend the rest of our lives basing our experiences upon them. We hold the confusion in our subconscious mind, in our belief systems, in our vibration. We have these inconsistent confusions in our bodies. So we spend much of our lives not feeling good. We develop a tolerance for not feeling good. We just assume this is the way it goes, because it's the way it has always felt to us.

Since we've lost touch with how we feel, and we don't really have a good sense of our internal guidance system, this tightens the fabric of fear, which becomes vibrationally dense in our bodies and creates a life of resistance. Separateness doesn't feel right. That's our indicator that we have lost alignment with our Soul, with our inner being, with our inner child.

But our inner being—that inner child, that Lightness, our Soul connection—is still there. Our intuition is still whispering to us, and we're still getting signals from our emotional guidance system. Our Soul just waits patiently on the sidelines, waiting to be invoked and invited in.

We have free will. We don't *have to* invoke our Higher Consciousness. We don't have to connect with that inner being or that playfulness or that Lightness. We don't *have to* realign with our Soul. We have the choice of spending our whole lifetime in negative vibration and misalignment ... or we can invoke our free will and use it to form desires to request realignment. Our emotional guidance system just keeps giving us indicators of how far we've gone from ourselves, and our Soul is waiting for us to wake up and ask for help.

Society reinforces the separation, which normalizes this whole ego experience of separation, even though it feels bad inside. Children come into the world feeling good, wanting freedom, having fun—those are spiritual qualities: freedom, fun, inspiration, feeling good. And what do we do as parents? What did our parents do? We say *No, no, no. No more freedom. You need to do what I say. No more fun. Come on, we need to get focused and clean our rooms.* We teach our children (as our parents taught us) that feeling good is bad, and that we need to use mind over matter and stop that freedom, fun, feel good stuff and get focused, so we can stay safe, productive, responsible, and socially acceptable. Here's an example:

After my daughter visited her friend's house, I received a call from the hosting mother saying my daughter had acted "full of herself" and the "center of attention." She went deep into her assessment of my daughter, and told me about all the people who felt the same way. She said she was just trying to help and I believe her intentions were to be helpful. Her interpretation of my daughter's self-esteem as inappropriate gave my daughter the message that she shouldn't feel *that* good about herself. Her view of how my daughter should conduct herself (she wasn't misbehaving!) was her idea of how the world should be, based on subconscious belief systems of separateness. Her talking to others about my daughter created more separation, judgement, and negativity around normal pubescent behavior.

Our society guides our children away from inner wisdom. We're not taught to listen from within. We're not taught to honor our feelings. We're not taught to freely express ourselves. We're not taught to listen to our inner guidance and do what feels good. Instead, we're taught to listen to our parents and teachers and relatives and those who are older than us, because they know better for us than we know for ourselves. At a very young age, we are immediately guided away from our inner wisdom. We are raised with rules and fear—society's fear, our parents' fear.

Some of us rage against their taking our freedom and fun (defiance), and some of us go into a place of acquiescence (victimhood). Most of us feel disempowered.

We adapt by developing different coping strategies and belief systems to make sense of the world around us because separating from our inner voice sends us off into the abyss. That's where we begin to feel separation from our Soul, from others, from Source, from everything. *I'm separate from you, but I am also separate from my inner knowing.* We are taught that others know better for us than we know for ourselves. As soon as we believe this, **our inner connection is broken**. We separate from our inner emotional guidance system and commit to a life that just doesn't feel good because it is based on the external world's operating system.

We download so many belief systems that revolve around separateness and disconnection from self. We learn how to be in the world from other people who have disconnected from their Souls, who are not aligned with the trueness of who they are. And we're learning it from outside ourselves, without bothering to ask our internal Souls whether it's the right thing or not. This is the human condition. We're taught from a young age to look outside of ourselves to feel good. And if we're not connected to our inner Source, our inner love and our inner knowingness, it becomes second nature to look somewhere else for our value and love. We look to someone else to tell us whether we're valuable or good, or whether we should or shouldn't feel good. We put together this whole concept of life based around a mental confusion of externally focused love, connection, worthiness, value, and responsibility.

Deeply Rooted Confusions

Early in our lives, we encounter some our most formative contrasts. These early contrasts build our belief systems for how the world works:

- Who and what is safe/unsafe?
- How do I process/bury emotions?
- What's good/bad about me?
- How does love work?
- How do you handle truth?
- Is the world kind/cruel?
- Is life easy/hard?
- Is my life lacking/abundant?
- Am I a creator/victim?
- Am I valuable/worthless?

Since we are separate from inner knowing, and society buys into separateness, many of our belief systems are dangerously far from the truth of who we are and how the Universe works.

When we're toddlers putting together our view of the world, based on vibrational input, we don't understand what's going on. We just put it together the best we can. If we have negative experiences, those negative experiences are vibrationally programmed into our body and mind. We are taught to look outside of ourselves to feel good, and to disconnect from our inner knowing. We buy into these distorted belief systems and thoughts because we don't have an adult mind to know any better. Our belief systems wind up looking something like this:

- When I grew up, my parents fought a lot, and that made me feel unsafe. And I found that if I was kind and loving toward them, I could help them feel better, and that made me feel safe. So I put together that **if I felt unsafe, I just needed to make the people around me feel better and then I could feel safe again.** So I become a peacemaker in my life.

OR maybe...

- I was praised when I did good things and that felt good, so I learned that I had to do good things in order to feel good. **Doing makes me feel good, so I go around now, looking for results to feel good about in my life.**

Perhaps...

- I did bad things and I get yelled at a lot, and felt like I was a bad kid. But if I was behaved, I got praise, and that made me feel good again. **Now I feel like a bad person and I look to others to tell me I'm a good person so I can feel good about myself.**

Possibly...

- My parents didn't pay much attention to me, so I began to feel like I wasn't worthy of love—I felt unlovable. Now **I live life thinking that I'm not really lovable and people wouldn't really love me**, and that just becomes my base belief system.

You see? This is how the toddler mind starts to put things together. These are deeply rooted vibrations that drive our thoughts and actions. They don't make a lot of sense with our adult minds. We wouldn't consciously think like that as an adult, because intellectually we know better. But because these beliefs were programmed into our subconscious minds and our vibrating body when we were very young, when we didn't have a rational mind to tell us otherwise, it became the basis for our belief systems. We will call these our deeply rooted confusions, which form our Tiny Mad Idea about ourselves.

Tiny Mad Idea

The downside of this deeply rooted confusion is that our whole life gets set up around a few key base confusions. The book *A Course in Miracles* calls it a Tiny Mad Idea about ourselves. This Tiny Mad Idea becomes the basis for all our relationships. Almost everything we think, say, and do revolves around managing this subconscious fear. And if all of our attention and energy revolves around this fear, then what will we be attracting in our life? That's right, more contrast to prove that fear to be true. And we wonder why we are on the hamster wheel!

If I have a base state of feeling **unsafe**, I make myself the peacemaker because I believe that peace is made outside of myself. In doing so, I've lost alignment with my true self, and I'm stuck with a base vibration of feeling unsafe. What am I going to attract into my life based on that negative vibration? I'm going to attract unsafe relationships or people that feel unsafe to me. I'm going to attract situations that don't bring me a sense of well-being; they bring me a sense of unsafety, because I'm vibrating at the base of level of unsafe. I will attract situations where I won't feel safe.

If I feel **unworthy** and **unvaluable**, I must do good things to feel worthy and valuable because I don't feel my Soul's inherent worthiness. I feel useless unless I *do* something about it. Doing makes me feel valuable, so I'm going to attract a life of *doing-doing-doing* just so I can feel valuable, which will make me feel very depleted. I probably won't spend very much time taking care of myself because I need to keep doing so I can feel good because feeling good happens from outside of myself. I feel unvaluable and I set up a life where I attract situations that reinforce that I'm not very valuable unless I'm doing. And even then, I don't feel valuable for very long because, in reality, my value has nothing to do with what I do.

If I feel like a **bad person,** I look for others to show me I'm good, and set up life with a number of strategies to prove I'm good. However, because my base vibration is *bad person*, I'm going to attract relationships and situations that show me my negative qualities, that reinforce this belief that I'm bad. I will filter everything from the perspective of being a bad person.

If I believe I'm **unlovable** or unworthy of love, then I look for others to love me so I can feel love. I think that love comes from the outside, rather than from my own inherent connection to my Source. If I feel and vibrate at the base state of unlovable, I'm going to attract relationships where people aren't capable or willing to show me love. I spend my life feeling empty.

If I believe I'm **not enough**, then I look for any person, opportunity or situation to prove that I am enough. I think that there's never enough of anything, and I live my life in scarcity. I attract situations that prove that I'm not enough, and financial situations where I don't have enough, and other people never feel like enough when they're with me.

This is how we set up our lives. We set up our lives with these deeply rooted confusions, and then we react to these confusions for the rest of our lives. This is not alignment with our Soul. This is not alignment with our Source. These Tiny Mad Ideas are not true. And they feel bad. Really bad.

The truth is that I am love, I am beauty, I am worthy, I am goodness and I am the essence of this well-being that flows through me. Period.

Negative Vibrations Expose Deeply Rooted Confusions

With these negative base vibrations, which we set up when we're young, we pinch ourselves off from Source. Deep down, we all know that we can't get our value or well-being from the outside world, but we have all these negative vibrations that reinforce an external focus on a day-to-day basis.

Now we know that these **deep confusions and negative vibrations are just CONTRAST programmed into our mind and bodies.** We have negative emotions constantly because these deep confusions, negative vibrations, and subconscious contrasts were programmed in at a very young age, keeping us from being in alignment with who we really are. And we have negative emotions whenever we feel this, because it's not aligned with our feel-good Soul vibrations.

We can stop and observe the negative emotions, and be thankful for them, because they're showing us where these confusions exist. **Our negative emotions are our red flags of where we need to dig down into the vibration to find the confusion.** Isn't that amazing? We keep avoiding the negative emotion by having a glass of wine or distracting ourselves with Facebook, but they're the red flags saying *Hey! Hey you! Look here. Take a look here. Dig a little under here.* We want the negative emotion to go away, but our non-physical inner Source loves us so much that it will keep raising the red flag until we dig a little underneath the surface to find the deeply rooted confusion below.

All we have to do is open the treasure box and shine the Light of consciousness to release the negative vibration. We dig down, we open it up, and we let it bask in the Light. We let it bake in the sun. We bring it love and space. We let it air out as long as it needs to air out. It's been sunk in there for like forty years … a dark, musty treasure box. Once we dust off the jewels within the treasure box, we start to see our true selves. We get to peek at the essence of who we are, and we realize we aren't those negative vibrations, and we aren't those deep-rooted confusions. We get to see the true essence and beauty of this treasure that's been hidden because we were confused and living our lives at the surface. If we follow the negative emotion down to that deep negative vibration, we see that we just got too far away from ourselves. We got caught up in the external. But in reality, what we can find is, *I am love and I am worthy and I am a good person and I am completely lovable, and I don't have to do a damn thing to feel good and worthy l because I AM THE LIGHT!*

If we give ourselves the space to feel into the negative vibration, it will eventually show us the important information that we were missing about ourselves. **It may feel like you are going to DIE when you feel the deeply rooted confusion.** It feels so terrible. Why else would you be running from this deeply rooted vibration your entire life? That's okay to feel terrible for a little while. It's <u>temporary</u>. Take your time and feel it. Once you have completely felt it, you have brought it up to your conscious awareness. It's now in the LIGHT! It is no longer creeping beneath the surface, haunting you with your unworthiness, unlovableness, bad-person-ness. Now you can look around your life to see what—in your relationships with others or self, or career, or life purpose—is out of alignment due to how you have set up your life according to your Tiny Mad Idea about yourself.

This is a shift in perspective, so it doesn't mean you have to clean house of all the things that aren't aligned. In fact, it's best to just walk around for a time period and watch the movie of your life. Allow yourself to witness how you set it all up, based on your Tiny Mad Idea. Recapitulate the past and start dreaming up an unbounded future.

It is helpful to feel some compassion for yourself. You did such an amazing job in your life, considering the beliefs you held of yourself. Feel that, and honor your journey and the contrast that was necessary to get you here. We don't need to psychoanalyze everything with the ego-driven mind. We just need to feel it and know that it's just contrast that was built into us, and we don't need it anymore.

Deep Confusions Create Expansion to Life Purpose

You might be asking yourself: Why would we have contrast built into us? Why can't we just come into this world as happy, free, loving, fun beings and then go have a happy, free, loving, fun life? Because the Universe is meant to expand. And the way the Universe expands is for us to create variety and expansion in the way we think and the way we live. The deeply rooted confusions are contrasts in our lives, which were built in when we were children. They are there to help us to create those deep, momentous desires that lead us to growth. That's why we just need to witness and feel the deeply rooted confusion and contrasts and MOVE ON to those desires!

Personally, I grew up feeling like a bad person, and that made me want to be a really good person, which brought me to do really good work in this world. It made me want to enLighten and align with myself, because I didn't like feeling like a bad person. I wanted to love myself. I had to face all my negative emotions, FEEL all the negative vibrations, unearth all of my own confusions, bring them up to my awareness, shine Light and love and compassion on my journey, and gradually shift into a more positive momentum of desire in my life.

Because I wanted to feel like a good person, I projected that I wanted everyone *else* to feel like a good person. I wanted them to love themselves and feel compassion for themselves. I wanted them to align and feel good all the time. I developed the drive and desire to awaken every single person on this living earth so they could see the beauty of their Light. That Tiny Mad Idea that I wasn't a good person, that little contrast that I had beautifully programmed in at a very young age, set off rockets of desires for me to want to be a good, valuable, loving, kind person. That Tiny Mad Idea allowed me to become the unique expansion of myself that I had the potential to be. That Tiny Mad Idea sets the stage for our life's purpose. The contrast was installed so we can manifest and create momentum around that which we care about, which is based on those early experiences.

The uniqueness of this contrast sets each of us in a direction of clarity of how we want our lives to be, how we want to create and manifest in our lives. That's why each of us is so very different; because we had different parents who had different confusions, so we were able to put the world together in our own unique way. There's so much variety in our contrast, and that creates different directions for our rockets of desire, which allows our paths to look and feel different, and allows us to expand the potential of the Universe, and the potential of humanity. No two struggles, no two people, no two purposes are exactly alike. We are all completely unique and have our own unique desires and gifts to offer the world.

It's necessary to give those deeply rooted contrasts the space to surface with compassion, without getting stuck in the victimization of the struggle. We can say, *Wow, that was living deep inside of me. Holy cow! I can't believe I lived with that for so long. Oh that poor 7-year-old me.* Sit with that compassion for the 7-year-old you. *Man, you had to go thirty years with that feeling before you woke up and realized that was just a confusion!* Then we can feel the momentum of not wanting to feel it anymore. Some of us just need to feel, *Oh yeah, that's how I DON'T want to feel. Let me focus on how I DO want to feel. Let me create a world of what I DO want.* Then we master what we *do* want.

This confusion was installed early in life so we could set off in the direction of our purpose, of our unique gift to humanity. Remember, our Higher Consciousness—our Soul, our non-physical reality, our Source, the Universe—works through contrast, to help us see what we're not seeing, to help us realign with who we really are, to help us gain clarity, to direct us into alignment, to direct our desire and our manifestations toward deeper alignment with our Soul. **Our Tiny Mad Idea catapults us toward our life purpose.**

However, we must remember that there may be a reason for some people to hang out in their contrast instead of refocusing toward their desires and life purpose. We get very impatient if we're awakened and see people sitting in their contrast, because we don't understand it. We're like, *Look in the other direction! Just look in the other direction. There's Light. Just look toward the Light. Create some desires and move on!* We need to honor and respect those who decide to spend time in their contrast. They're just getting their lessons. They are taking a little bit longer to get their clarity ... and they'll get it in another lifetime if they don't get it in this one. We don't need to get stuck on people who are getting their lessons and who are gaining clarity through contrast. We can just respect that they're in lesson. *They're in contrast mode. I've been there. And while I'm happy to be on the other side, my contrast added variety and expansion in my life and it probably will for them too.* We needed to spend time in our contrast, so why not allow them the opportunity to use their free will to spend time in their own? Yes, they may develop illness and disease, and they may have to lower their vibration so that they can get to the point of desire for something different, but we can allow them that opportunity to experience their contrast.

We can honor each other's contrast. We're just getting lessons so we can develop clarity. Sometimes people wait until the very end of their lives to finally receive the clarity, through their disease or through the contrast they've created. That's okay, too. We just need to get our clarity. Some people get it early, and some people get it later. Some people have to sit in contrast for longer than others. Let them be in their contrast even though it's uncomfortable to watch. That's their process and they know what's best for them. Really, they do.

Life Lessons

Our deep confusions and early contrasts allow us to focus and get clarity on our life lessons. They send us in the direction of our life lesson work. *Wait, what the heck is our life lesson work? I didn't know I had a life lesson!* Wouldn't it be great if we came with little instruction manuals that said, *By the way, here are your emotions. Here's what they mean. Here's your life lesson and here's how you work on that.* We didn't get the instruction manual … but here it is now! We all come to life to work out our lessons. Our Soul wants to expand. As our Soul expands, the Universe expands. To have that expansion, we work our life lessons.

If we felt unworthy, then we're building worth in this lifetime. If we felt unloved, then we're working on giving and receiving love. If we felt bad, then we are here to find our goodness. On every level of confusion, we are simply looking to get back into alignment with our Soul's oneness with Source.

Life Lesson Spiral—a Journey to Our True Self

We carry leftover vibrations from the past (past lives or early childhood) to play out our lessons in this lifetime. Throughout life, we are given our share of challenges and partners to assist in providing contrast. The resulting subject matter is what we play out so that we can discover who we really are.

While it may seem like we are continuously working the SAME issues over and over, we are expanding our consciousness and revealing who we are as we build awareness around the issues. It's like a spiral or onion of consciousness and we are working our way toward the center to discover our true self. The outer circle of the spiral is where we start in our lower consciousness. As we raise our consciousness, and go further inward on the spiral, we develop a better sense of what is external versus internal, and we grow more aligned with our Soul. We may continue to revisit the same subject matter (relationships, emotions, life situations) but each time we hit the issue, we are digging deeper on the spiral of our life lessons. Each trip around the spiral allows us the opportunity to expand the way we think about the issue until we eventually begin to find out who we really are from our internal resolution of the issue.

We realize: *I am not my mother. I am not my anger. I am not my roles in life. I AM loving. I AM worthy.* Here's an example based on the subject matter from my life:

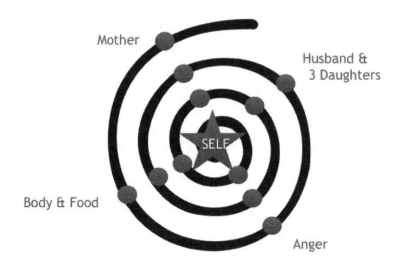

Outer Circle of the Spiral

Mother: One of my master teachers in life has been my mother. She presented my earliest contrast, and therefore was my first stop on my life lesson spiral. On my outermost layer, and lowest point of consciousness, my mother was my nemesis. She was always thwarting me, controlling me, and demonstrating how I didn't want to be in life. At this first stop on the spiral, I blamed her for all my woes. She was the reason for the angst in my life. I defied her and threw my anger toward her.

Body: Next stop on my lowest point of awareness were my issues with myself. I was overweight at a young age, and at 9-years-old, I developed very low self-esteem and a distorted body image. I loathed my body and how I looked. I developed an eating disorder by 13, along with a belief that if I could just be skinny, people would like me and I would like myself, and then I could be happy.

Anger: My emotion of choice was anger. I blamed everyone for every problem in my life. It was my go-to emotion and usually ended with my being violent or controlling.

Family: My husband entered my life in grad school. I played out all my issues with him: mother issues, body image issues, anger issues. He served as a reflection of my "ugly" qualities, my shadow side.

Middle Layer of the Spiral

In this middle layer of the Life Spiral, as I worked through the issues presented in my life, I was able to start seeing that they weren't about other people. It was about my inner thoughts and vibrations, and how I lived my life. The players and the subject matter helped me to continue to grow and build awareness of what was my stuff versus what was due to others. And while I still got caught up in the illusion of externalizing my emotions, I was quick to bring awareness to my responsibility in absolutely everything I came in contact with. At some level, I knew I attracted it, so even when I was lost in the outer world, my intuition was screaming at me to come home.

Mother: When I dropped some of the blame and anger toward my mom, I was able to see how I was participating in the relationship. I began to change how I interacted with her. I broke my dependencies on her. I stopped expecting her to change. I created some boundaries between our lives so we could stop the madness. I did a TON of forgiveness prayers (more on this later!) so we could begin to release some of the toxicity and karma. While the relationship hasn't yet made it to warm and fuzzy, I feel at peace with the integrity of my relating with her.

Body: After abusing my body for years, using food for comfort and numbing, I developed gut and autoimmune issues which were screaming for healing. I began a journey of mindfulness around my eating, and healed my gut. I ate foods that worked *with* my body. Over the course of ten years, I slowly and systematically eliminated gluten, dairy, refined and processed foods, sugar, GMOs, and pesticides. I started yoga. My body regained energy and I started working with my temple rather than against it. I began to listen to the whispers of my body, which told me I was starting to lose physical alignment, so I didn't have to have major physical issues slapping me upside the head.

Anger: As my consciousness began to rise higher, I began to see my responsibility in all situations. I started to see how I was causing many of the issues in my life. Blame and anger soon gave way to acceptance and allowance. My fire shifted from anger to passion for what I desired in life.

Family: As I worked through my issues and saw myself heal, my intuition guided me toward having children. The Universe gave me THREE DAUGHTERS to serve as constant contrast providers so I could continue to grow and raise my consciousness, and develop deep love, patience, and self-understanding. My old patterns, built in low consciousness, didn't work with these bright light beings that were beaming their divine qualities at me. So the consistent contrast from my girls was my inspiration to shift more deeply into my Heart.

Inner Layer of the Spiral

I'm still working this inner layer, but I can tell you that I truly understand that I cause and attract everything. My karmic buddies, or Master Teachers, don't trigger me as deeply because I recognize that I'm co-creating with the Universe. Every issue that shows up in my life is a lesson for me to see where I'm not aligned with my Soul. In fact, it doesn't scare me to feel the deep, dark aspects of life anymore, because I trust that the negative emotions are just telling me something that my Soul needs me to hear. Negative feedback from someone doesn't feel like life or death, because I have an internal awareness of who I am. I dictate my perspective of myself, not others. But I understand that if negative circumstances or feedback come into my life, then I've attracted it for a lesson … so I listen. I listen to everything that comes my way, because it's there to teach me something. My subject matter, and the players in my life, have helped me discover who I am. My spiritual practice and connection is strong, and it guides me through life every day.

Dark Shows the Light

We often make contrast or darkness a bad thing. We resist it because we don't acknowledge the gift it brings to us on our Soul's journey. I once had such a beautiful lesson about the need for contrast in order to show the Light:

I live in the Northeast, in upstate New York, where in the winter it is cold and dark. There's just not a lot of sunshine at that time of year, and the cold makes you contract and go inward. You can feel it in every cell of your body, in your bones.

I came to Southern California in the middle of winter, and it was so warm! The sun was shining so bright, and the mountains were so expansive. As I drove my children to school, I came up a hill and saw the ocean, and it just went on and on and on. As I drove home, I went up a hill and saw this mountain range that expanded so far out. I got to the beach and could feel the grounding of the sand and the Lightness of the wind and the sun. The elements in San Diego pull you up. Even if you're in a negative vibration, the elements pull you up to the higher vibration of nature. So each day is just beautiful and expansive.

If I were to look at the other side of that, though, each day feels the same. There's not a lot of variety because the weather is pretty much 70 degrees every single day. The sun is always shining and bright. I'm not, for one second, suggesting that having Lightness and brightness is boring or dull, because it's not. But it doesn't have a lot of variety built in.

If you think about what it's like to live in the Northeast, there is so much variety in the weather, and as a result, because we are connected to the elements, we journey through emotions that reflect the climate. In fall, it is colorful and cool and smells like fall. We feel the transition from light and warm to cold and dark. Winter is sometimes bitter cold, sometimes snowy and bright, sometimes dark and gloomy. As we watch much of nature die or hibernate, we go inward and feel our own darkness. In spring, it is wet and stormy and smells like spring. We emotionally feel the transition of cold and dark to light and sunny. In summer, it is 90 degrees and bright and humid. We feel more expansive, sociable, and alive!

Having lived in upstate NY my entire life, what I realized is that *outer* darkness requires us to dig deep within ourselves and clear out our *inner* darkness. In deep winter, we must find the Light and the fire within, and shine it brightly so we can feel the Light, because we can't be dependent on nature or the elements to do that for us. We can't even be dependent on other people to do it for us, because everybody is in the darkness during the winter. You know it because nobody even comes out of their houses. They're just hunkering down and waiting for the

Light of spring to come. What's built into us in the Northeast is that ability to dig inward for the Light. To do that, we must first uncover the Light by shedding as much darkness as possible, and releasing as much heaviness as possible, to let that flame flair up and warm us from within.

Being in California gave me such a deep appreciation for the dark, for the contrast of the elements. And ultimately, it gave me an appreciation for the darker emotions that come along with the contrast. If during the dark winter of contrast, we can dig deep and find the Light of who we truly are, then we can continue to hold that Light in any climate, in the presence of any darkness. That's a pretty remarkable skill.

There's so much rich variety in who we are, because of the contrast that was built into us to help us discover who we really are. Can we honor that unique contrast? Can we recognize our paths as a sacred school for our Soul's journey? If we can honor that contrast, the deep confusions, that Tiny Mad Idea, then we can release it … and stay in the Light. Permanently.

Releasing the Need for Contrast and Darkness

In December of 2012, people thought the Mayan Calendar said the world was going to end. This was just a misinterpretation of the ages. We were leaving the age of darkness and coming into the age of enLightenment. The Golden Age of EnLightenment began in 2013. This means that, spiritually and energetically, **the age of learning from darkness, suffering and pain was over. The age of enLightenment is about learning in Light, ease, joyfulness and freedom**.

If we play with that and try that on right now, we can look at our own lives and say that our contrast from our childhood and that early negative vibration that was programmed into us has done its job. It has created the variety in our lives, and we don't need that anymore. We can honor it and release it.

All we need to do is set the intention to release the old. Release the need to learn through contrast, deep confusions, and darkness. It served us for a while. It gave us variety. But we don't need it anymore. I encourage you to set the intention to release some of those old patterns and vibrations that have lived within you. It served its purpose to show us our purpose, mission, and direction in life. Now we have that direction, and we can release all the stuff that led up to the clarity. We can let that contrast still be the lesson—but without all the baggage and negative vibration that came with it. We're working in the Light, with our Higher Consciousness, so all we have to do is set the intention to release the old baggage. Recognize that the contrast served us beautifully. We can honor it and release it with love and appreciation. Our clarity is gained. We can replace it with purposeful intention and action moving forward.

I don't need to walk around feeling like a bad person or feeling unworthy anymore. I know that I am good and do good. I can still hold that purpose and mission, the clarity, without feeling bad, without feeling unworthy or unloved.

Do you see that you can drop that negative vibration and all the baggage, while still holding the life lesson moving forward? This is New Paradigm Energy. We're learning through our joy and love, not from suffering and angst. Our emotional guidance systems can still inform us that we've veered from Soul without all the stories that are stuck within the older dense vibrations. Some people call it releasing the old karma, or clearing out the etheric records (the energy from all our lifetimes).

All you have to do is set the intention to release the old energy that you carry around, and because of the Law of Attraction, we *can* release it. Ask for the release and it shall be wiped clean. It's your choice, however; your free will to actively release old dense vibrations (karma). You can keep the lessons and release the negative vibrations. I encourage you to do so.

Alchemizing the Dark with the Light

Once our consciousness shifts to see that the dark or contrast showing up in our lives is a way for us to learn lessons and set clear desires and direction, we can begin to work with the energy that reveals itself to us. We don't see it as a threat that we must resist against. Instead, we see it as the next puzzle piece. We explore the contrast with curiosity, and question its message in our lives. We allow it.

Witnessing the contrast without engaging in negative thought or emotion creates an environment of NEUTRALITY, so we can have a more Soul-based experience of life.

We can practice neutrality once we recognize that **the dark works for the Light, and that the contrast is just a tool used to reveal our Soul to us**. Contrast and darkness are not bad; they just ARE. Neutrality allows us to stay out of judgment/ego, and focus only on the lesson itself.

When we shine the Light of our conscious awareness upon the dark contrast that has shown up in our lives, an incredible ALCHEMY happens. The Light transforms the dark into the golden awareness of truth. We watch ourselves wake up, and we watch our lives transform. We watch the alchemy of the dark into Light.

- Having a parent who was angry and controlling made for a miserable childhood (dark contrast), however with introspection, desire, and awareness (Light), it transformed me into a loving, present mother (alchemy).

- Having a confusion about my body image (dark contrast) was an unfortunate existence, but with personal growth and prayer (Light), the transformation toward health and healing for myself and others was life-changing (alchemy).

- A friend's divorce felt like her tragedy (dark contrast), but with support, hope and love (Light), she transformed into a much more joyful expression of who she is (alchemy).

- A friend's struggle with domestic violence was horrifying for her (dark contrast), but the qualities of strength and self-worth (Light) that she built within herself as a result of that experience transformed her into someone who is extraordinarily helpful to other women who are ready to wake up to their strength and self-worth (alchemy).

While the dark contrast is unfortunate, the Light and awareness combined with the dark contrast ALCHEMIZES the two into something bigger, brighter, and more Divine. Is it possible to have achieved these effects without the dark contrast? Yes, but not until we woke up to our true potency and set intentions for the extraordinary.

Maintaining neutrality is a practice of non-judgment of the contrast, non-engagement with the negative energy, and stepping back from the storm that has descended. It allows us to see the gift in the contrast, even when the contrast is heavy. Once we see this gift, we can release the karma, and forgive all the people who dressed up in those dark cloaks to play the part of contrast for us to have the transformations our Soul desired. As you will read later, forgiveness (and the Violet Flame!) helps to alchemize much of the unnecessary angst that we hold when we focus on the contrast.

In Summary...

At some point in our childhood, we experienced deep separation from Source, from others, and eventually from ourselves. Because we experienced this so early, before we had rational minds, the separation didn't make sense to us so we formed deeply rooted confusions that wired into our subconscious mind. These deeply rooted confusions set the filters through which we view and experience life. All of us have different confusions based on our karma, belief systems, and family environment.

We can view these deeply rooted confusions as the means through which we discover our life lessons. Whatever we overcome in life informs our work in the world. Our life lessons expose the truth of who we are so we can move toward our life purpose.

We are not the contrast. We are not the relationship issues. We are not our failures. We are the Light. The darkness and contrast shows us the Light of who we are. If we can work with the dark contrast, and transmute the energy from resistance to desire, we alchemize the situations into rich treasures. We don't need to continue to generate negative experiences. We can now learn in the Light.

Journaling Meditation Practice: Deep Confusions, Life Lessons, and Purpose

The following is a journaling, meditation and prayer exercise to help gain clarity on what contrasts and life lessons have formed you, their value and purpose moving forward, and how to clear up the negativity and karma. Grab paper and a pen, and make yourself comfortable, in a seated position, for a journaling meditation.

Our Higher Consciousness speaks to us through our intuition and inner voice, and as we are connected to our breath, we sink in to that inner voice. During this meditation, read the questions, and as you stay connected to your breath, allow the answer to spontaneously show up for you. Try not to engage the thoughts or the mind, and avoid going into the fear that you don't *know* the answer. If you do go into that fear, you won't have access to the answer, because that's not the part of your brain that we're using. We're using our intuition, our inner guidance system. We want the thoughts to arise from your Heart center. Sink into the deep trust that all the answers exist within you, and that clarity is waiting for you to ask the question.

1. Feel your inner being with Lightness

Allow yourself to **observe your inner being or inner child** when you were young, before the separation into the ego occurred. Sit and watch what it felt like to be joyful and free, to feel inherent worth, love and safety. Begin to feel the vibration of that inner being. If you can't remember it, just imagine what it might have felt like when you were aligned, totally and completely in the flow of love and well-being.

Feel it deeply in your body and **notice how good it feels**. Watch it play out. Notice where, specifically, you feel it within your body. Notice the sensation. Notice what thoughts arise and what visualizations you have. Write down your experience of that Lighter inner being—thoughts, visuals, and vibrations in the body.

2. Feel your first most formative contrast

Breathe into the chest at the Heart, clear the mind, and come back to that experience of your inner being. When you're ready, allow yourself to **surface your first contrast** or a **period of**

your life that was full of contrast. Try not to engage it with the mind, just pull it up vibrationally and watch it for a moment.

Notice whether the vibration in your body begins to change as you continue to play out the situation or that period of your life.

- Watch the people involved.

- Watch your reaction to the situation.

- Bring your focus into how that period or experience feels in your body. Where do you feel it? Is there pressure, sensation, heaviness? If so, where?

- How would you label the vibrations or emotions? Intensify them if you can't feel it strongly enough. Feel the negative vibrations more intensely, recognizing that they're just vibrations. There's nothing to be afraid of, though it feels like fear.

- Write down the contrast that started those negative vibrations in the body, and how it feels.

3. Identify the stories or belief systems formed by that contrast

Now coming back into the breath, bring the breath into the chest. Notice whether that negative vibration is still there.

- Are there any stories or belief systems that you put together in your life around the confusion and the contrast that you experienced?

- How did the contrast form the way you related with people—with the world?

- How did the contrast set up your direction in life?

- How did it create a series of decisions for you as you moved onward in life?

- How did the contrast create confusion for you?

- Write down your thoughts.

4. Identify your life lessons

Now come back into your breath at your chest.

- How did your confusions form your lessons in life? What lessons grew out of your confusion?

- What were you supposed to learn in this lifetime, for you to transcend those confusions? What were they teaching you?
- Journal when you're ready.

5. Identify the purpose for your life that arose from your life lessons

Coming back into your breath, breathe into your chest.

- How did these life lessons provide clarity for your purpose? They showed you what you don't want in life. What clarity did they bring for what you *do* want in your life?
- How has your lesson shot forth rockets of desire for you to transform and expand your consciousness and your experience in this lifetime?
- Write down your thoughts.

6. Gratitude for the contrast

Coming back into your breath, allow yourself to see all the gifts and seeds of desire that have formed as a result of the contrast you created in your life. As you see all your gifts, bring up the feeling of appreciation and deep gratitude for this path of contrast, for the confusion. Allow yourself to feel the appreciation of the journey, recognizing that it's just an ongoing journey with no specific destination—just a series of contrasts to help us develop deeper desire. As you feel appreciation and gratitude for that journey, stay with the breath centered in the Heart.

7. Self-forgiveness

Forgive yourself for anything that you may still hold against yourself, using an ancient Hawaiian forgiveness prayer (I'm sorry, I love you, Please forgive me, Thank you) to release karma and negative vibration. Releasing yourself now, whispering softly, repetitively:

"**I'm sorry**, I'm sorry, I'm sorry, I'm sorry, I'm sorry. **I love you**, I love you, I love you, I love you, I love you. **Please forgive me**, please forgive me, please forgive me, please forgive me, please forgive me, please forgive me. **Thank you**, thank you, thank you, thank you, thank you."

As you inhale, feel the Light coming into every cell of your body. As you exhale, feel yourself releasing all the burdens that you've carried on the journey because you just didn't know you could release them with your free will. Breathe out through the mouth.

8. Forgive others

Now, think about all the people in your life that helped create the contrast for you to get your life lessons. They lowered their vibration and put on the dark cloak in order to serve you in this lifetime so you could grow and transform and transcend any karma or negative experience.

We'll say the Ho'oponopono forgiveness prayer for all of the people. Picture each one and say:

"**I'm sorry**, I'm sorry, I'm sorry, I'm sorry, I'm sorry. **I love you**, I love you, I love you, I love you, I love you. **Please forgive me**, please forgive me, please forgive me, please forgive me, please forgive me, please forgive me. **Thank you**, thank you, thank you, thank you, thank you."

9. Clearing the karmic slate.

If you will now, verbally state your intention to release all the negative vibrations that have lived within, asking for any other life lessons to be revealed gracefully, with ease and Light.

"Divine, I now release all of the negative contrast, the negative vibrations, the negative karma, the ancestral karma. Please bring in the Light and allow me to release, to forgive, and to make peace. I ask for the Light to come in and bring me my lessons through grace, ease, and love. Please help me to Lighten my vibration and create intention and desire with clarity. Please, Divine, thank you. Amen.

Release Daily Resistance

*Most of us are as eager to be changed as we were
to be born, and go through our changes
in a similar state of shock.*
-James Baldwin

My life used to come with very strong dramatic lessons until I learned to ask for subtler lessons to come with ease and grace. Since my inner listening is a bit more refined, I don't need to get hit upside the head with my lessons anymore. I can receive them with grace, ease and subtleness, because I've created the space in my life to actively and consistently listen to what is being brought to me. When I'm out of alignment, I can feel resistance building in my body because I've slowed my life down and eliminated the noise. Until we develop that refinement, though, we get our life lessons at first subtly, and then they get louder and louder until they bang us upside the head.

Often, we are too busy to listen for those life lessons. So much of the spiritual path is about slowing down and creating space to hear the subtle messages that come our way. Personally, I had to eliminate every commitment that served my ego, so I could stay in the flow. I learned to let my Heart schedule my life, not my mind.

Cleaning House

I received one of my abrupt life lessons six years ago. A week after my third daughter was born, we received a phone call from the hospital that her newborn screening came back with markers for a potentially fatal genetic metabolic disorder. If she were to go more than just a few hours without eating, she could die. I was in a bit of denial: *Oh, she won't have this disorder.* To this, the nurse said, *Please just wake this child up every couple of hours and nurse her. Don't let her go more than a couple of hours without eating because SHE COULD DIE.* A week later, we got the final results that she did, in fact, have this potentially fatal disorder.

So we woke her up to breastfeed every two to three hours. If you've nursed an infant, then you know that the feedings can take up to a half hour because you don't know when the baby has had enough to eat, so there wasn't much sleep between round-the-clock feedings. On top of that, I was juggling two other toddlers and managing potty training, terrible twos, treacherous threes...

Needless to say, I didn't sleep for the first two years of her life. I was getting more and more depleted because I wasn't able to replenish my body physically. The more I kept trying to keep all the balls in the air and continue life as *normal*, the more depleted I got, and the more depleted I got, the less breast milk I was producing, and the less milk I was producing, the more at risk my baby was for dying. My own self-care and replenishment (to keep my breast milk supply up) would determine whether she lived or died. This made self-care a life-or-death scenario in my life. Quite a big contrast for me, but it was such gift.

I could have gone into suffering and victim mode, and I'm sure I did some of that, but what happened in the months that followed changed my life forever. I realized that I couldn't serve on the board of directors for organizations anymore. I couldn't bring my toddlers to Kindermusic. I couldn't drain myself with playdates. I couldn't continue the friendships that took more than they gave. I had to basically clear my entire life of anything that did not nourish me, or did not provide an immediate return on my energetic investment (spiritual ROI!) ... because my daughter's life depended on it.

Wow, right? What if all of us could get such a dramatic lesson to show us the importance of self-care and self-connection! **Every time we have a big contrast, there is a huge gift that's waiting underneath it for us.**

Ego Attachments

What if we were able to evaluate each responsibility and obligation that we have in our lives as if it was make-or-break like that? What if each thing that we were doing, each responsibility, was evaluated as a life-or-death situation? Or, at the very least, as a feel good / feel bad?

That was the blessing that I was given, and it cleared my life of all the external hamster wheel attachments and responsibilities that weren't aligned with what felt good. If it felt good, it fed me. If it felt bad, it drained me. So I was trained very quickly to become more purposefully aligned. In the transition into alignment, I had to release the *doing* that was based on my ego's attachments.

- Being on a board of directors made me feel important, smart, and valuable. Instead, I had to find those emotions within.

- My toddlers' enrichment activities made me feel like a good mom. Instead, I had to help the kids develop the ability to play low key on their own, versus all the *doing* that I was putting in their lives, which was distracting them from being comfortable with their stillness. I needed to feel like a good mom in the stillness, too.

- Playdates got me out of the house so I could distract myself from the monotony and disconnection of my life. Instead, I needed to teach myself to slow down and stay home when I needed it; to stay connected with myself.

- Cleaning, cleaning, cleaning made me feel productive in my nothing-to-show-for-my-day stay-at-home world. Instead, I had to look at what it meant to be a stay-at-home-mom and how to feel my value without all the *doing*. My house needed just one cleanup a day. And I derived my value from self-esteem, rather than results.

- My friendships helped me feel like I was a good person. Instead, I had to see my goodness outside of my constant interactions. I found stillness and comfort in being alone and taking care of myself, instead of taking care of others.

I had to clear all of those external attachments so I could focus on rebuilding myself so my child could stay alive. And once I did, my life became inward and Heart-based.

When I got healthy enough to start letting things back in, I was able to very clearly evaluate whether something was going to be life-giving for me, or life-depleting. It was based on whether the thing that I wanted to do was something that served my ego or something that served my Soul. Because I was so depleted and undernourished, it was very clear whether an activity would throw me into energy reserves or fill my tank. I could visualize and try on the activity, and figure out whether I would feel good doing it, or not. *Is this doing based on my fears and deep confusions? Is this something that I'm going for because it makes me feel worthy, valuable, lovable, and important (ego-based reasons)? Or is this something that feels aligned with my Soul and will nourish me and others?*

So many people have said, *Oh, I'm just too busy during the day to check in with myself and do all this feeling. I can't fit this into my life.* For me, having that experience years ago, I say, What is more important than our connection to ourselves? What could possibly be more pressing than connecting with ourselves to explore the path that serves us? Yes, it needs to be built and requires mindfulness, but why not, if it'll lead to a more joyful existence?

If connecting with self, settling in, quieting the mind and connecting inward doesn't feel good, then there may be a deep confusion or misalignment that's trying to speak to us. We can look at what deep-rooted contrast has created that feeling, and why connection with self doesn't feel good. It just means there's a non-alignment.

We've confused ourselves by thinking that all of our *doing, doing, doing*—endless doing—is the point of life. We've created an externally focused, doing-based life. However, from the spiritual perspective, many would say the point of life is to feel peaceful, at ease, joyful, and playful. To feel free. In fact, feeling freedom is one of the highest qualities for many on the spiritual journey. Freedom to connect with self. Freedom to have our time be *our* time. Freedom to create and manifest, to connect with other people, to serve others. When we're working fifty hours a week and coming home to a million family obligations, and then maintaining the upkeep of personal lives, there's not a lot of freedom there. It's a life of doing. Not so much living and enjoying.

This doesn't mean all *doing* is *bad*. It just means that the ego-based doing doesn't serve us, and usually depletes us. It makes us feel less potent and purposeful in life.

Soul- vs Ego-based Doing

Many of us don't go deeply into the Heart to be able to sense whether something is going to be Soul-based (feels good) or ego-based (feels bad). The difficulty in determining whether an activity or decision is Soul-based is that we haven't refined our feeling nature.

Some people like their lives full of doing-doing-doing, and as long as they feel happy and connected with self and are living in the present joyfully, then that's perfect. Go do-do-do, because that doing is coming from the Soul. But if the doing is *not* aligned with the Soul, if it feels like an obligation and you have suffering and resentment because there's no time for yourself, then you are in ego-based doing.

Perhaps you are doing to support a Soul-based value, but you're not conscious of that choice, so you suffer and go into ego about it. Most of us get disconnected from the value that brought us to the doing, so we live a very disconnected, resentful, and suffering life because of it. For example:

- I wanted to own a horse, but cleaning the stables stinks (literally), so when I clean the stables, I can either suffer and complain because I'm not present to the fact that I'm supporting my value of the horse, OR I can I stay mindful of my love for the horse and focus on my love for the horse while I'm cleaning up after it.

- I love my children. Having children added true value to my life, so while I'm cleaning up the house and making the meals, instead of complaining and focusing on the small parts I don't like about having children, I am staying present to the vibration of my love for my children.

- Let's say I am a business owner and care about bringing this business out into the world, but there are the tedious tasks related to the business that give me a headache. I can take on the tedious tasks with love, appreciation, and connectedness, because this is all an expression of what it means to bring this business out into the world.

Do you see how often we refuse to own <u>all</u> the aspects related to the value that we are looking to express in life?

Suffering from Ego-based Doing

Sometimes, the underlying value of our *doing* is based in our deep confusions. We feel deficient—unworthy, unvaluable, not good, alone—so we developed a lot of ego commitments to show us the contrary. For example, *I'm serving on the board because I thought it would make me feel valuable, but because my value can't come from the outside world, I'm just getting annoyed and resentful.* Or *I have children so they can love me unconditionally (so I could get my love from the outside world), but as they grow up and defy me, I feel unloved and angry at them for not fulfilling my expectation.*

We must evaluate all of our *doing* and ask, *Why am I doing this? What value does this support?* We can either re-embrace the value we are going for, or we can evaluate whether there's space in our lives for that commitment if it's not a Soul-based commitment. People have fears about releasing commitments (friendship, professional, family), but releasing something when you are working to realign with the Heart will often be win-win.

Most of us see ourselves as a slave to our commitments: *I committed to do this, and now I HAVE TO do it.* Yes, that's true, follow through is important, but it's also important to consistently evaluate what *doing* belongs in your life and what needs to be shifted. For example, if you don't like cleaning your house and you feel resentful about cleaning toilets, then get a housecleaner or learn to live with a messier house. We have a lot of beliefs and assumptions about what we *have to* do in our lives. So much is a *have-to* for many people, so they suffer their way through their lives.

Suffering gets so deeply programmed into our patterns that even our Soul-based commitments turn into suffering. Many of us have well-worn belief systems and neural pathways toward suffering. Suffering is so important to be aware of in our lives. If we are negative and suffering, then we will attract situations and people that vibrate in suffering. Suffering attracts more suffering. I've known many people who have made a lifetime out of suffering, and they like it that way! *Great! Go for it!* But if you have a habit of suffering through life, and you want more alignment, then it's time to shift the vibration.

If I commit to help with my daughter's school play, then when I'm running around town searching for the *perfect* tiara, I can go into suffering or I can focus on the value that led me to the commitment in the first place (supporting my daughter at school, or driving around town doing something special with my daughter). Do you see? It's all about the perspective and the reasons why we're *doing*. I spend a lot of time helping people look at their *have-to's*, all the things that they feel obligated to do in their lives.

I'm a mother of three young daughters and I am constantly washing dishes and making meals. It can consume the whole day. I used to obsess about needing to get the house cleaned and spend pretty much my whole day cleaning up and barking for other people to clean up until I realized, *Oh, okay. I don't have to set the expectation that my house needs to be clean 24 hours a day when I have three kids.* I realigned to what felt realistic. When I'm trying to get the kids out of the house in the morning, the dishes will wait neatly in the sink until lunchtime, and then I do all of the dishes at once. I had to readjust my expectations of living in a super clean house with three children. We can, for example, adjust our expectations to getting the house neat *enough* and do one sweep later in the day—rather than twenty sweeps a day while feeling resentful and getting mad at our children because they didn't do this and they didn't do that. (This is why it's such a relief to go into someone else's house and see that their house is completely trashed. *Beautiful. My house is trashed right now, too.* There is no need for us to put on a show for each other.)

This same scenario applied for my husband in getting through all his emails at work. Clearing out the inbox is not realistic. There always about 50 *urgent* emails waiting in his inbox. So he had to accept the fact that the inbox is never empty. He needed to keep it prioritized and work his obsession to clear the inbox while running an organization. He could try to clean it out and stay up to midnight, but that would be an ego decision to sacrifice sleep and self-care. The ego may set an expectation that's not based in reality, that's not based in the Heart of someone's best interest.

When you have three daughters, there is constant contrast in life. My consistent expectation that there should be peace and harmony in my day is completely unrealistic. *Why would I expect that? Why would I expect that there would be a moment where someone wasn't complaining about something?* That is a completely unrealistic ego-based expectation that keeps me suffering and barking all day long. Instead, I shift into the Heart and realize that kids have conflict, and this is natural. I can learn to accommodate and work with the conflict, rather than expect it to go away and suffer about it..

We're often a slave to our own expectations of what life *should* look like and *should* be. So many of us are upholding completely unrealistic expectations of our *shoulds*. This is where we need to step back and witness all of these patterns and start questioning them—bringing them to mindfulness, and to consciousness. *Why do I believe that? What's bringing me the most headache?*

On our spiritual path, we want to create space in our lives for freedom. That means we want to evaluate the obligations and expectations we have for ourselves. Anything we feel obligated to, or resentful or suffering about, we need to make a change. We can make a list of those things, evaluate each activity, and ask ourselves:

1. Why did I get myself into this? What value was I going for?

2. Is this a Soul-based value or did ego get me into this?

3. What can I do about this activity to feel better about it? Is this something I want to keep in my life, and truly embrace because it supports Soul values? Or do

I need to look at how I got myself into this situation (i.e., what was my underlying confusion), and determine how to ethically release this activity so I can be better aligned?

Once we do this work, we start to create space in our lives...inward space. As we settle into that space, the peace and grounding that is cultivated bleeds into the rest of our lives.

Creating the Inward Space

Personally, my morning process four days a week is to get the kids on the school bus, sit down with my cup of tea, gaze out of my windows into my beautiful backyard, and connect to my breath. I have developed a ritual of breathing into a state of presence. Once I'm present, I feel all of my emotions bubble up from the week. I feel each and every one of them, and as I feel them, they naturally release out of my vibration. Then I do my spiritual practice and go into silence. When I'm done with the stillness, I work with my clearer, higher vibration to manifest what I want to create in my life. Four days a week, I'm creating inward space. A couple of hours to just sit with myself.

Most people don't want to sit with themselves because it doesn't feel good. They sit down and feel all the negative stuff bubble up. They don't know what to do with it, so they hop on the computer or busy themselves with *doing* to make the bad feelings go away. This is only because they don't know how to release the negative vibrations. They haven't yet mastered their vibrations and they don't know what it feels like to **find comfort in the stillness**. Once we start releasing all of the ego-based *doing*, we can recreate that relationship with ourselves through inward space.

People say, *I don't have time for that type of self-reflection and connection*, but I will tell you, once you create that rhythm in your life, once you develop that connection with yourself, you get so nourished and hooked on it that it becomes the staple of your life. Life gets scheduled *around* self-connection. *I'm sorry, I can't volunteer because that's my inward time and that time is golden. Or, I won't be able to do an 8am meeting, how about 10am?* That's sacred time, and all of life gets scheduled around it.

But first, we have to get totally hooked on that daily time to ourselves. It needs to feel good enough that we are drawn to it. It's not a *have-to*! It's a yearning. It's like creating a yoga practice. Some people have to force themselves to go to yoga until they get hooked, and then they see, *Oh, wow. This is amazing. It feels so good!* Once they feel how amazing it is, life gets scheduled *around* yoga. But yoga is still *doing*, so we can create the inward space that's not dependent on a teacher, or a studio, or another person.

Once we have that inward connection, we don't want activities or obligations to get in the way of it. It's too important, so we begin to restructure life around our connection to ourselves, which allows us to start to mindfully create the life our Soul is yearning for! This is where life gets juicy.

Stillness to Manifest Our Heart's Desires

The inward space allows us to reflect on our values and determine whether our outward manifestations reflect our highest values. We start to release the situations that drain our prana (life force energy) and our connection to self, and we create rhythm around self-nourishment. With the self-nourishment, we become crystal clear about what serves us and what doesn't. And with that Soul-yearning clarity, we can manifest brilliant situations that support living a vibrant life.

If we have a job that eats sixty hours a week, we start to look at how to be more efficient or how to recreate our work situation so we can get more money in less time. Why couldn't we work less and bring in more money? Why can't we be more efficient? Why can't we better organize our time or prioritize our tasks? Of course, we can. We can use the Law of Attraction to create whatever scenario we want! We just have an old-school model we were trying to squeeze ourselves into. (Many spiritual people will have unique work situations because their freedom is their most important thing in life!)

People thought it was crazy that I was packing up my family and going to California for two months. They were like, *Why? What? How? How did you even do that?* For me, I know that my body does not like the cold and I like more sunLight. As I sat with that, I realized I *could* just leave the cold during the winter! I started creating momentum picturing myself in the warmth during the winter. Because our lives were already aligned—our kids were in a school that valued adventure and connection to self, my husband was working from home and had a job that supported his connection to himself, I was in an industry that supported connection to self … so creating a situation that was more comfortable and aligned with ourselves was easy, because we've been setting it up for years. The Universe was able to easily orchestrate that manifestation because I truly believe that what I desire is totally possible.

If there is something in your life that doesn't serve you, manifest a new scenario that *does* serve you. If part of what you're doing doesn't serve you, see if it would serve someone else to do it so you can free your time to do more of what you love. We have a lot of rigid belief structures about what's possible and what we *should* be doing.

I was offered a "prestigious" job (for a yogi). It totally aligned with what I saw myself doing and would be purposeful, but it would require more hours for less money, and less time supporting my highest values: inward space, my children, creativity, self-expression, and manifestation. So I had to do a cost-benefit analysis on what my ego would be getting out of having this prestigious position, how it could further my purpose in life by serving others, how it might help/hinder my creativity and self-expression, whether it would encroach on my inward space and self-connection, how it would affect my connection to my children and husband. Would I be getting a bigger benefit for my time versus the cost? I evaluated it all and gained clarity on all the Soul and ego qualities in the position. In the end, I decided it was too many hours, but I went forward with it anyway because my intuition told me that it served my Soul's purpose. And do you know what happened? I was given a less prestigious position, with less hours, and all the purposeful work, at the same pay rate! Beautiful clarity and manifestation.

This is the evaluation we can be doing in every moment of our lives. *What value would I be getting out of that? What's my highest value? Would I have to sacrifice my highest value? What do I care about in my life? What would I be losing versus what would I be gaining?*

Imagine living with this level of mindfulness every moment of every day. Imagine how much happier we would be if we were either owning what we were doing or releasing it so that we could have more time doing what we want to do.

We can evaluate all of the belief structures that tell us we *have to* do something because we trust that the Law of Attraction can put together whatever we want, however we want it to look. If we do truly believe that, we can start releasing the way we've set up life until this point.

Practice: Journaling on the Doing

Take a horizontal piece of paper and create the following six columns.

1. **Activity:** This is a list of the obligatory or suffer-y activities that you have going on this week, this month, or in general in your life. You'll know what to put down there. It's not about simple activities like showering (unless showering is a big deal for you, which in my life, it is!). These are the activities that feel heavier, that require evaluation.

Example: My activity is having coffee with Jane.

2. **Value:** What value are you going for by doing this activity?

Example: If I have coffee with Jane, then I'm a good friend because Jane doesn't have friends and I want to be a friend to someone who doesn't have friends.

3. **How it feels:** How does this activity feel in your body? Positive or negative? Good or bad? This is the feeling underneath the activity.

Example: When I try that on in my body, it feels negative.

4. **Why it feels that way:** Why does it feel positive or negative? This gets to what you were going for when you committed to it.

Example: This feels negative because I don't share values with Jane. She judges people and gossips a lot and it's tough for me to navigate to topics outside of negativity.

5. **Ego/Soul:** Is this an ego- or Soul-based activity? Perhaps it started as Soul but shifted to ego?

Example: The reason why this is an ego activity for me is that I want to be a good person and I think a good person chooses to be friends with people who don't have friends. I've set up the situation in my life so I can feel like a good person, so she can feel loved. But in reality, this situation isn't aligned with my Soul/interests/values, and every time I do it, I feel worse because I could be covering up Jane's lessons around building healthy relationships.

6. **Shift required:** What shift is required in you to make this commitment feel good? This will either be a shift in perspective or a shift in the activity itself.

Example:

1. Stop initiating coffee and be honest about my feeling about the friendship.

2. Set an intention to attract a better situation that honors both of us.

3. Change my perspective on Jane. I can change my perspective and just own the fact that I want to feel like a good person doing a good deed. I'm owning the ego-based attachment that I'm going for. (It's okay to stay mindful if we are not ready to make a major shift! It's also totally fine to say, *Oh, I'm eating a piece of cake. I'm covering up some emotions, but I'm going to be mindful about eating this cake until I'm ready for change.*)

This exercise is an opportunity to truly own what we're doing and why, so we can feel more joyful day-to-day.

Deeper Exploration of Resistance

Once we stop all the *doing*, and create some inward space, we begin to process all the resistance that has built up in life. This is a heavy vibrational clean-out period, but it doesn't last forever. Stillness allows the resistance to surface and the clean-out is pretty simple. Once we release resistance, we pave the path for allowing all that is. We pave the path to feeling good.

Imagine that you have a vortex of energy around your body. If you get too far from center (at the Heart), you lose your alignment and move outside of that vortex. It doesn't feel good to get away from yourself and get misaligned, right? It doesn't feel good to be outside of our vortex, so the closer we are to center, the better we feel. When we maintain distance from center and venture outside of our vortex, we experience resistance. The only way to feel better is to release the resistance and feel our way back to center. Our ego keeps the resistance in place until we mindfully decide to stop resisting, and use our emotional guidance system to bring us back to the Heart.

Resisting the Beach Balls

I'm going to take you into a visualization metaphor. Try to imagine that you're floating in your own personal swimming pool. You're floating on your back with a set of beach balls. In your society, you don't see beach balls in anybody else's pool, so you believe your job is to take each beach ball and shove it underneath the surface. The beach balls represent the negative vibrations that are happening in our body. The balls are the misalignments, the experiences or vibrations that are outside our vortex. We hide them beneath the surface, right?

Imagine yourself laying in a pool with a bunch of inflated beach balls that you're trying to keep underneath the surface, because when you look around, you don't see anyone else's beach balls on the surface of the pool. You've made a life out of taking these beach balls—these negative vibrations, these misalignments—and continuously pushing them below the surface, under your body.

Now, when you push them below the surface, what do you feel? What does it take to keep all of those balls below the surface? You feel **resistance**, right? You're resisting against the beach balls because their natural action is to pop up above the surface and blow away with the wind. But you

don't want to do that, because you've been taught that beach balls must not be seen, they must live below the surface.

And the truth is, you're not conscious of what specific beach balls are living below the surface. In fact, you're not aware of many of them until the resistance gets really intense and loud. Until, for example, they're causing pain or discomfort underneath your ribs, neck or hips. You notice the <u>effect</u> of the resistance, but you may not know that you are subconsciously pushing those beach balls down. There are some that you're more aware of, and there are those that you're *not* so aware of.

Every one of them creates resistance, which causes discomfort. They create dis-ease. The ease of just floating on the surface of the pool is disturbed by the necessity of keeping these beach balls underneath the surface.

As life goes on, you accumulate more beach balls, and it takes more and more effort to keep them below the surface. You can feel your physical body getting contorted, right? Your neck is pushing against the resistance and it feels pain. You may feel pain in your shoulders, your arms, knees and hips. It takes a lot of effort to keep these misaligned beach balls in place. You feel built-up tension—anger, resentment, or sadness—with more balls to keep in place.

This is what it feels like to be in our human bodies. We've taken all of these negative vibrations and emotions and continue to resist against them, keeping them underneath the surface. If one pops up, we quickly push it back down, because, you know, God forbid you're at work and a negative emotion that's been there for twenty years pops up! *No, no, no, no, no, no!*

We were never taught what to do with these things. We look around and we don't see anybody with their negative vibration beach balls popping up, right? The norm has become a process of continuing to keep the resistance in our bodies below the surface.

Releasing the Balls—Feel It on Its Way Out!

So what do we do with all these beach balls? All we need to do is let the beach ball pop up. Release it. Pop! We can look at it and say, *Wow, that's been living underneath my shoulder this whole time?* It's that easy.

We have been putting so much effort into resisting these negative emotions, these pesky beach balls, but all we need to do is LET THE DAMN THING SURFACE! When we go into our inward space and let the ball surface, we will feel it. We may feel like we are going to DIE! Yes, it doesn't feel good to let the gunk surface after pushing it down for ages, but once we let it go and sit in it, we recognize that we were running from a vibration. Feeling it releases it.

Once it releases, it may take some time for it to blow out of our pool. It may circle around us a little bit. And when this happens, we can simply witness it. **Feel the vibration**, watch the pattern, keep releasing it with our breath, and allow it to float around as long as it needs to, knowing that when it's ready, it will blow away.

This is what we mean when we're talking about really sitting with ourselves, connecting with ourselves, listening to what the resistance in our shoulder is telling us. Feeling the vibrations even though intellectually we have no idea what the vibration is about. It won't make sense intellectually, because it's often an old, leftover vibration from when you were like five years old!

Often, we look around our lives and make up stories about what we think the vibration is from in our current life, the past, or even in past lives. We need to BLAME it on something or someone, right? Really, the story doesn't matter ... unless it assists you in releasing the resistance. So if you want to go into a past life or your childhood and find a story that gives you a reason why this beach ball has been sitting underneath your shoulder your whole entire life, it's totally valid to do so—but only if that story assists you in releasing resistance against the beach ball. The reality is that resistance has been living in the body and it's ready to come up to be released—that can be the end of the story!

Life should feel good all the time, right?

We all go through those periods of negative vibrations or emotional dips. Unfortunately, as a society, we believe that we shouldn't have an emotional dip, a rough week, or a rough day. We go around expecting that our lives should be glossy and beautiful and sunny every single day. We expect our bodies to give us peak energy every day (*no room for being tired!*), and we think that we should be the best version of ourselves in every moment. Pretty high expectations, eh?

Really, if we're on the spiritual path, then we're asking these beach balls to come up to be released. As they come up to be released, we must feel the resistance and negative emotion deep down into our bones, and allow it to release. This is not a process for the meek! It takes courage and requires a great deal of self-awareness and self-care to journey through this tunnel of resistance. The spiritual path is not for someone who just wants to float around in denial of all this stuff that's happening underneath the surface of the pool.

If there's resistance in our emotions, thoughts, or body, then we are open to the beach ball coming up. We're open to looking at it, feeling it, and allowing it to float around us in the pool for a little while until it's ready to blow off. Throughout this process, life may not feel cheery, beautiful and sunny every single day.

We must adjust our expectations and allow the beach balls to start coming up. We must set aside this contorted belief that life is supposed to be perfect and easy-going and simple. It's not supposed to be that way. We're *supposed* to have this contrast, but we continue to believe that there shouldn't be any contrast in our lives. Ideally, we are meeting this contrast with NEUTRALITY—not judging or resisting—as we release the beach balls.

We can look at these beach balls from the perspective of our chakras, too. We have these energy centers in our body (Chapter 2), and we may feel the resistance (pain or discomfort) in a specific area of the body, which will be our signal that we have some deeply rooted low vibrations stored there. The yogic perspective has elements (earth, fire, water, air, and ether) and colors (rainbow) and even planets connected to various chakras in our body. There is resistance, with lessons attached, that we come to this world to explore, which correspond with the energy centers within our body. Resistance is there, vibrationally, to draw our attention to it. As we bring awareness and breath (prana, life force energy, chi) into those parts of our bodies, we allow the Light and dislodge the resistance.

Relationships and Ball Exchange

We live with this resistance in our lives and keep our beach balls under the surface. And then a friend, or a relative, or a spouse pulls their pool right up next to yours. They've got their own set of beach balls in different parts of their body. They may have more beach balls, or fewer. The balls may be organized in different areas of their energetic body.

Soon, you start exchanging some beach balls. Your partner or your friend is throwing his beach balls in *your* pool and you're throwing some of your balls over to *his* pool, and next thing you know, the fabric of your lives are intertwined. You have a mix of each other's beach balls in both pools. Over time, it's hard to know whose balls are whose, right?

At first this exchange feels good. You're sharing the burden of your balls because he is taking on some of the resistance load for you. He has thrown some of his balls over into your pool and while they create a new burden for you, they are *new* balls and it's creating variety in your life, so you're happy to take them on. There is a new mix of resistance now.

Shall we make this a little bit more tangible so we can see what this really means? Let's say a friend is typically depressed and feeling unloved. They are pushing some beach balls down under their chest (Heart chakra #4). They have some resistance and negative vibrations around being loved. You took those balls on as a friend, to show them that they're loved because you've got a lot of love flowing—you're not pushing many beach balls down at the Heart—so it was easy for you to provide love for them. So you've placed yourself in their life as the person that gives them support and love, because they haven't been able to access that for themselves. Turns out that they're so far outside of their vortex when it comes to love—they're so disconnected from their Heart and their own Source of love—that you're in a *critical* exchange with them now. You started this exchange feeling like you're giving them something they need, so you can feel useful in all your *doing*. That was your part of the exchange. Except after a while, it starts to feel like there's a dependency, since you've taken on one of their heavier beach balls. Now *you* hold the responsibility in *their* life to give them love, because they're so far away from their Source, they're so misaligned in this area, that they feel like they are going to DIE if you withdraw the love. You see the problem with the exchange?

Another type of ball exchange: Jason has a lot of anger (in the upper belly—Will chakra #3), so to help balance out his beach ball of resistance toward reality, Sheila has become very accommodating in helping to make life more comfortable for Jason. Sheila, acting as the accommodator, tiptoes lightly around Jason's blame and anger, and walks on eggshells to help him feel happier and show him the bright side. In exchange, Sheila has a safe and secure home, because she has trouble providing for herself due to low self-worth (Root chakra #1, and Will chakra #3). Now they have this kind of dance, a beach ball exchange of covering up anger in exchange for a *safe* home.

Even though the beach balls have been exchanged, and each person temporarily feels better because they are sharing the resistance burden, there is still imbalance and resistance being pushed beneath the surface. Now there's dependency along with the negative vibration. There's still negative emotion because neither person is hanging out in their vortex—where there wouldn't be *any* resistance.

Relationships Without Ball Exchange

When we're aligned with our Heart, we don't need to do a ball exchange to get our worthiness, because when we're in our vortex and connected with ourselves, we're in the stream of self-worth. When we're in our vortex, our relationships start to take on a different nature. There's not a lot of dependency. There's not a lot of exchange on anger, suffering, or lack. It's not based on the exchanging of beach balls.

Typically, in relationships however, we exchange beach balls, create more resistance, and begin to feel even more dependent, powerless and outside of our vortex. We're not connected to our own Source energy and the exchange gets muddled.

When we start on the spiritual path, we have these beach balls releasing out all over the place! You're feeling the resistance surface and you're witnessing it and you're kind of … a big fat MESS! But as you get closer to your alignment and have fewer balls underneath you in your pool, you start to feel Lighter and brighter, with a higher vibration. This sounds great if you live in a vacuum, but this can be tricky if you're in a relationship with someone who is not, at the same time, releasing their own beach balls. Maybe as you are surfacing their beach balls—that you have been carrying for them for like twenty years!—their balls pop back over to their own pool, and they don't like it. Hmmm, yes, some contrast may occur.

If you're in a relationship where you've been giving someone love because they can't feel their own alignment and Source, as you get more aligned, you recognize that being the sole Source of love for that person is not serving them. You're covering up their lack of alignment and you don't want to be the cover-up that is keeping that person from their inner joy and love, so you compassionately release their beach ball to allow them to find their alignment.

It takes a great deal of consciousness to compassionately shift the relationship. We have to feel our way through it. Every interaction needs to be guided by intuition, by what feels good. Our Heart will guide us if we stay out of ego, and stay inward in our feeling nature. We can allow the other person to be who they are. We allow reality to be what it is. If they are experiencing negativity and resistance toward you, that's okay. It's their choice to have that experience in life. Abraham-Hicks said the most profound thing that helped me gain clarity here:

> ...You do the simple work of paying attention to your own vibrational offering... You save yourself the enormous and impossible task of controlling the behavior of others. When you remember that the varied behavior of others adds to the balance and well-being of your planet—even if they offer behavior that you do not approve of, and you do not have to participate in the unwanted behavior, and will not unless you give your attention to it—you become more willing to allow others to live as they choose.

We can watch their behavior like a movie, in neutrality and in witnessing state, without vibrationally engaging with the negativity. We can even honor that there is a purpose in their negativity, for them and for others. Perhaps the purpose is to help *us* set off a rocket of desire for something different in our lives.

We can try on each of life's scenarios moment-by-moment, day-by-day, in a very present way so that our inner emotional guidance system can shift our actions and reactions, which lets the partnership evolve to serve both people involved. While we all want a rule for how to deal with "negative people"—*The way to deal with negative people is 'x'*—in each moment, we can check in and see, *Okay, I'm starting to awaken to this pattern. I'm starting to witness it. It doesn't feel good anymore. Well, what would feel good? What response to her negativity would feel best?* As long as you're in alignment, your Heart and your vibration will tell you the best thing to do.

We have a choice to *resonate* with others' vibrations, and therefore let them set the momentum, or we can work to strengthen our own positive vibration, which will set the vibration for those around us. If someone who is in lower vibration in our lives wants to stay in low vibration, once you raise your vibration, you may not **resonate** with each other anymore. This person wants to stay angry and blame the world. You don't feel angry anymore. You just don't **resonate** in that vibration. So stay positive, and find your own positive vibration momentum by focusing on something other than the contrast. Create your own happiness, peace, or other high vibration. In time, the other person may begin to resonate with you because your strong momentum may start setting the resonance. Or it may become so obvious that you are on different wavelengths.

Maybe people see that you're Lighter and brighter, so they think that you would be in a good position to carry more of their resistance. So they start throwing *new* beach balls into your pool! We begin to notice other people's balls popping into our pool *all of the time*, and because we're not distracted by our own beach balls, and because we are closer to our Source, all we can see is everybody else's beach balls. It's like, *Oh my gosh, dude. I'm not taking that on for you. Just release it already!* The nature of our relationships changes.

We must set the intention to *stop receiving the balls*. To stop enabling. To stop the dependency. We can do this as compassionately as possible. It's just not natural; it doesn't feel good in our bodies to take on the beach balls anymore, because if you're in your vortex, your perspective and consciousness has shifted. When you're in your vortex, you don't take on other people's resistance.

We stop receiving the beach balls, while still allowing the person to do what they wish with the balls. We allow their resistance to exist in life. It exists. It just is. It's their lesson, it's their journey, and we need to allow that. We allow their beach balls to come up to the surface ... but we don't take the balls and cover them up.

If someone is very upset or angry with me and wants to lash out, they may lash out. I don't rage and resist against their resistance, because I work to be in a place of neutrality and mindfulness—I recognize that their resistance is going to want to attract resistance out of me. As I pull back and allow that, I also refuse to take their beach ball or cover it, so their resistance is exposed at the surface. This is how we can be of service to other people by simply being the mirror, the reflection, of their resistance. If we allow their resistance without feeding into it, and hold compassion for them (because we know how vulnerable it feels to have our beach balls exposed at the surface), we give them the opportunity to reflect on their resistance. They can't make it about us because we just got out of the way and served as a witness, so they can see their lessons. And we know that seeing our lessons is just part of the human process, so we don't feel pain or angst when other people's resistance is up. We celebrate it! *Oh, wow. Look. They're getting the contrast. Maybe they'll get the lesson this time!* We celebrate other people receiving their contrast and seeing their resistance because that's how we grow, transform and release the negative vibrations out of our bodies.

In Summary…

Our ego's attachments get us involved in so much *doing* that we don't have space for *being*. Looking at what we are doing, and why we are doing it, allows us to align life with the Heart. When we are in alignment with the Heart, life feels better. There is less suffering and obligation. It's Lighter and more joyful.

To release the resistance that builds up in our daily lives, and manifest a life that is in alignment with the Heart, we must first create some space and find stillness. This provides the environment to feel all the resistance, identify what beach balls are lingering beneath the surface, and finally release them. When we do this regularly, we can release the beach balls in our relationships and move into more purposeful exchanges with those we love.

Recorded Meditation Practice: Releasing the Balls

You can access a guided meditation to help you work with releasing the Resistance in the body at: www.enLIGHTenWithKim.com. Click on **Community Resources** and **Book Meditations**, log in for free, and find the meditation called **#5 Chakra Resistance Clearing Meditation.**

Take Back Your Power

A clay pot sitting in the sun will always be a clay pot. It has to go through the white heat of the furnace to become porcelain.
-Mildred Witte Stouven

As we journey along on our spiritual path, we begin to see all situations as completely perfect when they show up in our lives. Everything that shows up has Divine timing, arriving at exactly the time we need it—the resources, the blessings, <u>and the contrast</u>. We have deLight and gratitude in the blessings and miracles that we're experiencing. We have similar gratitude for the contrast because when the contrast shows up, we've attracted it, and we take complete responsibility for pulling it in. As we pull it in, it's exciting to see what the Universe has packaged up for us to learn in that very moment. We see everything as an effect of the Soul's journey through this extraordinary life, through this vessel of the body.

We begin to see our responsibility in attracting EVERYTHING that has shown up in our lives. And that responsibility for everything brings with it empowerment and potency. We see how our thoughts and vibrations can create our Mastery. Responsibility feels good and powerful … the ticket to the life we always dreamed of.

The Power of Responsibility

I'm going to take you on a little journey to show you what this empowered responsibility might feel like in a situation. The first perspective is coming from a place of responsibility, and the second is victimhood, or non-recognition of attraction.

Let's say your spouse has decided that they are leaving the partnership. As the contrast comes into your awareness, it puts everything on pause and you step back. As you step back, the first thing you do is take full responsibility for having attracted it. You look at the contrast and start to dissect it. You look at the different aspects of it. As you unwrap and dissect it, you begin to feel into the contrast that showed up. As you feel through the negative vibration of the contrast, you search for the ways that you're responsible for attracting it into your life. While the situation may be painful, you know how to feel through every wave of negative vibration to get the lesson and release the vibration. In time, it actual feels good to see, 'Wow, I attracted this marital breakup. How did I do that? Whoa! I hadn't even seen myself doing that. I'm learning so much about how I do the world.'

It's like a mystery to be solved, and you have reverence toward the situation because the contrast is the clue that's been sent from the Universe to help you learn something that you weren't able to see about yourself. You spend some time with the contrast because you need to look at it from every angle and feel into it. You keep looking deeper and deeper for the responsibility you had in vibrating that into your life, because you know that it's a gift being sent to help you learn and see something that you weren't seeing before. You celebrate the learning because it has helped you figure out what you <u>don't</u> want. You know that this is giving you complete clarity on what you don't want, so you hang out with that learning and feel what you <u>don't</u> want. You let yourself feel it, because you're not scared of it. You don't think you're going to get stuck in it, and you know you're not going to die, even though there are days where it feels like it.

You know when you are done exploring and feeling it because you've done this so many times before. You begin to shift the momentum of what you don't want and that feeling of not wanting it. You refocus your energy toward what you <u>do</u> want, because what you do want is so clear. Clarity is gifted to you through the contrast and the feeling into what you don't want, and now there's clarity on what you do want. As you refocus the momentum on what you do want, you get really excited because the clarity feels good. You didn't have that clarity before the gift of the relationship breakup, before the contrast arrived into your life. You now have a new trajectory of passion and excitement and clarity that you didn't have before.

You play with that clarity and begin to feel the vibration of what you do want, and you match your whole being to that clarity. Every cell of your body gets vibrationally matched to that vision of what you want, and you begin to savor that vibration. You begin to dance with it and explore it and feel it. In every cell of your body and every second of every day, you feel the joy and excitement of what you do want, until you can vibrate it so effortlessly, as if it's already occurred. In fact, you almost don't need it to occur, because your current vibration makes you feel so good. There's really no difference. You can feel the vibration of having had it, and the only thing that's missing is the material manifestation of it. It feels like you're 3/4 of the way there. If it manifests, great. If it doesn't, well, you still have the clarity and the vibration that you're sitting with. It feels good and your vibration is high.

Okay, so that situation started with contrast but ended feeling really good. As you may have noticed, there wasn't much mention of the spouse or the other person involved in the situation, because it was a personal experience. It was *your* experience. **You were 100% responsible for the situation.** You called into the world what you wanted to experience. Our contrast doesn't have much to do with the messenger.

Now we're going to try on that same situation from the perspective of ego and the mind:

*Your spouse decided that they were going to leave you. You feel that contrast, and it feels awful. The awful feeling is so deep and you feel so powerless and weak and sad, and the vibration is super low. All you can do is think about the contrast of your spouse leaving you. As you think about it, you feel even more horrible. You build a mountain of heaviness and lots of momentum on the horrible feeling. Then you start to get angry, because anger feels a little bit better than being powerless and miserable. You start brewing on **how wrong they were** to do what they did and how much you can **blame them for creating this contrast in your life**. You start picturing and visualizing these arguments that you can have about how **you are right** and **they are wrong**. In fact, you may engage in that argument of how you're right about how **they shouldn't have done something**, and your **expectation** of what they should have done. If you do have the opportunity to exchange with this person, you start throwing your beach balls in their pool and they start throwing their beach balls in your pool. You can get some other people's pools involved.*

In the end, it feels a little bit better because sitting in that vibration of powerlessness, weakness and sadness didn't feel good. Anger and blame felt better. But now you've got quite a messy situation, because you don't know whose beach balls are whose. You don't know whose negative vibrations are whose, and you've just pinned your negative vibrations all over each other. As you leave the situation, you feel powerless, negative and just plain crappy.

Then you start to attract more of those crappy, bad-feeling, low-vibration situations into your life. You keep proving the negativity, because there are more people to be angry at and to blame and exchange negative vibrations. You keep attracting more of that because you haven't seen your responsibility in this at all. It's all everybody else's fault, so you're going to keep attracting situations where you will have those negative vibrations with other people, and you'll feel low about yourself because really, your base vibration is low and negative. You turn to your go-to vices—wine, overeating, drama. You're really just trying to raise your vibration, but you're doing so from the ego, and you're not seeing your responsibility. You don't own your vibration and you're trying to pin it on everyone else. You just go to deeper anger and judgment, because that feels a little bit better than sadness or depression.

That's where that story ends: feeling crappy and creating more crappy, and feeling more negative and attracting more negative, and pinning everything on everyone else and starting to see the world as 'I'm a victim and other people create negativity for me in my life.'

Now you can see the difference between feeling the contrast, taking responsibility and owning your contrast, and shifting into desire ... versus feeling the contrast and going into anger, blame, judgement, and keeping yourself confused in the external world.

There is power in seeing our responsibility in the world. We want our power when we want to manifest something positive, but we often want to ignore the unconscious negative manifestations that we don't like. The reality is that **we have to see our responsibility <u>for it all</u> in order to harness the Law of Attraction**. We don't need to include self-blame and punishment in our responsibility. We can stay neutral and in the Light as we dig through our life situations so we can maintain our potency.

Karma

Karma, or the Law of Cause-and-effect, means that every action that we put into the world has a reaction. Every vibration we put out there will boomerang back a similar vibration. Karma is a kind of energetic and vibrational build-up or accumulation of what we have been attracting into our lives.

Our karma comes from various sources. We carry karma forward from our **past lives**. We have karma along our **mother's family lineage**, along our **father's family lineage**, and we have our **current life's karma**. There's karma built into geographical locations, among heritages, in communities and countries. We've experienced all kinds of relationships and exchanges of beach balls and negative vibrations along the way. Karma lives vibrationally in us until we can bring it to the surface and consciously process and release it.

Our past experiences, from this life or past lifetimes, gather energy which lives within our energy field or vortex. We can view these vibrations from past lives/experiences, or from early in our current life, as leftover vibrations. They're vibrations that we can tap into at will. Many of us have believed that if we've had these negative vibrations in the past—negative relationships or negative karma—then we're stuck with the karma in the present. The current spiritual understanding is, *Hell no, you're not stuck with it!* In fact, we can use forgiveness, the Violet Flame, and the Law of Attraction (rockets of desire!) to pave new pathways, to create new vibrations. Perhaps we have leftover negative vibrations from unlearned lessons from our childhood or our past lives. Perhaps, there are beach balls that we've exchanged, that we haven't cleared up from past lives or childhood. We are not plagued with the past. It may be that those are the well-worn pathways in our vibrations, and it may be what's familiar to us, but it is not, in fact, our destiny for our future. The beach balls will stay with us until we clear them from our energetic vortex, and decide to focus our energy in a new direction.

Also in that vortex of who we are, are all the positive aspects and vibrations from the past. Positive Karma! We can tap into whatever vibrations we desire.

Many of the eastern spiritual traditions will say that we continue the path of karma, in the cycle of birth and rebirth, taking new bodies and playing out our karma until we uncover who we truly are, until we know that we are the Light. Deep in the teachings of these ancient traditions, there is the recognition that once you know you are the Light, you can align with the Light and release the drama created from the human ego's karma. You can release all the karma you've accumulated. That is what is available right now. We are entering the Golden Age of EnLightenment, and we are all filling with high vibration Light that is completely accessible to us. It is up to us to decide to release the pattern of karma, and to stay aligned with our Light, setting new high-vibrational intentions here and now. So much Light is now accessible on this planet that we don't need to stay in those negative vibrations and old patterns. They are done, and we can use our intention to mindfully release karma, to mindfully release the old patterns and negative vibrations.

The Light that is currently coming into this planet is pushing our inner darkness up and out. We are going to find ourselves stuck in some temporary negative vibrations as we move toward alignment, as we align with the Light, love and well-being of who we are. We'll feel the negative come up to be released, and we will make stuff up, saying, *I'm stuck in this negative vibration and I was doing so well, and I thought I got past this, and why am I here in negative vibration!* We'll suffer about it. But in reality, when that negative vibration comes up, it means we are pulling in so much Light that all we have to do is look at that beach ball as it's coming up so we can mindfully release it. Do you see that we're *not* stuck with it? We just get confused when we're feeling that low vibration, because we resist against it.

What if we can simply wake up now and recognize that we are the Light and we don't need these negative vibrations to learn anymore? Instead of continuing the cycle of taking this karma from lifetime-to-lifetime, we're ready to release that tango that we've been doing with the same people. *I don't need to tango with my mother in the next lifetime to realize I am the Light and she is the Light. I don't need to struggle against my body, because I know it's my sacred vessel of Light.*

For a while, my daughter and I were continuously banging up against each other. The more she resisted me, I would resist back and she would need me more. Being the yogi that I am, I had her Vedic astrology chart done to map out her karma. The chart said that she has past karma with her mother and resists her mother, but needs her mother more than anyone else. There it was in black and white, that which I knew, but it gave me a story to get to a place of allowing and acceptance. Once I saw our storyline, I just allowed it all, did prayers of forgiveness, and the relationship shifted. Now I understand that she and I have a special connection, and the resistance has lessened. I accepted it and it released.

If we need to go into the past life stories or even make something up that sounds plausible, fine. The idea is to release the resistance that we have in those relationships and those karmic relationships.

Forgiveness Clears

The way to release these negative vibrations, these beach balls that we've been exchanging (all of the blame and judgment), is through the spiritual tool of forgiveness. The vibration of forgiveness allows us to break those negative vibrational patterns or karma with people, to release the ties, cut the cords, and realign the relationship back into the Light without all the low-vibrational, karmic, egoic ties. Think about it: There are no issues in the Light. Issues only come about when we are in the ego resisting what-is. To release the effects of the ego, we use forgiveness.

We all have egos, and those egos get us tangled up with deeply intertwined beach balls. The spiritual tool of forgiveness allows us to release the beach balls back to the original owner—*I release the "beef" I have with you, please release the "beef" you have with me, and let's release ourselves for whatever "beef" we hold against ourselves.*

Or more formally (from Howard Wills): **I forgive you. Please forgive me. Let's forgive ourselves. Please Divine, Thank you Divine. Amen**

Forgiveness allows us to return back into the vibration of love, acknowledging that we were caught up in the ego game. All we have to do is become aware that it's a game, that we've put on the dark cloaks for each other, and it doesn't serve our

Soul to continue. Bringing awareness to the muddied situations gets us into a place of allowing, where we can release the negativity. Forgiveness goes from the Heart in one person to the Heart of the other person. It's almost like your Soul is stepping in as the parent, guiding the ego to release the negative emotional charge. You're allowing the negative vibrations to melt away through the vibration of forgiveness.

Because this is spiritual work, it doesn't need to be done ego-to-ego, face-to-face or person-to-person. It can be done Soul-to-Soul, as we're letting the Soul take the reins. Our egos get us into such a mess because we see ourselves as completely separate and externalized beings. The Soul is always clear and high vibration, so if we allow ourselves to pull the Soul into a situation, then it will help us to release the resistance between us and other people. As we do that, we begin to Lighten our vibration, and we get to jump back into our vortex of high vibrational energy. We hand the steering wheel from the ego back to the Heart.

Our Soul has no problem with the other person's Soul. On a Soul-to-Soul level, we have that understanding that we were just playing those roles in each other's lives; but on the human level, we need to release those vibrations between us, because we don't have the understanding of how the Universe works. Our Souls get it, but our minds usually don't. Forgiveness gets us into the vibration of allowance by helping us to let go of the resistance.

I once heard a saying: **Not forgiving someone is like taking poison and expecting the other person to die**. Our resisting someone is just hurting us. It hurts no one but us, really. Releasing our resistance in our relationships allows us to realign with who we really are. The more we align with ourselves, the less we will need to keep revisiting our lessons.

In Chapter 2, we talked about moving up our vibrational ladder. Forgiveness is a tool to move up our vibrational ladder. It helps us release ourselves from past hurt, from past resistance, from negative vibration, from the judgment, and from the pain. This hurt and resistance is stored in our physical bodies, energetics, and emotions. It's stored in our mind.

If we have accumulated of all our earthly experiences and associated vibrations, we can use forgiveness to begin to release the negative vibration and resistance that we've gathered, whether it's been through past lifetimes or our current life.

Forgiveness exists in just about every religious tradition. For ages, we have known that we must forgive to release the energetic burden in relationships. Forgiveness prayers are essentially saying: *I align back with my spirit and the Light, and I know that this entanglement really is not who I am, and I know it's not who you are, and I forgive myself for that and I forgive you, and I hope you forgive me. Because I'm sorry. Game over. This karma game is over. We don't really need to do this. I'm not buying it anymore. I know I'm Light. I know you are Light and a Master Teacher dressed up in a dark cloak. Sorry, I got entangled there. I'll take my beach balls back and I'll use forgiveness and release it all.*

PLEASE NOTE: If the word 'forgiveness' doesn't resonate with you because some people have incorrectly associated the concept of forgiveness as *I'm letting you off the hook,* or *it was okay what you did,* you can work around this resistance by replacing the word with <u>release</u>. Instead of *I forgive you,* you can say, **I release you. Please release me. Let's release ourselves. Please Divine. Thank you Divine. Amen.**

Everyone reading this book right here, right now, has the opportunity and knowledge to shift out of this cycle of karma, and align with who they really are. The path to get there is the path of feeling good, and releasing past resistance and karma. It's wired into our emotional guidance system to do just that.

Just because you're ready to forgive and release, doesn't mean all the people in your life will be too. Not everybody is going to see life this way. You may be in a tango with someone who likes to savor their contrast. There are many people who may be early in their life cycles, and wanting to hang out in their contrast. That's okay. Just because you're not savoring your contrast anymore doesn't mean they can't hang onto it for another lifetime or two, right? You've had lifetimes of savoring the contrast and drama and pain and suffering. It's delicious for someone whose path is meant to be slow and savoring of the dark contrast. We felt that once, and we don't need it anymore for our life path. We can just align with the Light and keep aligning with ourselves, but for other people, this lifetime may be about having some heavy-duty contrast, and that's okay.

General Forgiveness Prayers

As discussed, a general forgiveness prayer we can use (created by Howard Wills and provided by Mirabai Devi) is:

"I forgive you. Please forgive me. Let's forgive ourselves. Please Divine, Thank you Divine. Amen"

OR

"I release you. Please release me. Let's release ourselves. Please Divine, Thank you Divine. Amen"

A longer prayer from Howard (and Mirabai):

"[Person's name], I forgive you for all the ways that you have hurt me, physically, emotionally, mentally, psychically, spiritually, sexually, financially, or in any other way, knowingly or unknowingly, in the past, present, or future through thought, word, or deed; through [words to describe their negative words or actions and to describe your feelings about this person's negative words and actions], please forgive me for all of the ways in which I have hurt you, physically, emotionally, mentally, psychically, spiritually, sexually, financially, or in any other way, knowingly or unknowingly, through thought, word, or deed, through [words to describe your negative words or actions toward them]. Divine, please help [person's name] and me to forgive each other and to forgive ourselves. Please, Divine. Thank you, Divine. Amen."

Self-forgiveness Prayer

Everything that we experience in life is a reflection of a vibration that lives within us. Sometimes our biggest adversary is ourselves. Our Soul's relationship with our ego needs cleansing. Many of us are very hard on ourselves, and our issues with the world are reflections of our issues with ourselves. *I judge myself and I'm hard on myself, and I projectively judge others and I'm hard on them, and I experience them as hard on me. So if I release myself of the self-judgment and learn to be more compassionate with myself, then I will naturally be that way with others.* Change starts from within. Say the following prayer with your hands on your Heart.

From Howard and Mirabai:

"[Self], I forgive you for all the ways you have hurt me, through [list all the ways you've hurt yourself]. Divine, please help me to forgive myself and to be forgiven for all of my mistakes, hurts, and wrongs to myself and to others. Please Divine, thank you Divine. Amen"

Issues that we have with ourselves are based on the ego's judgment of self. Self-forgiveness can release the ego's grip on our own self-image, expectations and our past.

Another prayer that I use daily from G. R. King's St. Germain book series:

"Divine, release me from every mistake I've ever made, and replace those mistakes by such Ascended Master Sacred Fire Blessing and Perfection and Happiness to the rest of life that I never think of them again. They can never be existing anywhere in the Universe and no one else can be touched by them!"

Family Lineage Forgiveness

As discussed, we receive karma from our family as well as ourselves. We take on karma from our mother's lineage and our father's lineage. Here is a story about my family's karma.

I grew up in an Italian family. My grandmother loved to feed us. You were supposed to eat a lot because that was a compliment to an Italian grandmother. You ate a lot to show her that you loved her food, and so she could feel good about herself and be happy. But the other value that my grandmother had was beauty and being skinny ... so you were supposed to eat a lot and stay very skinny so you could be beautiful through her eyes. Those were my grandmother's values, and that was what she upheld in her life. She was a beautician. She styled people's hair and helped make them beautiful so they could feel good about themselves. (Note: *externalized beauty to feel good*) My mother grew up with this perfectionism about her body and her looks, and never left the house without makeup on, and spent her life dressing other people and making them look beautiful.

So I grew up feeling like I needed to have the perfect body to be beautiful. At the same time, I had developed an attachment to food, which made me feel comforted and happy. Needless to say, I struggled with my body, food, and body image. Until my thirties, I had to work through every layer of beauty, food, and feeling good.

- What is beauty?
- Is a perfect body realistic?
- How do I learn to feel good outside of eating?
- What is the purpose of food? Can food feel good?
- How do I break my addiction to food as an escape?

I worked through all the emotional and spiritual aspects of releasing these long-lived family issues. Then I had two daughters, and it took me a while to learn that *if they don't eat, they aren't going to die!* because as an Italian, you think that if the kid is not eating, they're going to die. It's just programmed into you. It's programmed into your whole heritage (lineage belief systems!). I finally recognized that, released the fears, and found ease around feeding my two daughters.

Then my third daughter came along, and one week after she was born, we got that call from the Department of Health, saying that she had a genetic metabolic disorder—if we didn't wake her up every three hours to eat, she could die. It didn't take me very long to step away from this situation and see it as the effect of the karma of my female lineage. The karma shot straight into the DNA for a genetic mutation! I could see the lineage karma, the lineage lesson, and because I saw the big picture, I didn't go into victim, *Oh, woe is me. Woe is my daughter.* I saw how this way of thinking went deeper and deeper until it got into the DNA of our lineage. (If this seems far-fetched, research how the environment—emotions, energy, etc.—dictates our DNA. Epigenetics. It's fascinating.)

That was my first true lesson in understanding what ancestral or lineage karma was. We carry the energies or the vibrations from our lineage, from our ancestry. My mother's lineage had food, body, and anger issues. My father's side had tons of alcoholism and victimization. There are some heavy denser vibrations that live in my lineage and also beautiful vibrations that we carry along our lineage. My mother's lineage gave me strength and willpower of thinking I could achieve anything. My father's lineage gave me my sense of humor and ability to be laid back and have fun and not take everything so seriously.

We all have these qualities that get passed down to us. If we're not mindful, if we're not living a conscious life, then we just continue that lineage all the way down to our children and their children and their children. If we're living a conscious, mindful life then we step back and we say, *Hmmm, is this something that I want to continue, or can I bring myself closer to who I am and bring myself into the Light to transcend this karma?*

One of the many gifts our family and children give us is that they reflect us back to ourselves. Our spouse will serve as a mirror as well. The people in our lives are here as a reflection to show us what energies we're perpetuating in the world.

Here are some family lineage forgiveness prayers (Written by Howard Wills; provided by Mirabai Devi):

Family Lineage Forgiveness Prayers

Prayer to cleanse relationships with all women (left side of upper body and right leg):

"For all of the women who have ever hurt me, I forgive you, all of you. Mother(s), mother-in-law(s), daughter(s), daughter(s)-in-law, sister(s), sister(s)- in-law, aunt(s), grandmothers, friends, ex-lover(s)/ex-wife(s), partner(s), wife. I ask that you all please forgive me. Divine Light, please help us all to forgive each other and to forgive ourselves. Let us all forgive and release ourselves for our hurts, wrongs, and mistakes to ourselves and to others. Please, Divine Light. Thank you, Divine Light. Amen"

Prayer to cleanse relationships with all men (right side of upper body and left leg):

"For all of the men who have ever hurt me, I forgive you, all of you. Father(s), father(s)-in-law, son(s), son(s)-in-law, brother(s), brother(s)-in-law, uncle(s), grandfathers, friends, ex-lover(s)/ex-husband(s), partner(s), husband. I ask that you all please forgive me. Divine Light, please help us all to forgive each other and to forgive ourselves. Let us all forgive and release ourselves for our hurts, wrongs, and mistakes to ourselves and to others. Please, Divine Light. Thank you, Divine Light. Amen"

Another Lineage Forgiveness Prayer:

"Divine, for me and my entire lineage throughout all time, past, present, and future: please help us all forgive all people, help all people forgive us, and help us all forgive ourselves. Please, Divine. Thank you, Divine. Amen"

Full Power Prayer:

"Divine, please help me forgive all people, help all people forgive me, and help us all forgive ourselves. Please Divine, Thank you.

Divine, for me and my entire lineage, throughout all time, past present, and future: Please help us all forgive all people, help all people forgive us, and help us all forgive ourselves. Please Divine, Thank you.

Divine, for me, my spouse(s), all our family members, all our relationships, all our ancestors, and all relationship with all creations and life forms, throughout all time, past present, and future: Please help us all forgive all people, help all people forgive us, and help us all forgive ourselves. Completely and totally. Please Divine, Thank you.

Divine, please help us all love each other and love ourselves, be at peace with each other and be at peace with ourselves. Please Divine, Thank you.

Divine, we give you our love and thank you for your constant love and blessings. We love and appreciate all your creations, and we fill your creations with our love. We love you Divine. Thank you for loving us. We love you Divine. Thank you for loving us. We love you Divine. Thank you for loving us. Thank You Divine, Amen.

Divine, please open, bless, empower, expand, lead, guide, direct and protect me, my family, all humanity and all of creation, throughout all time, now and forever. Please Divine, thank you Divine. Amen."

Group Karma

In addition to family ancestral lineage, groups can carry karma and vibrations as well. The Deep South of the United States still carries the karma or vibration of slavery. Germany may feel the vibration of the Holocaust. South Africa may feel the karma and vibrations of Apartheid. Japan has the karma of the Fukushima nuclear radiation spill. Even if a situation resolved a generation or two before, the group still carries the residual negative vibrations. If you know someone who is in the lineage of a Holocaust survivor, you'll know that even though they didn't live through the Holocaust, it still lives within them—the field of epigenetics has studied the genetic impact of the Holocaust on the lineage of survivors. A whole culture or a whole community can carry the vibrations of that which came before us. It's palpable in some cultures. The vibrations also live through their stories and belief systems. These are the elements of karma that go deep into our vibrational belief structures.

We can use forgiveness to cleanse a group, a family, or ourselves personally. We can go so far as to cleanse the entire collective consciousness, because as we cleanse ourselves, we do it for everyone.

Let's make that more tangible from group dynamics. If I come home to my three daughters and husband with a negative vibration, whether I take it out on them or not, I will automatically begin to negatively shift the vibration of the family unit within seconds. In fact, I could probably shift it before I even pull my car up into the garage. My three daughters are all very energetically sensitive, so if I am even a little rattled, I can watch their rattling. It's a vibrational ripple … like I'm throwing pebbles into the pond and watching those ripples vibrate out.

Our vibration creates a ripple effect. After I create negative ripples in my family, if I cleanse that with forgiveness and release all those negative vibrations, I can create a positive vibration ripple effect both in the present moment and through our lineage and through our lifetimes. I can cleanse myself and create that positive vibrational ripple … or I can choose to stay in anger and negative vibration, and create THAT ripple. That's my responsibility. That's my choice. We all have that choice.

100% Responsibility for Everything

In the book *Zero Limits*, Joe Vitale writes about a Hawaiian shaman and therapist named Dr. Len. He was called into a psychiatric prison where people were very violent to each other. Most prisoners were on many medications. It was a terrible work environment, and there was significant staff attrition. Instead of meeting with each inmate and working through their personalities, egos or emotions, he took each of the inmate's charts into a private room by himself and focused on each of their heinous crimes. As he took the crimes into prayer, **he cleansed himself** of each of the crimes using the Hawaiian shamanic forgiveness prayer called the Ho'oponopono: **I love you. I'm sorry. Please forgive me. Thank you.**

One inmate had murdered someone. Dr. Len felt the vibration of murder, hooked into that vibration of the collective consciousness of murder, and cleansed himself by saying, I love you. I'm sorry. Please forgive me. Thank you.

Now, why would he cleanse it in himself? Because he too was part of the collective consciousness, the collective minds of humanity. He too felt the ripple. Since he attracted himself into the hospital, and had the spiritual awareness, he saw his responsibility to do the spiritual work. This shamanic perspective on forgiveness is that **we all have 100% responsibility for absolutely everything that we attract into our lives—even if we didn't directly cause it.**

Within three years of Dr. Len doing this work in the prison, he began to shift the vibration of the hospital. The administration was able to close the whole high security section because people had shifted so significantly that they could be in lower security areas, and they didn't need the amount of medication or surveillance they'd needed before.

Last week, my daughter was causing problems in my house. I was doing the best I could with her, so there wasn't much I could do differently in my opinion. As I stepped back, I said, *I have responsibility for her behavior whether the situation is about me or not. What's the lesson? What's the truth? What is the Universe trying to communicate to me?* I said my forgiveness prayers, worked with the Violet Flame, and the situation shifted immediately.

If we look at our responsibility—and stop doing the whole blame, right/wrong judgment, *you made me feel bad thing*—we can look and say, *Oh, there's something coming my way. I attracted this. How can I bring it into the Light now?* Dr. Len did not commit those murders, but he could still cleanse himself of the crimes on behalf of the people in that hospital.

Recently, I had a few difficult days. I went to work to teach a yoga class for thirty students, and as I entered the building in my negative state, I immediately locked egos with one of the most negative people that I work with. (We were resonating at the same vibration!) This snowballed into a negative situation with yet another person. Within minutes, I had a big mess on my hands. I went into the bathroom to cry and said to myself, *Okay, I am responsible for this mess. I created it. I attracted it. I see all my responsibility here. I surrender. Please help me, Divine.* When I came out of the bathroom and went into the yoga room, I laid in child's pose to get grounded, to take care of myself. After a few breaths, a friend came over, touched my back with love, and showered me with a compliment from the previous week. She did that without the desire to take my pain away—she was in a place of gratitude. Because she was in her vortex of gratitude for me, I immediately felt it wash over me.

So by going into the bathroom to release my emotion and see my responsibility, I changed my vibration. Even though I was still struggling, the mindful responsibility shifted my vibration enough to change the trajectory of my experiences. Responsibility attracted a beautiful interaction with a friend, which then transformed my experience. *And do you know what happened?* By authentically sharing this whole story immediately with the 30 students, I was able to help them access the same emotions and lessons in their lives. Everyone was touched by my lesson because I stayed real and authentic.

Our inner work affects every human being on this planet. As we shift our vibration, we start sending more positive ripples. If we forgive and release everybody that has done anything negative to us, and send those loving vibrations out into the world, then all of those people are going to get a wave of goodness, love and high vibration coming to them.

I was once doing forgiveness work on my ancestry, clearing out my lineage. As I did so, I got a text from one of my Soulsisters, someone that I knew I had a Soul connection with. The text said, *Are you sending me Light or praying for me right now? I had a picture of you and I felt a huge wave of Light coming my way.* I knew she and I had had a connection prior to this life (or something!), but as I was doing ancestry forgiveness, she could feel the Light pouring toward her. That was such a beautiful display for me, and a huge lesson on the power of forgiveness to heal and cleanse past and present relationships, and the energy that connects us all.

Recently, my husband was in a place of resistance, and was angry at me about something he projected I was doing *wrong*. He was so fired up that, within minutes, all three daughters were mad at me about something. I had all four family members firing negativity at me. I stayed in neutrality and forgiveness, and started doing the Violet Flame like it was my job! A white tube of Light and, *I AM a being of Violet Fire, I AM the purity God desires.* Over and over and over again. Within 5 minutes, the energy shifted and we sat down for a nice dinner!

I hope that you're now inspired to find your responsibility in everything, and use forgiveness to help cleanse and clear out your vibration, as well as the vibrations of your family. I trust that as you do so, you will get that Light shone straight back at you. As we do this work, our spiritual team is on the other side of the veil, celebrating our enLightening process. As we ask to be released from someone's grip of anger, and as soon as we release someone from our grip of anger, we are being assisted from the spiritual realm, by our spirit guides, by our spiritual team, by Source. But we have to ask for it because we have free will. We have to continue to ask with momentum of desire.

If someone cuts me off in the car, then I say, *I forgive you. Please forgive me. Let's forgive ourselves. Please, Divine. Thank you, Divine. Amen.* If there is an issue with my family: *I ask for forgiveness on behalf of my whole female lineage, my mother, my sister, my daughters. Please help us forgive all people. Help all people forgive us. Help us all forgive each other and forgive ourselves. Please, Divine, thank you.*

These are the prayers that we can use to mindfully and willfully release the beach balls, release the negative vibrations that we hold with people. If we use our free will and intention to forgive, then we will feel an immediate release of our vibration.

Here's the exciting part: We have been asleep for lifetimes, and this is the lifetime for us to wake up and come deeply into alignment. There is an army of Light waiting passionately for you to wake up and recognize that you are of the Light. The Universe is waiting so anxiously to take your order, to fulfill your desires and show you your potency. There's not just one General Manager; there is an army of general managers that are celebrating on the other side saying, *Oh my gosh, they get it! They see it! They are on their way! Yay!* They're cheering you on, and they're right here to support you, for you to call on them, for you to shoot your rockets of desire, for you to get clarity. They're waiting. They're waiting to deliver you back to yourself. They're waiting to assist you as soon as you ask. Ask, ask, ask! The Universe is waiting for you to mindfully release the old stuff! Release away! *Divine, I completely release all karma and negative vibrations from the past, present, and future. I ask to completely merge into the Light for enlightenment and ascension, here and now.*

Do you believe that this is possible? You wouldn't have picked up this book if you were not on the path of the Light, if you were not ready to release the dark, if you were not called to release this whole pattern of karma and learning through negative vibration. You have everything you need to let it all go, and to align with yourself and the Light.

In Summary...

The most powerful tool we have is the potential to see our responsibility in everything we attract into our lives. This requires us to stay out of our deep confusions so we can see life as a series of lessons, rather than failures. We can shift our perspective around responsibility. We can learn to *celebrate* when we see our responsibility in the contrast because we know that gives us the power to change our circumstances. The power of responsibility is the key to the Law of Attraction.

We have accumulated karma—through our personal, family, and group thoughts and actions—which can be cleared through the spiritual tool of forgiveness. When we see our responsibility to clear the karma through forgiveness, we are free to choose new vibrations and manifest new situations.

Practice: Forgiveness Meditation

You can access a guided meditation to help you work with forgiveness at: www.enLIGHTenWithKim.com. Click on **Community Resources** and **Book Meditations**, log in for free, and find the meditation called #**6 Forgiveness Meditation.**

Build the Bridge Back to Self

Come forth into the Light of things.
Let nature be your teacher.
-William Wordsworth

Recently, I was counseling someone who was unhappy and unmotivated—just completely disconnected from herself. Our conversation went like this: *Well, it sounds like you're disconnected from yourself. You really don't like yourself.* And she goes, *Yeah, self-acceptance and self-love, blah blah blah.* I just cracked up. It was so funny because it wasn't long ago that I had the same sort of reaction: *Yeah, I know. I need to love myself. How do I even do that? How do I get to a place of self-acceptance and self-love?*

Self-love sounds like this great concept, but how do we move from this intellectual knowledge of self-connection, self-forgiveness, self-acceptance, self-understanding, self-love ... to implementing it in day-to-day life?

We have discussed feeling our vibration and working with our emotional guidance system. Often, though, we are mostly in the hamster wheel of the mind and it's hard to connect with what's going on beneath the head. There's so much background noise in our mind, body, and energetics that we can't decipher what our emotional guidance system is telling us.

To pave the path to self- connection and awareness, it's helpful to develop an understanding of what energies are creating distraction and imbalance. To build this understanding, we will examine the ancient traditions of Yoga and Ayurveda to decode our minds and vibrations, and to help us get to a point of self-care and self-acceptance, the building blocks toward self-love.

Connecting with Self

We can look at the opportunity to connect with ourselves from a very practical perspective by developing an understanding of how our unique energy systems flow. This self-understanding can help us learn how to form a compassionate connection with our bodies. Once we develop the understanding of how our energy flows, we can then begin to quiet some of the background noise that tends to get in the way of truly listening to the body and calming the mind. There are unique elements and energies shifting through our bodies, and because these energies feel like they have a life of their own, we often feel like we're being energetically and emotionally thrown around in life.

This is where we start feeling like victims of our busy mind, or the disease that we've created in our bodies, because the bridge between our mind and our well-being does not appear to be a linear path of cause-and-effect. Our mind sees things as isolated points in time. The ability to link cause-and-effect and see how our thoughts or energetic patterns are actually *creating* the negative circumstances or disease is difficult because there's some time between a cause in the mind and an effect in the body. And even when there's *not* a lot of time between the cause and effect, we usually don't acknowledge the relationship between what we're thinking, doing, and saying and that which we're manifesting.

Being connected to ourselves, and understanding and accepting how our unique energy system works, helps us in the process of the Law of Attraction. Mastering our vessel is incredibly helpful in mastering our vibrations toward intentions.

Connection to self is a process of self-understanding (to calm the mind), which leads to self-acceptance (to get us into a place of allowing), which leads to self-forgiveness (to help us to release into our natural flow), which brings us into our vortex of self-love. Self-connection takes us back into our Heart, which enables us to manifest our desires.

Conscious Intention for Self-Connection

We can use our intentions to create this inner-connection to get back into the flow. If we set our attention on the external world and expect things outside of us to make us feel good, then we are going to stay in misalignment and disconnection from self. **If we set our intention to connect with ourselves, then our conscious awareness will attract more opportunities to connect with self.**

We must start with the simple intention to **want to** connect with ourselves. We must want to love ourselves more, to understand and accept ourselves as we are. Many of us feel like that's a useless intention. *I'm connected to myself, I live with myself everyday. What's the use of self-connection and all that self-love?* We're not even motivated to want that in our lives, and it may not seem very useful. Isn't that hilarious? It's true though, right? We want to *do-do-do*. We want to be productive and get results, but the mere intention of wanting to connect with self seems kind of frivolous. We don't feel motivated to connect with self, which shows that we need to develop **deliberate** intention for self-connection, otherwise it's a long road.

We can have so much potency and bliss if we just become more connected, attuned, and aligned with ourselves. The more connected, aligned, and compassionate we are with ourselves, the more we are able to be compassionate, aligned, and blissed out with others, because the external world is just a reflection of what's going on in our internal world. If we're out of balance and out of touch with ourselves, then we are going to be out of balance and out of touch with others. Even if our intentions are externalized—*I want to connect more and feel more love with others*—that all has to start with our connection to self. If we don't have that connection with self, it's practically impossible to connect with others authentically and joyfully.

You may say to yourself, *Well, I go to yoga and I get massages and I eat healthy. I'm doing well. I'm connected to myself and taking care of myself. I have good self-care.* That may, in fact, be true. However, what we're doing externally may not be true indicators of what our intentions and focus are. For example, I may be going to yoga and getting massages and eating healthy because I don't like my body and have an expectation that my body *should* be skinnier, *should* be in better shape, *should* feel less pain, and *should* have more energy. If I'm going at self-care with expectations for a result, then that's different than going for self-care as a means of connecting with myself for the process of enjoyment in the present moment. Do you see? The same act of yoga could be a way to meet my own expectations of myself, or it can be so I can have a breath-related experience of myself in the present moment, and just feel my Soul because that feels good.

Our awareness in the present moment helps us bring consciousness to what we do: *What am I doing? Why am I doing it? What am I looking to get out of that?* Or how we are feeling: *How am I feeling? Do I feel good? Why am I doing this if it <u>doesn't</u> feel good?* Often, we're not focusing on our own present moment enjoyment to feel good. We're going for results. We're going for expectations. We're going for other people's approval. We're looking to get those deep confusions met from the external world.

A focus on self in the present moment allows us to rebuild an inner relationship that we may have abandoned many years ago. When we reconnect with self, it's like saying, *Oh, abandoned self, I'm here again and I'm sorry for not paying attention to you or caring about how you felt for the last <u>thirty-five</u> years. I'm here now. What can I do for you? What do you need? What can I do for you that will help bring you back into balance?*

If we can approach ourselves in this way—as if we've abandoned that child and then woke up one day and realized, *Oh, crap, I've been ignoring and neglecting you!*—our Soul, our inner selves will gladly welcome the care, because coming back to self feels good.

Yoga and Ayurveda Pave the Way Back Home

The best way that I have found to reconnect, develop a better understanding of self, and rebalance internal energies is through the practices of Yoga and Ayurveda. These practices provide an incredible mind/body/spirit approach that is based on profound ancient tradition.

Yoga

Yoga is the yoking or unification of the mind, body, and Soul—a merging of these layers with Source. I always talk about yoga with the small "y" and Yoga with the big "Y."

Yoga with the small "y" is how we define it in the Western world, which is the actual practice of physical postures (asana). Many of the yoga poses are ancient and have been practiced for many years, so every time we practice asana postures, we are energetically tapping into the ancient collective consciousness of yoga. Yoga with the small "y" is mostly the physical poses.

Yoga with the big "Y" is the practice of self-exploration, introspection, and alignment as a means of building Higher Consciousness and awareness in life, and ultimately having a deeply spiritual experience through merging body, mind, emotions and energy with Source. It's about looking at your level of fear or love in life, allowance versus resistance, and karma and life lessons. It's about how you nourish your body, how you exercise and take care of yourself. It's about your breath and life force energy, prana. It's about living from the Heart. Your connection and full merging with Source.

There are many different systems of Yoga. Putanjali's Yoga Sutras defines the eight limbs of Yoga (Yoga with the big "Y") as the following:

1. **Yamas** are ethical standards for how we conduct ourselves in life. Five Yamas are:

    - Ahimsa: reverence, love, and compassion for all (nonviolence)
    - Satya: truthfulness, integrity
    - Asteya: generosity, honesty (non-stealing)
    - Brahmacharya: balance and moderation of the vital life force (celibacy)
    - Aparigraha: awareness of abundance, fulfillment (non-greed or possessiveness)

2. **Niyamas** are the areas for self-discipline and spiritual observances. Five Niyamas are:

    - Saucha: simplicity, purity (cleanliness of mind, body, and spirit)

- Santosha: contentment, acceptance (peace with self and others)
- Tapas: igniting the purifying flame (perseverance, persistent meditation)
- Svadhyaya: sacred study of Divine through scripture, nature, and introspection (self-reflection and introspection)
- Isvara pranidhana: whole-Hearted dedication to the Divine (contemplation and surrender to Source)

3. **Asanas** are the postures that promote physical health and stamina. We build an aligned and strong spine to increase energy flow and sit upright for longer meditation.

4. **Pranayama** are breathing techniques for managing life force energy.

The last four limbs are methods for working with the mind so we can attune to Source.

5. **Pratyahara** is the withdrawal of your senses from the material world in order to still the mind.

6. **Dharana** is concentration, in which you strive to achieve one-pointed mental focus.

7. **Dhyana** is meditation, which extends your uninterrupted concentration to transcend the mind.

8. **Samadhi** is merging completely with the Divine to access full truth, bliss, and consciousness. This is the ultimate focus of the yogic path.

Ayurveda

Ayurveda is India's ancient science of life and longevity. It is over 2000 years old, and was handed down through ancient Vedic texts. It's a very practical approach to the mind, body, and spirit. Together with the practice of Yoga and meditation, Ayurveda provides a comprehensive perspective on wellness, health, and healing.

Ayurveda looks at the human as a mix of the elements—ether, air, fire, water, and earth. Each of us is born with a unique mix of all of these elements in our bodies, set forth by planetary alignment and our karma when we were born. The combination of the elements in our bodies make up our dosha (elements) constitution.

- **Air** and Ether make up the **Vata** dosha.

- **Fire** and Water make up the **Pitta** dosha.

- **Earth** and Water make up the **Kapha** dosha.

This Ayurvedic view of the doshas helps to develop deeper self-understanding of our unique energetic system. The dosha categorization is valuable to help us figure out what's going on so we can navigate the energies better, stop throwing ourselves further out of balance, and find some internal peace.

So, how does this relate to the Law of Attraction? To master the principles of focusing our attention, raising and aligning our vibration, and staying mindful and present, we work with the energies of the body, mind, and emotions. We must return the elements in our bodies back to their original state of balance to be in true alignment—body, energy, thoughts, emotions, awareness—with a blissful state of love. Clearing out the background noise in our systems allows us to hear the guidance to regain balance, alignment and well-being. For example:

- If you have a lot of **anger and judgment**, then there may be too much fire in your system. You can cool and ground some of that fire, so you can have more clarity and align with the energy of love.

- If you have a lot of air built up in the mind and you find yourself worrying and experiencing **anxiety, fear, and mental looping**, then it's valuable to slow down and ground the air with some earth so that you can have peace and clarity of mind.

- If you find yourself frequently **depressed and sad**, there may be too much earth energy, so it may be valuable to add movement and fire. This will add vitality and energize you to raise you up to higher vibrational emotions.

You can see how critical it is to work with the energies of the body, mind, and emotions if you want to create more of what you want in your life. We are made up of the elements, and we inadvertently throw our systems' elements out of whack by disconnecting from how we feel, without knowing how to get back to a state of balance. Ayurveda can give us the framework for: how our bodies function with respect to the elements, how the elements work in our minds, and how to bring the elements back into balance.

Over time, through mental, physical, emotional, energetic, and environmental stress, we fall out of balance. **Stress creates an imbalance of our inner elements and ultimately leads to illness.** Illness (mental or physical) can be reversed by bringing the elements back into balance.

We were born with a unique balance of elements (prakruti). This is the original state of elements in our body at birth. Every person's prakruti is different. Throughout life, we become imbalanced, and our imbalanced elements (vikruti) show up in our physical, mental, emotional, and energetic layers of the body. The goal is to get ourselves back to our original unique prakruti balance of elements in our bodies. For example, Mark was born with a lot of earth in his body, but he began a career in the fast-paced, high stress, financial management industry, which involves a lot of risk, quick decisions, and competition (all fire-based attributes). While he was born with a lot of earth, his job has brought imbalanced fire, which has created a ton of stress on his mind and body. To get Mark back to his earthy state of balance, he will have to make some lifestyle changes—such as slowing down between meetings, daily meditation and yoga, time in nature, creativity, time with friends—to cool and ground his energies to reduce the fire.

For me personally, when I found Ayurveda, my body was severely depleted. In fact, every time I would go to my weekly Chinese Medicine Acupuncture appointment, they'd say, *Yep, you're severely depleted.* And a year later, *Yep, you're still severely depleted.* Every healer I went to (and I went to almost every one in my town!) would confirm that *I was broken*, that I was in such a deep hole that there wasn't much I could do for myself. Needless to say, I wasn't able to create a vision for my self-healing, and this cycle of handing over my self-care to other people was creating a sense of being defeated by my own body. I was expecting healers to *fix me*, which made me very disempowered and disconnected from my self-knowledge of how to heal myself.

Through Ayurveda, I was able to see all of my quirky physical and mental symptoms described so simply and beautifully in one model. I was so relieved. It showed me I wasn't broken. I was just *out of balance*. My fire element was overheated, my air was too light and dry, and I was lacking earth to ground me. With a deeper exploration, I was able to very intuitively start to figure out where I was throwing myself more out of balance, and where I could bring myself back *into* balance. That is some of the most empowering information. Even if you decide to mindfully continue to throw yourself out of balance, it's good to know how to work with the energies of the body so that we don't feel broken, so we don't feel like *there's no way out*. We know there's a way out, and once we commit ourselves to creating more balance, we have the information available to do so. Thank you, Ayurveda!

Now, keep in mind that all giving and receiving to self comes from the Heart chakra. If we set the intention to care for ourselves, it's an act of love, self-love, to listen to what's going on in our body and act accordingly. If our body is screaming that it's in pain and we ignore it or cover it up with our vices or medications, then we're going to feel undernourished and neglected. **As soon as we can lovingly listen to our body, and fulfill the need (rather than covering up the symptom), our body will lovingly accept the well-being and HEAL. A consistent vibration of self-love through self-care can do a lot for our healing process.** To do that is an act of love toward ourselves ... *and* toward humanity since our external connections are based in our relationship to ourselves. Keep that in mind as we go down into the nuts and bolts of Ayurveda. This is a spiritual practice of self-care and self-love, and as we balance our energy, we build the connection to self, to Source, and to others.

Practice: Discover Your Ayurvedic Constitution

On the next page, you will find a chart to help you figure out your Ayurvedic Dosha Constitution. Circle one per row and total each column. (Note: The assessment tool below was *derived* from Dr. Frawley's Constitution form, a much longer form.)

	Vata (Air)	Pitta (Fire)	Kapha (Earth)
Hair	Dry, coarse, sparse	Oily, fine, soft, balding	Thick, oily, wavy
Skin	Dry, cracked, vein-y	Oily, freckles, flush, acne	Wet/moist, thick, smooth, light/pale
Weight	Bone-y, skinny	Muscular, moderate build	Heavy, holds extra weight, obese
Height	Lanky, tall/short, bone-y	Moderate	Short, stocky
Temp	Feels cold to the bones	Runs warm or hot	Feels cool but insulated
Eyes	Small, unsteady	Medium, piercing	Wide, large
Build	Small/thin, flat, hunched over	Strong, moderate	Broad, large, thick, padded, round
Legs/feet	Small, thin, dry	Medium, soft, oily	Large, thick
Energy	Energy spurts, short duration	Moderate, overheats	Slow to start, long duration
Appetite	Erratic	Strong, irritable if hungry	Constant, low
Urine	Not much, colorless	Colored, burning, profuse	Moderate, white/milky color
Feces	Hard, dry, infrequent, gas, constipation	Frequent, colored, burning, tends toward diarrhea	Moderate, regular, pale, occasional mucous
Immunity	Weak immune system	Moderate, prone to infection	Strong, prone to congestion
Diseases	Nervous system, joint pain, mental issues	Fevers, infections, inflammation	Respiratory illness, edema, mucous
Mind	Quick, indecisive, overwhelmed	Intelligent, critical, demanding, perfectionistic	Slow, steady, dull, doesn't forget
Emotions	Anxiety, fear	Anger, irritable	Attached, depressed
Sleep	Light, insomnia	Moderate	Heavy
TOTALS			

Ayurveda and the Doshas

Let's go through the qualities of each of the elements and focus on how you can make changes in your daily lifestyle to create more balance. Creating balance at the energetic level will affect all other aspects of your body, mind, and emotions. Since the body is a product of your thoughts and emotions, you can shift your health and well-being through working with the mind. If you can balance the mind and emotions, you can bring yourself into your vortex and have a higher vibrational experience in life!

With the numbers from the form, you will find that one or two of the columns were higher than the other(s). For the numbers that are highest, see which of the descriptions that follow are most accurate to nail down your Ayurvedic Constitution type. Please note: We all have a mix of all the elements, however people can score high on one dosha (scored a high number in just one column), dual doshas (high in two columns), or tri-doshic (evenly across three columns). As you read through the descriptions on the next page, note where you reflect certain elements so you can start to view yourself in terms of what element is working through your mind, physical body, and emotions. The general qualities of each of the Doshas are shown below. Items with * are the qualities unique to the specific dosha.

Also note: You can visit an Ayurvedic Wellness Counselor or Ayurvedic doctor for a deeper understanding of your constitution. You can also find more books from Dr. Frawley or Dr. Lad to explore the doshas more in-depth. Sometimes it takes deeper exploration to determine what specific elements are working through you because your mind, body, and digestion may be demonstrating different elements. For example, you may have a lot of Pitta fire in your mind and digestion, but more Kapha earth in your body structure.

Physical and emotional traits and imbalance qualities for each dosha are as follows:

	Vata	Pitta	Kapha
	Cold	Hot*	Cold
	Dry*	Oily	Wet
	Mobile	Mobile	Steady*
	Light	Light	Heavy*
Element	Air (Ether)	Fire (Water)	Earth (Water)
Function	Move	Transform	Sustain
Body	Thin, tall/small, long-limbs, low stamina	Medium build, muscular, freckles	Large build, padded joints, high endurance
Mind/ Emotion	Creative, expressive, inspired, playful	Sharp, strategic, intellectual, clarity	Easy-going, kind, loyal, forgiving, consistent
Digestion	Gas, bloating, constipation	Heartburn, diarrhea	Heavy, undigested stool
Imbalanced Emotion	Anxiety, worry, inconsistent, overwhelmed, forgetful	Angry, jealous, critical, demanding	Sad/depressed, lethargic, greedy, resists change
Other Imbalance	Insomnia, dizzy, moving pain, Nervous system issues, Mental health issues	Infection, inflammation, migraines, skin rash, eyes/ liver/ gallbladder	Head/chest congestion, excess mucous, fluid retention, swelling

Vata Dosha: Ether and Air

Vata is like the wind. It is **cold, dry, lightweight**, and **always moving**. The primary function of Vata in the body is **MOVEMENT**. Movements include all bodily fluid, heartbeat, breathing, metabolism, elimination of waste products, relaying stimulus to the brain and response back to organs or tissues. If Vata is imbalanced in the body, it can show up as insomnia or dizziness, vertigo, pain, issues with the nervous system, or difficulty in the large intestine. If Vata is imbalanced in the mind or emotions, it will show up as worry, anxiety, fear, and feeling overwhelmed, spacey, forgetful, or inconsistent.

Vata balanced	Vata IMbalanced
Adventurous, spontaneous	Insomnia, fear
Creative, multi-tasks well	Gas, constipation
Innovative, energetic	Dry skin, ears ringing
Trendy, fashionable	Lower back pain
Impulsive, quick learner	Anxiety, ungrounded
Intuitive	Phobia, nervous

In a balanced state, Vata dosha in the mind/emotion is very creative, expressive, inspired, and playful—you can feel a lot of air and movement in those qualities. But once imbalanced, all that air and movement can create instability and a lack of grounding, which results in lots of worry or overthinking. This worrying makes problems seem worse than they actually are, because of the looping nature that occurs. Vatas can be overly sensitive and overreactive. They can take things personally. Because of that oversensitivity, they're prone to premature or inappropriate action, which just creates more problems—oversensitivity leads to overreaction. Vatas will lose a lot of prana, or life force energy, through the excessiveness of the imbalanced Vata mind. It's exhausting in the Vata mind!

Imbalanced Vata can manifest fear, alienation, anxiety, nervousness, insomnia, tremors, palpitations, unrest, and mood shifts. Manic depression is one of the aspects of Vata imbalance—

during the manic state, a lot of ungrounded energy is expended with incredible creativity and expansiveness. As a result, the loss of prana leads to a crash, because when you've expended so much, the system must close down and contract, which can be expressed through sadness.

Due to their sensitivities, Vatas experience sensory disturbances and disturbance of the mind. They should be careful about what they expose themselves to (e.g., mass media, loud noises, disturbing stories, distasteful odors, intense gatherings).

From a childhood perspective, neglect and abuse can create a predisposition for Vata imbalance in the mind.

There are many options to ground the Vata dosha:

To balance, do:	Avoid:
Meditate, yoga, breath work	Not breathing properly; overexercise
Keep a regular routine and rhythm (sleep, work, eating, self-care)	Too much traveling; inconsistency in routine
Eat warm, grounding, nourishing fresh food	Late nights or too much technology (TV, phone, computers)
Sesame oil on head and feet before bed	Exposure to severe dry and/or cold climates
Get plenty of sleep	Overworking; too much sex; exhaustion

Breath: Go into a slow deep breath in and out through the nose, focused into the low belly, hips, legs, and feet. This brings prana down into the lower body to connect to the earth element.

Physically: Vata can be grounded through connecting senses to the earth: eating root vegetables, gardening, laying on or walking in the sand, leaning up against a tree, gazing at or climbing the mountains. It can be warmed with a hot bath, warm food or tea, wool clothing, and warm climates. Cold salads/foods (especially in the winter) can be hard on Vata digestion.

Movement and yoga: Vatas need to feel strong and grounded. Their yoga practice should be very slow, and build strength. (Most modern yoga is fast and unbalancing to the Vata body and mind.) The Vata will want to keep busy and moving because it's almost painful to slow down, but ratcheting down the movement is really important.

Body: Abhyanga, the act of oiling the body with an oil that supports the specific dosha, is also a spiritual act of self-love. Cover the body in warm SESAME oil, sit for twenty minutes for it to soak in, and then take a warm bath or shower to rinse the excess. Warm sesame oil can help ground and warm the Vata body and nervous system.

Rhythm: There are times of day and seasons that will throw off the Vata element. If you have extra Vata in the mind, you may find yourself more ungrounded in the fall and early winter. The Vata times of day are 2 to 6 (AM and PM), so these would be times you might feel more **un**balanced so do some self-care to create more balance. You may wake up between 2 AM to 6 AM with insomnia (if so, oil the top of your head and bottom of your feet, or bathe before bed!). You may lose energy between 2 PM and 6 PM, so scheduling a short nap or simply laying down to rest and get grounded could be life-changing.

Emotional introspection: Vatas can calm the anxious mind by observing their fears, grounding unruly thoughts back to reality, and staying connected to their breath so they don't float away! It's important for the Vata to find stillness and get connected to the earth for grounding.

When identifying Vata symptoms, find the specific **quality** that is out of balance. If you are experiencing too much **lightness** or **movement** (flighty, nervous system, fear), you may need to **ground yourself** and **find stillness**. If you have symptoms of **cold** (joint pain, cold to the bone), you may need to **find warmth**. If you have symptoms of **dryness** (dry skin, dry stool as constipation), you may need to balance it with more **oil externally or internally**.

Pitta Dosha: Fire and Water

Pitta is like fire. It is **hot, oily, lightweight,** and **moving**. The primary function of the Pitta or the fire element in the body is to **TRANSFORM**. The fire element digests food, emotions, thoughts, big changes, and deep transformation. It is responsible for the eyes, liver, gallbladder, food assimilation, and body temperature.

Pitta balanced	Pitta IMbalanced
Natural leaders, risk takers	Irritable, anger, frustration
Loves challenges, charismatic	Perfectionism, dominating
Competitive, athletic	Heart problems, high acid, inflammation
High expectations, practical	Liver, gallbladder, eye issues

If Pitta is imbalanced in the body, it can show up as infection and inflammation, skin rash, acid reflux, migraines, and liver and eye problems. These symptoms are related to too much fire built up in the body. If Pitta is imbalanced in the mind or emotions, it will show up as anger and resentment, jealousy, criticism, controlling or demanding nature, and perfectionism.

The Pitta's strength is that they're sharp, strategic, and clear-minded. They are transformative, strong producers of results, and like to get things done.

If there's too much fire in the mind and body, they need to cool and ground it. The Pitta imbalance in the mind shows up as aggression and hostility, over-judgment and criticism, and the need to always be right. Pitta is related to the intellect, so they're very smart, but out of balance they can be very *right* about everything, which requires someone else to be wrong (blame).

Where worry and anxiety consume the Vata mind, the Pitta mind is in judgment, opinions, shoulds/shouldn'ts and expectations. In extreme, they may get violent and domineering. You don't want to get in the way of a Pitta when they're on fire, especially if they're doing a project, since they have a tendency to become competitive. When hungry, they may bite your head off!

Too much competition as a child or too much conflict in childhood will often create an imbalance of Pitta in the personality. The way to balance Pitta is to cool and ground the mind, body, and emotions. Here are some tips:

To balance, do:	Avoid:
Daily meditation	Overexercise
Coconut oil massage, cool showers	Overheating in the sun
Eat before starving and irritable	Alcohol, spicy food
Rest your eyes and calm intensity	Long hours in front of computer or TV
Get to sleep before 10:30pm	Competitive sports, jobs, relationships

Breath: Pittas can use a cooling breath by curling the tongue lengthwise, breathing into the tongue to the upper belly and exhaling through the curled tongue to bring coolness to the Will/fire chakra in the upper belly. This works great at work, when the temper has flared up and cooling is needed, instead of stuffing that emotion down and pretending it doesn't exist. Cool the fire whenever possible.

Physically: Pitta can be grounded through connecting senses to the earth: eating root vegetables, gardening, laying on or walking in the sand, leaning up against a tree, gazing at or climbing the mountains. It can be cooled by taking a walk in the cool air or spending time in creativity. **Salty, spicy foods are not recommended** for Pittas because it drives up the heat in the body. The more heat in the body, the more anger and imbalance in the mind.

Movement and yoga: Pittas need a cooling and gentle movement that creates flexibility of mind and body. A quick walk in the cool air can be enough to cool the body. Their yoga practice should be steady and relaxing. While Pittas may be attracted to strengthening hot yoga to burn off their fire or anger, this will often throw them further out of balance. The Pitta is already strong and hot so their yoga practice needs to be cool, gentle, flexible, and grounding. (Most of the intense vinyasa yoga classes are throwing Pitta's fire out of balance.) Add coolness and gentleness to the body.

Body: Abhyanga body oiling for Pitta would be warmed coconut oil to help ground and cool the fire element.

Rhythm: Pittas may find themselves ungrounded and fired up in late spring and summer, when the sun is hotter. The Pitta times of day are 10 to 2 (AM and PM), so they can be prone to **im**balance during that time. The Pitta will probably overheat (emotionally or physically) between 10 AM and 2 PM when the sun is highest in the sky. (Non-Pitta minds can use this as the intellectual time of day; non-Pitta bodies can also use the strong digestion of these hours for their largest meal.) It is best for Pittas to remain cool and balanced during this time. The Pitta mind will also start getting critical and overstimulated around 10 PM to 2 AM, so in the nighttime, Pittas should cool and ground the mind before bed and get to sleep before the 10PM mind-revving hour.

Emotional introspection: Pittas may want to focus on *being* rather than doing, see their enjoyment outside of results, and find joy in being present. They can introspect on their judgments of self and others, as they spend a lot of time in that opinionated mind! Working to release the anger, judgment, perfectionism and blame is an important step in finding emotional balance.

When identifying Pitta symptoms, find the specific **quality** that is out of balance. If you are experiencing too much **heat** (anger, acid reflux, inflammation), you can **cool your mind** with meditation or music, **cool your digestion** with some lemon water, or **cool your skin** with some aloe or coconut oil. If you are too **oily**, eat **dry** food. If you are experiencing too much **lightness** or **movement** (busy, over-achieving, do-do-do), you may need to **ground and find stillness**. Calmness and coolness should be the aim in your relationships as well as your foods.

Kapha Dosha: Earth and Water

Kapha dosha is like a thick, watery substance (much like the consistency of mucous!). Kapha is a stabilizing element. It is **cold**, **wet**, very **steady,** and **heavy**. The primary function of the Kapha element is to **SUSTAIN**. Kapha helps in the binding process and provides bulk to the body, lubrication, moistness, fertility, stability, strength, resilience and memory. This is the heaviest and steadiest of all doshas.

Kapha balanced	Kapha IMbalanced
Compassionate, loving	Weight gain
Great memory	Disheveled, slow mind
Thorough, patient	Depressed
Trustworthy, loyal, sentimental	Over-emotional, greedy
Deep thinker	Careless, lazy, attached
Strong stamina	Upper respiratory congestion

If Kapha is imbalanced in the body, it will show up as head and chest congestion, and mucous or fluid retention. Energetically, Kapha is slow moving and gets stuck in inertia—transitioning off the couch can be troublesome. If Kapha is imbalanced in the mind or emotions, it will show up as sadness and depression, dullness and poor perception, greediness and attachment, and resistance to change.

In a balanced state, Kapha dosha in the mind/emotion shows up as easygoing, kind, loyal, forgiving, and consistent. In the body, a balanced Kapha is very healthy and has a very healthy immune system.

Because of the Kapha tendencies to be steady and heavy, there is a lack of drive or motivation. They are resistant to change and can get attached to keeping things exactly the way they are. They struggle with excessive attachment to people, situations and their *stuff*. Kaphas can lack motivation and sink into depression and clinginess. They can be passive and dependent, and will often want to be taken care of.

Kapha's emotional disturbances can result from excess pleasure, enjoyment and attachment, too much sleep during the day, a lack of exercise or a diet heavy in sugar or oily, heavy food.

The Kapha, as a child, may have been overly indulged or emotionally smothered by parents. To balance Kapha energy, it's important to create more fire, strength, stimulation, and movement.

To balance, do:	Avoid:
Meditate daily	Overeating, emotional eating
Rigorous and stimulating regular exercise	Cold weather or food
Stay awake later; wake up earlier	Inactivity, sleeping too much, lethargy
Eat light, hot, spicy food	Ice cream, sweets, pizza, dairy

Breath: Kapalabhati breath creates fire and movement. With the mouth closed, inhale through the nose, and originate an active exhale from the upper belly with force. Releasing the belly creates a passive inhale. Continue pumping the breath in this way, ensuring a thorough inhale. This pumping of the breath through the nose to the upper belly is effective in creating stimulation, fire, and movement for the Kapha. (*Find examples on YouTube for further instruction. And make sure you check in with your body to see if it feels good because it can be destabilizing if you have another element present.*)

Physically: Kapha can be warmed and stimulated by moving vigorously, exercising outside, spending time in the sun, and pursuing creative endeavors. Spices can add heat and pungency to meals to help stimulate digestion as well.

Movement and yoga: Kaphas need lightness, strength, and stimulation. Modern vinyasa yoga works well for the Kapha because it creates movement and fire in the body. Being on the floor and creating stillness in the body can worsen imbalanced Kapha, because they're already very grounded.

Body: Abhyanga body oiling can be done with sunflower, corn, or mustard oil to bring lightness and stimulation.

Rhythm: Kaphas are less balanced in late winter and early spring, due to the cold and unmoving nature of the seasons.

The Kapha time of day is 6 to 10 (AM and PM). Vata/Pittas may find this time of day grounding and stabilizing. Kaphas may experience slow energy and mind between 6 AM and 10 AM, so they can wake early and start with vigorous exercise in the early morning to get things heated and moving. They can focus intellectual work and digestion during Pitta hours of 10 AM to 2 PM if their mind feels dull. The 6 PM to 10 PM timeframe is when most people eat dinner, when digestion is slow, so a light early dinner and some late evening movement can help counteract the heaviness of the evening.

Emotional introspection: Kaphas may want to loosen their emotional attachments and energize their mind to help create balance and counter the effects of sadness. They can create motivation, new thoughts and ideas, and ways of being, instead of being stuck in the lack of change and movement. Movement and fire in the mind are critical for the Kapha.

When identifying Kapha symptoms, find the specific **quality** that is out of balance. If they are experiencing too much **heaviness** or **steadiness** (unable to move or change, greediness, sadness), they may need to stimulate the body with exercise, stimulate the emotions with Bhakti yoga devotional chanting, and stimulate the mind with learning. If they are experiencing too much **cold** (mucous and congestion), they can warm the system with spicy foods, warm the body with body oiling, or Nasya oil (a special blend of herbs and oils to drip into the nasal passages for warming and clearing). If they are too moist or wet, they can eat **dry** food. Warmth, change, movement, and stimulation should be the focus of their energy balancing.

Regarding all the doshas, please note: In our society, Pitta (results and strength) is typically most valued, but there are incredible qualities in all of the elements/doshas. Kaphas are kind and loyal friends, and will come to work and do the most consistent job every day. They are very dependable if given plenty of direction. Vata spontaneity and creativity creates expansiveness and lightness, and while they don't get much done, there is value in the qualities that they bring. It's important to learn where you are strong to celebrate the qualities, and to know where you lack the other elements so you can start to create self-acceptance and inner balance for more joy, peace, well-being and manifestation!

Restoring Our Senses

Dr. David Frawley suggests that if we develop a strong awareness around our senses, we can nourish ourselves by restoring prana, rather than depleting ourselves by *spending* prana. It's important to look at every activity in our body and whether it's nourishing us or depleting us, whether we're gaining prana or losing it. We know that based on how we feel, so we must develop that connection with self to figure it out.

We can use our senses as a way to balance ourselves rather than mindlessly allowing our senses to be focused on the experiences and stimulations that continuously rob us of prana.

Food and digestion

Our food should have sufficient prana (live, organic, plant-based food, pesticide-free, GMO-free) and be appropriate for balancing the qualities of our dosha. Our hydration and oil intake must properly hydrate our body. Eating with mindfulness will aid our digestion which requires significant energy. Without proper digestion, undigested food and by-products can create a significant amount of waste (ama) in the system, which lays the foundation for disease.

Breathing

When we breathe, we pull in prana, life force energy, and oxygen which is critical for metabolism, detoxification, immunity, and many other functions. However, most of us are barely breathing. We have shallow, quick breath. Extend the breath and deepen it to pull in more oxygen and prana to revitalize the body physically, mentally, emotionally, energetically, and spiritually. Awareness around breath will help us to connect with ourselves.

Balancing internal elements

As discussed with respect to the doshas, we can be mindfully balancing the elements within the body, depending on our dosha and how we feel. We are always looking to balance the quality that has imbalanced. To know what's out of balance, we must be attuned to how we are feeling—what feels good and what feels off. Once we have that level of attunement, we can balance with more clarity.

Managing Sensory Input

We can prevent the expending of prana by avoiding sensory impressions that drain us—doomsday media and TV, negative posts on social media, negative stories, gossiping, dysfunctional relationships, and toxic family interactions. These all drain our prana. We want to look at every situation and relationship in our lives and determine if it helps nourish prana or drains it, *Is this yoga class filling me with prana or is it taking too much prana? Is this relationship taking prana or is it nourishing me with prana?* You'll know based on how you feel. Where you spend your time, how you organize your life, and who you spend your time with will dictate whether you're losing prana or nourishing yourself. This is critical.

Fire: You can nourish yourself with fire, sunLight, warm food, and campfire. What will drain you in the fire element is TV, computer, or concentrating your eyes.

Air: You can be nourished through your mindful breath (pranayama), breathing in clean air, going out in nature, and using essential oils that compliment your Ayurvedic dosha constitution. You can lose prana through toxic chemicals (new carpet, plastics, VOCs), too much smoke or incense, and pollution. Not breathing and not being attentive to your breath is another way to lose prana through the air element.

Touch: Self-massage using the dosha-specific oils will nourish your body and bring prana through the sense of touch. For Vatas and some Pittas, sex can drain your prana. Kaphas have a good storage of energy (Ojas) but Vatas can get depleted through sex.

Ether: We can connect with the auditory element of ether through music, singing, Sanskrit chanting, finding silence, and listening to nourishing stories. We lose prana through negative stories, going to bars, loud restaurants, negative thoughts, and music with negative lyrics or jarring sounds.

Ideally, we strive to conserve and pull in prana as much as possible. When my high-risk third daughter was born, I naturally cleared out all of the things that drew prana and did not nourish me because I intuitively knew that my prana was so low. People may think that's selfish, but really, we should be filling ourselves with prana at every moment and releasing the experiences that rob us of prana.

We can channel prana by giving love and service to other people only if we are doing it from a place of love and connection to self **when our cup is already full**, not as a means to get our self-worth through serving others or to fill our cup. **We give from the OVERFLOW, not from the reserves.**

By knowing your dosha type, you're able to start looking at the elements in the body and developing the inner wisdom of how to balance the element showing itself to you. Restoring ourselves through rebalancing can be simple and profoundly effective. **We are the observer of our energies, and we can use our intellect and our will to create more balance within our bodies and our minds, so that we can become more aligned with our Soul.**

Meditation Practice: Mantra for Balancing Elements

Sanskrit is an ancient language based in vibration. When we speak Sanskrit words, the sound that you make translates vibrationally into what you want to attract. There are many different seed mantras that we can use to balance out the elements in our bodies. This is sound for healing. Below are the suggested mantras for Ayurveda body types, based on Dr. Frawley's recommendations. You can try on each mantra and then go into a silent meditation with the mantra that feels best.

OM (all types): clears the mind, opens the channels, and increases Ojas or the juice of life. It is the sound of affirmation that allows us to accept who we are and open up to the positive forces of the Universe. Om is the sound of prana, the sound of Inner Light that takes our energy up the spine, and awakens the positive life force, the prana, necessary for healing to occur.

RAM (Vata): (pronounced like MOM with an R). RAM an excellent mantra for drawing the protective Light and grace of the Divine down. It gives strength, calm, rest, and peace. It strengthens and fortifies the Ojas, that deeper, juicier energy in our body, and it helps support the immune system.

HUM (Kapha): helps in dispelling negative emotion. It creates fire and stimulates the perceptive powers of the mind.

SHRIM (Vata and Pitta): (pronounced SHREEM) can be used for promoting general health, beauty, creativity, and prosperity. Shrim strengths the plasma and the reproductive fluid, nourishes the nerves, and promotes overall health and harmony.

HRIM (Vata and Kapha): (pronounced HA-REEM) can be used for connecting with Divine feminine energy. It is a mantra for cleansing, purification, and transformation. It gives energy, joy, and ecstasy, but initially causes detoxification, atonement, and realignment.

Repeat the mantra that feels best and take it into a silent meditation for 10-20 minutes by focusing your mind on the sound. You can start by chanting aloud, and then allow it to go into a whisper until the sound disappears, but continues to repeat in your mind. If you lose the mantra, just prompt yourself to go back to it.

Ayurveda and Self-Acceptance

Most of us are plagued with our own self-judgment, expectations, and *shoulds* for ourselves. We spend so much time believing we (or projectively, others) should be different than we are. And through this, we create A LOT of resistance in our experience of ourselves. Ayurveda helps us get to a place of self-understanding, which can then lead to a place of surrender—releasing the resistance against ourselves—so we can start to work with our energies to move forward.

I hope you now have a better understanding of what type of energies are flowing in your body and mind, because these very energies are what we're working *with* or *against* every moment of our lives. These energetic tendencies are what determine the difference between someone who typically goes into depression versus someone who flares into anger. It's not something we need to judge or make right or wrong. It just IS. It's how our body works. It's where our energy goes. It's a shift of the elements. Symptoms of imbalance show us where and how we are misaligned. That's it. We don't have to judge it. We don't have to make it bad. We can just use it as a point of contrast that we can look at it as, *Whoa. Where did that come from? What's going on, self?*

Once we begin to understand why things are happening in our mind and body, we accept ourselves more. We become better able to forgive ourselves because we stop confusing ourselves with our imbalanced emotion—anger, sadness or anxiety. As we get some space from the imbalance, we can witness it and simply see it as energies that are sweeping through our bodies or emotions.

With the Ayurvedic understanding, we're given the opportunity to realize that **the imbalanced energy is not who we are**. We are not the waves; **we are the watcher of those waves** ... even though we get swept up into them sometimes.

It has taken me years to get to a place of self-understanding, which has brought me to a place of self-acceptance. As I build self-acceptance, I find that my acceptance of all my stuff—the madness, the messiness, the deep love, my crazy fire—gives other people permission to accept all of *their* stuff. Then this avalanche of surrendering to what-is can permeate through life, creating ease and fun, playfulness about the way we do things.

I remember my yoga teacher sitting in the front of the room with her little belly showing. Her shirt was up a little bit and she was sitting there, looking comfortable with herself, *with her belly showing.* As I looked at her and her belly, I thought, *Aw, what a pretty little belly that's hanging out.* Being in the presence of what I interpreted as her self-acceptance helped me look down at my little poochy belly with a little more acceptance. I was able to feel her self-acceptance and translate it vibrationally and say, *Why am I not able to look at my belly with that much love, but I can look at her belly with so much love?* It was such a simple and poignant experience for me, because what I saw was that I don't judge other people for their bellies (I celebrate their muffin tops!), but for me, it doesn't FEEL good in my body. I don't like to feel the nerve endings around my belly. It started an introspection and **deep desire to accept myself as I am**: *Okay well, let me work to be able to have that level of acceptance (that I was projecting she had). What would that take?* Being in the presence of someone who accepts all their qualities is empowering. Based on how I grew up with a deep lack of self-acceptance, witnessing self-acceptance was like a breath of fresh air.

When I speak publicly about my dosha imbalances—and expose my deep acceptance of my anger, hives, over-reactivity (and other qualities that are commonly judged)—people respond positively to the acceptance. **My acceptance of myself sets resonance for their acceptance of themselves.** We can shift so much by coming to a place of surrender, acceptance, and understanding of how the elements flow in our body. Resistance creates persistence of negative imbalances, whereas allowing and acceptance creates a deep sense of self-compassion.

Recognizing the Elements

With each of the elements comes a positive quality and a limiting quality. We can look at the elements as bringing a gift, as well as contrast or a limitation. **Working with the full embodiment of an element, we can see the limitation as being the other side of the gift, instead of only filtering life as a series of limitations**, which is what many of us do.

I'm going to give you a sense of how the elements work in my body. I have Vata air and Pitta fire, which means I lack the earth element. Now, it's not that I don't have any earth element. I just don't have a lot of earthy-ness in my constitution. I am missing earth's qualities of steadiness and heaviness in my body and my mind.

What I know about myself is that if I wake up before 7AM, I'm pretty much useless for hours. If I can sleep until 7:30AM, the Vata time of day is fully over (2-6AM) and I am waking in Kapha earth hour (6-10AM), so I can have a much more grounded start to my day and throughout my morning. I can either force myself to wake up when it's not working for my body, or I can have the self-knowledge and understanding that waking up at that hour just doesn't work for me.

I get a burst of energy between 10 AM and 2 PM (Pitta hours!), and then after 2 PM (Vata hours again!) my energy quickly plummets. I used to just push myself all day long, because I would look around and see everybody else pushing themselves. I thought, *Okay well, I must be weak or just useless if I can't function after 2 PM*. I would get overtired in the afternoon, my fire would flare up, and then I would find myself yelling at everyone from 3 PM on, because I was crashing during afternoon Vata hour (worse from 2:30 PM to 5 PM). I ran this cycle most of my life, until I learned to be more compassionate and work with this energy. In working with this energy now, I try to wake close to 7:30 AM and give myself until 9 AM to move slowly. I make sure I finish any intellectually and physically demanding activities before 2 PM (and I can usually do this very efficiently because I'm using the fire hours of the day), and I complete mindless activities in late afternoon if necessary. I plan my day around my energy not being strong in the afternoon, so we have "quiet time" in my house for an hour and a half every afternoon from 3:15-4:45 PM—all three kids and I go into our rooms for stillness and rest, reading, playing with a cat, or going inward to recharge. We don't have extracurricular activities or outings at that time, unlike most of society. When I rise again at 5 PM, I am perky and ready to tackle my evening. We are <u>all</u> refreshed to spend time together again.

My life is structured around my energy patterns, and I completely honor them. With excess Vata, my body can get irregular (constipation, unable to sleep, tired, and emotionally reactive) if I don't have a routine to keep me grounded.

By resting, listening to my body's needs, and nourishing myself, I'm a happy, kind mom in the evenings. My kids know that they have to leave me alone for quiet time in the late afternoons in order for me to feel balanced (they have nicknamed my exhausted alter-ego "Mommy Monster"). They value my rest, because I do! Due to the combination of my Vata and Pitta elements, I know that I can get really tired, and when I get tired, my fire element flares up. I used to judge myself so much for that, and now I know the rhythm and energy waves of my body, so I just go with it.

It's important to see what the *ideal* rhythm of your day looks like, and what your energy patterns are.

- For people who have just Vata, when they get tired, they crash and go into loopy, hamster wheel anxiety mode. Vatas may wake between 2 AM and 6 AM with insomnia if they are super ungrounded, or they may feel exhausted between 2 PM and 6 PM.

- If you're a pure Pitta, then around 10 AM to 2 PM, you may flare up with anger or resentment, or feel judgmental and perfectionistic. If that's the case, then look at how to structure your day so you can cool your fire (a lunchtime walk in shade). Pittas may have a hard time getting to sleep between 10 PM and 2 AM because they get overly critical, analytical, or judgmental—so having a cooling (non-media) nighttime routine is crucial.

- Kaphas may feel very heavy in the morning, from 6 AM to 10 AM, or in the evening from 6 PM to 10 PM, so they may need to schedule movement into their early morning or late evening routine, and avoid heavy foods at that time. If sadness kicks in during those hours, then adding stimulation will balance a dull mind or body.

Because I have Pitta and Vata, I am very goal-oriented and like to see results, but the Vata in me doesn't have the energy to follow through! I have to make sure that my Pitta doesn't commit to more than my Vata energy can provide. There's always the evaluation, *Okay, I know I'm ambitious, but I don't want to burn myself out.* I do so much to conserve prana, so I can make the most of my energy reserves.

My Pitta puts myself out there, but my Vata keeps me plagued with self-doubt. My Pitta strength and leadership are always putting me in front of groups, going to that next level of my growth and achieving a transformation. Then my Vata is saying, *Stop. Go hide in a cave, please.* I'm always working those two energies into some level of equilibrium.

My Vata nervous system overstimulates easily. I feel everything, so I don't put myself in a lot of group situations anymore, where I will be on the receiving end of scattered energy. I can present to big groups because I'm setting the tone and resonance for the energy, so I can keep the energy high and positive. When I put myself into situations where there are large groups and lots of small talk, I feel completely drained. If I've been taking on other people's vibrations because I haven't practiced self-protection (connection to my breath, visualizing a bubble of light around me, invoking the violet flame), then I need to plan to nourish myself afterward. I just accept the fact that I get overstimulated and rattled, and I plan to have that downtime in the afternoon. Extra planning is required during the holidays or busy times of the kids' school year to make sure I stay balanced.

My Vata digestion is weak, so I get constipated. If I lose my rhythm or if I'm not able to cook for myself, my body gets off track. I used to ignore that and then just push myself, because *I should be able to do what other people do!* I would go on weekend vacations and do things that threw off my rhythm, threw off my body and my emotions. Now, I travel for two months and I make that my home. I cook my own food and I'm able to bring my rhythm into my travel. I don't usually put myself in situations that will get me severely imbalanced, but if I do, I make sure I have my sesame oil, special foods, and other comforts to help me stay in rhythm when I'm traveling.

It's so beneficial to acknowledge our dosha limitations, accept them, and work with the energies we have (rather than depleting our prana and getting out-of-whack). Self-care and working with the energies, rather than against them, is critical to our mental well-being and ability to maintain our prana. The more we maintain our prana and stay with our inner alignment, the more we can manifest our desires through our acceptance and allowance for the energy we have.

The last thing that has taken me years to come to peace with is my menstrual cycle. For women, we naturally have our elements of air, fire, water and earth completely shifted throughout the course of a month. Men will have shifts every three months, I've observed, but for women, it's every month with our cycle. Every week of our month is different. (Gentlemen, listen up! You have a woman in your life that you may need to understand, and chances are they do not understand it themselves!)

It has taken me many years to come to peace with the elements and how they shift my whole energetic system during my monthly cycle. For those of us who are super sensitive, we get thrown around through the month, so working with the elements of the body throughout the month, throughout the seasons of the year, throughout the time of the day, we can know, *Oh, my body's shifting in this direction*, and we can take steps to balance accordingly, allow the shift (instead of railing against it), and release the fear and resistance.

Each person's unique dosha combination will dictate how they experience the shifts during the menstrual cycle. After menstruation comes the Kapha earth time of the cycle which goes through ovulation (this is my happy time). After ovulation is the Pitta fire time (this is when I unintentionally bite people's heads off), and menstruation is the Vata air movement time of the cycle (this is when I'm completely wiped out on the couch for three days).

My PMS used to sneak up on me like Groundhog Day EVERY SINGLE MONTH. Like I have amnesia that the firestorm is coming. So now, what do I do? I have an app on my iPhone that alerts me when day seventeen of my cycle comes (Pitta FIRE phase), because that is "Mommy Monster" crazy-lady time of the month. I get a little warning notification, and my children get the warning too, and I build mindfulness about the fire element to catch it and cool it early. The notification helps my whole family to work with the fact that fire is about to descend on Mommy's body. We make light of it because we work with what is coming into my house of four females. My hope is that it will help my girls build awareness around their bodies in puberty (a mom can wish!).

Self-Understanding Leads to Self-Compassion

If we can accept that we are a messy mix of elements, then we recognize that others have their *own* mess of elements, and come to acceptance of ourselves and each other. That is when we can start acting more compassionately. As we act more compassionately and lovingly with ourselves, we begin to work with the energies, laugh at the quirkiness, and drop the judgment to build peace within. As we become more compassionate within, we can see the elements working through other people's bodies, minds and emotions. We can say, *Oh wow, look at them. I wonder what just set off their fire*, or *Wow, that person is really stuck in the mud. They need some more fire to energize them.* It becomes less personal, and more understandable and compassionate.

Once we start to understand and accept ourselves, we can get to a place of FORGIVING ourselves when we slip up—when we get caught in the wind, or we start to burn up in the fire, or we get stuck in the mud. We recognize that we got caught up in the elements and lost our balance. We forgot to **be the witness of the elements**, and got swept up. We thought we were the element—*the airhead, the angry monster, or the lazy thug*—rather than the witness to that energy working through our body. As we begin to release ourselves from all the judgments and the opinions of what we should be experiencing, we can forgive ourselves and move into a place of self-compassion.

There was nothing more liberating for me than to be able to say, *Wow, on day seventeen every month, my body and mind and emotions burn up.* As I worked with that and accepted it, I started burning things up less, because I anticipated it. I started giving myself a little bit more leeway and taking care of myself a little bit more, because I wasn't resisting the elements as I used to. I changed from, *Dammit, Kim. Do you have to yell at your kids? You suck*, to *Oh wow, Kim, you're getting a little unhooked. Go do something to cool yourself and get grounded. Sorry, kids!*

Now I don't get too caught up in the fire. I see it, I catch it, I forgive it, and I release it. But it's not always that straightforward—sometimes I have to sit with it and see what was going on underneath it and feel it and allow it. As I allow it, it dissipates. Then I apologize to the people who got burned by the fire that was pouring out of my mouth. It loosens up all the tension and awfulness of it, **because we're always doing the best we can.**

Shadow Side and Self-forgiveness

We all have a shadow side of our personality—that part of ourselves that we judge so much that we're not even willing to look at it, that part of ourselves that we can't even see because we dislike it so much. I've worked with enough people to know that there's a deep confusion around our shadow side that creates a lot of self-judgment, and because of that self-judgment, we have a hard time forgiving ourselves and leaving the space to heal our relationship with self.

If we could just lay down the bat that we beat ourselves with, we can develop some level of understanding and peace about the fact that we all have a shadow side, we all have a part of ourselves that's not in alignment, that creeps out, rears its ugly head, horrifies us and others, and then goes back into hiding. It's okay that we have it. We just need to observe it and see ourselves as more than our shadow. We are not *solely* our shadow side. We are not *only* that part of ourselves that we don't like. If we can observe it, watch it, feel it, and allow it to release, we can let go of the grip it has on us ... and maybe even laugh about it! The letting go and releasing is an act of self-forgiveness. It's also releasing the karma associated with it. It's releasing the negative heavy vibration, and that allows us to Lighten up our vibration and align with ourselves.

Once we can release all the baggage and judgment and beef we hold against ourselves, we find that we are truly aligned with our Light, with the brightest version of ourselves.

When my shadow side creeps up now—and many people have watched my shadow side creep up over the last couple of years (barking at an angry woman in the front of forty people while teaching yoga, yikes!), I think, *Oh wow, did that really just come out of my mouth?* But I understand that it's just an old pattern that creeped up out of my subconscious when I wasn't being mindful. I feel it and I look for my responsibility and lesson. (The lesson in shaming the woman was, *Don't get too big for your britches there, yoga teacher. Have some humility.*) Then I release myself. I forgive myself for not being perfect. When I've made peace with myself, I then make peace with the other person. (I apologized to her for my misbehaving. She couldn't forgive me immediately, but she started coming back to class a month later, and I gave her the royal treatment to make up!) Sometimes I can't make peace with them in person because they're caught up in the blame model, but I try to show them that I love them. The whole time, I do some Soul-to-Soul forgiveness: *I'm sorry. I love you. Please forgive me. I forgive you. Let's forgive ourselves. Thank you.*

No, we're not always going to be proud of ourselves, and we're not always going to reflect the highest qualities of ourselves, but that's just the way life goes. That's just the human condition. We don't need to pretend it's not that way. The more we let our bellies hang out, the more we give others permission to let *their* bellies hang out. *Oh yeah, you've got a little pooch? Great, I've got a little pooch too. You've got a little anger? Yup, I've got a little anger, too. You lose your mind sometimes with your kids? Yup, I do too.* It's not a way to sweep it underneath the carpet. It's an acceptance and a self-forgiveness so that we can make peace with it. This peace allows us to heal whatever needs to be healed.

I hope that through this book, you have developed more self-awareness and acceptance so that you can release yourself from all these burdens that you have accumulated throughout your life. You don't need to carry them anymore. It's okay. You can just let them sit on the table, let your belly out, and release all the stuff that you've held against yourself all this time. You can release and accept and forgive layer after layer after layer. This is not a hard process, because it feels good to let the burden release. That's how you know it's right.

Now, I have seen people who are not ready to release themselves because they haven't made peace yet. They haven't forgiven the other people. They haven't done what it takes to reconcile. When they do what they can to reconcile, then they can self-forgive. Maybe there are apologies. Maybe they haven't taken responsibility. We do need to take responsibility for the effect we have on people, absolutely. We need to make peace with other people ... but we also can release ourselves while we're doing that.

Personal Prayer Practice: Self-forgiveness Meditation

Place one hand on your chest and the other on your belly. Breathe Light into the hand on the chest, and exhale it down to the hand on your belly. Continue inhaling your breath from the chest to the belly, and exhaling from the belly to the chest. Create a wave of light with your breath. Say the following prayer (from Howard Wills and Mirabai Devi) from your ego to your Soul:

"[Self], I forgive you for all the ways you have hurt me, through [list all the ways you've hurt yourself]. Divine, please help me to forgive myself and to be forgiven for all of my mistakes, hurts, and wrongs to myself and to others. Please, Divine, thank you, Divine. Amen"

Continue saying this prayer until you can feel the forgiveness in your cells (just wait for it, it will come). Then say:

"Thank you for forgiving me. Thank you. I love you."

Elements and Relationships

Once you begin to understand your own vibrations and energetic imbalances, it becomes fascinating to watch them in other people through our relationships whether it's parent-child, husband-wife, partner-to-partner, friend-to-friend, or co-worker-to-co-worker.

Understanding the elements present in our relationships can shine Light on interpersonal dynamics and allow us to move more quickly into understanding, acceptance, forgiveness, and compassion.

As I've learned Ayurveda, I have also come to watch the elements as they flow or create disturbances in people's relationships. You can see how each individual's unique energetic elemental pattern meets their partner's elemental patterns. As you learn how to work with the elements within yourself, you can begin to navigate the elements in others.

Often I'll see a fiery Pitta woman partnered up with a steady Kapha man. She may be focused on completing her goals and achievements, and may get caught up in judgment, perfectionism, or anger, getting carried away until she is ungrounded. She partnered up with a Kapha male, who is steady and supportive, loyal and forgiving of all of those fiery emotional tendencies. He helps cool and ground that Pitta fire with his calming earthy-ness. He supports her transformative qualities and gets motivated by her. She becomes more grounded, thanks to his sustaining earthy qualities. She is very motivated and always working on projects, whereas he is laid back and lets her do her thing. They found each other because they (externally) balance each other out, initially—she motivates and inspires him, and he grounds and supports her. That works, until one person says, *Why am I always the one changing? Why can't you get something done?* Or the other one says, *Why does everything have to change? Why are you never happy with the way things are?* You can see how the fire and the earth dynamic may work to some degree, or they may clash.

Now what I always say is, *Dear Pitta friend, you're partnered with a Kapha. All of those wonderful elements that you cherish—his being a caring and kind father and a loving husband and a steady provider—have a downside. The other side of those positive qualities is that he is not going to want to change, or he won't be super motivated to do projects on the weekend. He may get stuck in lack of momentum, just as you get stuck in your anger.* By seeing the other side of the element, we can learn to be more compassionate with each other. *Oh, that's just her fire getting too fired up. How can I help my partner cool, or how can I be a mirror and reflect the need for cooling?* Or, *He is really stuck in the mud/earth, how might I accept that his earth doesn't want fire right now?*

What I've learned through my path is that the more we engage in our partner's shadow side or someone's more negative expression of their element, the more we cover up the negative effects of the element. If I'm in a relationship with a Pitta, and he wants to fight, fight, fight with me, and I engage him and fight back, then I will continue to feed his fire. But if his Pitta gets out of control and I'm willing to stay in the witnessing state and not engage (neutrality!), then he is left with the effects of his fire. His Pitta can't get confused with my energy. No exchanging beach balls. It can't get confused because I know it's just his Pitta firing up. It's not about me.

When we are able to see the karma and elements playing out, we can step back into the witnessing state rather than engaging in it, because we can see it for what it is (a buildup of an element's energy). This is how we practice NEUTRALITY. Watching the storm, setting our own boundaries, and serving as a reflection.

We can say, *Oh, it's that person's shadow side being expressed.* Or, *It's that person's fire getting a little too wild.* It really never has anything to do with us. When we're in relationships, we serve as mirrors; we are reflecting for the other person. That's our purpose for each other. We allow the person to grow and to evolve their Soul because we are on the other side, reflecting. If we're working toward our own place of self-acceptance, and are in those intimate relationships with an open Heart chakra, the giving and receiving energy allows us to be mirrors for each other.

Often, I will counsel a Pitta-Kapha. The Pitta-Kapha has a lot of fire and a lot of motivation, and s/he's very productive and successful. S/he's also very grounded and loyal and emotionally balanced. In fact, the Pitta-Kapha combination is a very healthy and successful combination of elements. This is someone who can function in this high fire society because s/he is balanced with the cooling, grounded earth element of Kapha, while being motivated and productive with Pitta fire. No matter who this Pitta-Kapha is married to, this person is often very independent and may wake up one day saying, *What do I need my spouse for? I can pretty much do everything myself. I have enough stamina and I'm pretty successful, and I'm healthy and I'm grounded and I'm loyal. (I am Superwoman, hear me ROAR!)* They are on their spiritual path, and one day they wake up and look at the other person and say, *What does s/he bring to my life?* This brings us back to the assumption that our relationships are there to *do* something for us. Maybe the service of the relationship is to be a mirror so we can regain our inner balance.

We often look to balance ourselves *externally* through our relationships. Some people will partner with someone (in business or romance) who has elements that they have less of. For example, a Pitta-Kapha (fire/earth) woman may marry a Vata (air) man for balance. She saw the expression, creativity and spontaneity of the Vata and thought, *I'd like more of that in my life.*

Or maybe a Vata-Pitta (air/fire) woman marries a Kapha (earth) because he grounds her and shows love and forgiveness even when she can't forgive herself.

Many of us will balance our elements through our relationships, and there is nothing wrong with it, however, it does pose a few issues that can be healed through understanding, neutrality and compassion:

- Once we get internal balance, we don't need to balance ourselves *externally* through our relationships anymore, so we will need to redefine the relationship to a more conscious expression of the partnership.

- Often we'll feel deficient and we'll look for something in the other person to complete us: *You complete me. I see our relationship as making me feel whole. I feel connected to you because you are giving to me what I'm not able to give to myself.* Clearly, that can pose a problem, because a relationship can't make anyone whole and complete in the long term. The relationship is set up for difficulty with unrealistic expectations for someone to make the other whole.

- Communication styles can be very different among the elements, so each person needs to bend to truly meet the other person in the middle. For example, I have a client who is Pitta-Kapha. She felt her Vata husband wasn't listening to her because they weren't able to connect. I asked for some examples to see how it played out. She said, *Every time I want to sit and talk and really work things out, he just keeps walking and moving around the kitchen and nervously washing dishes and moving around, and I feel unheard.* Her Pitta mind wanted to process issues and nail things down and his Vata body and nervous mind wanted to MOVE! So I said, *Well, he's a Vata. He needs to move. Just walk with him. Go for a walk and talk to him. Meet him where his element is. If you're all fire and earth, that's not going to feel good for him to sit down (earth) and analyze things (fire). He needs to move (air).*

We will often partner up with the element that serves us at that period in our lives. Maybe we feel deficient in a specific area, so we match up with that element that fills the hole. Do you see how this might set us up for deficiency in our partnership later, when we wake up spiritually and realize *I'm the Light and I am whole*, and *What am I doing in this partnership?!?*

Have your friend or partner fill out the constitution form (earlier in the chapter) and learn to understand each other's tendencies. Remember, everything can be healed through love and neutrality!

Awakened Partnerships

Your spiritual path and awakening may shake the foundation of everything. It can shake the foundation of your job. It can shake the foundation of your relationships. It can shake the foundation of your family. It has the potential to awaken the consciousness of every relationship, requiring you to reevaluate how you relate to everything, because your perspective has changed.

Relationships often assist us in our awakening process. While awakening changes the *nature* of our relationships, it's important not to throw out the baby with the bathwater. Just because you're questioning yourself doesn't mean that the relationships have no purpose in your life anymore. They have served as a mirror on a Soul-to-Soul journey, and they continue to have value. People in our lives aren't there to make us whole … their existence has value whether they are *serving* us, or not.

Love is our alignment with our Light. Love is the vibration of our well-being. Love is our connection to our Soul. Love is Source energy. It's *not* a currency that we exchange with people to feel worthy, loved or adequate. That is how we've confused love in our society. We believed we were not enough, and expected our partner to take some of those beach balls and make us feel like we were [good, valuable, worthy, loveable] - enough.

Love is our connection to Light and alignment. It's our connection to who we are. It's our channeling of that Source energy. That is love. This is how it looks in awakened relationships: *I'm connected to my Light and my Heart is open. I am giving and receiving from my overflow. I have so much Light in my Heart and I have so much of that high-vibrational energy flowing through me that I can simply beam that out to you without any need to receive anything back. You are aligning with yourself and connected to your Light, so when you give to me, there is no deficit. It's just an expression of who you are. And when my Light meets your Light, and our energies come together, it is a powerfully juicy synergistic ever-present experience. Divine, awakened, love. We* 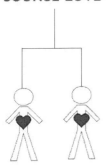 *each have our own vibrational overflow coming through the Heart chakra, and we both have that connection from our crown chakra up to the Light above us. Our Hearts can connect through our overflow of Light. The synergy of that coming together is so much bigger and brighter than what we can have alone, and that's the purpose of our partnership—that synergistic connection.*

SOURCE LOVE

What if that's what our relationships were built upon? What if we approached our relationships from a place of wholeness? How would that look? It's not an easy task as messy humans, with the ego and all these elements imbalanced. It is constantly challenging to work with the complexities of being in a long-term relationship with a person or a job. No doubt. Just as we let our bellies hang out and got to a place of self-acceptance of who we are individually, it would be valuable if we could let our bellies hang out in our relationships. If society could be more real about what it means to be in a human long-term relationship, we would see that it takes work, compassion, and willingness to take responsibility and sort out the beach balls.

Relationship Maintenance

We all have our egos, our shadow sides, our elements, and our subconscious minds working through our relationships. It's messy on our own, so add another human to the mix, and it gets complex. Add some kids to the mix, and it's even messier!

Part of our spiritual contract with our partner is to shine the Light and reflect each other's shadow or imbalances. Our relationships can be structured so that we can all wake up and align with who we really are. If we all take that approach in our relationships—*My purpose in your life is to help you align, and your purpose in my life is to help me align*—then we're in a mindful, Soul-based partnership, a spiritual contract.

In Chapter 7, you looked at your activities and *doing* to determine whether they are Soul- or ego- based. You can look at your relationship exchanges in the same way to decide whether your partnerships have more Soul- or ego- based exchanges. *Am I doing this for him to make myself feel worthy (ego) or because my cup is full and I want to be of service (Soul)? Am I unhappy in this situation because we don't have common core values (Soul) or because I'm suffering that she's not giving me what I want (ego)?* The situation, at the core, will feel good or bad, high or low vibration. Again, the relationship serves as a mirror for us to grow and change and recognize that it's not our relationships that make us feel good in life, it's our connection to ourselves. By shifting our perspective, our consciousness, and our vibration around the other person, the relationship shifts.

When we build self-compassion, we can then project it onto others, and be more compassionate to those in our lives. This is the goal of this spiritual journey within—self-compassion and compassion toward others—for a more joyful and peaceful experience of life.

My husband and I have been together about 18 years, married for 15 years. I don't expect him to be exactly where I am energetically or spiritually, and I do try to have compassion for his struggle in life. The more I have compassion for my awakening, the more patient I can be through his learning process. With that flow, we can both hold the joint vision for us to continue to grow and evolve our relationship, so that we can have an ever-evolving higher vibrational relationship.

Over the years, we have developed a rhythm and space for our connection and growth, so that life, work, and family don't distract from our partnership. For example, after the kids get on the bus, we will have tea in the morning and talk for about a half hour before he goes to work, so we can be present and keep our communication open. Every Saturday night for the last five years, we've had date night: four hours of time to be present with each other. Sometimes the first hour is an argument about the stuff that has built up over the last week, and that's okay, because then we have three hours to work through it. Often these dates are meant to give us time to work through the accumulated emotions and vibration that have built up.

Every six months, we "dump the purse" of our relationship. You know when you dump out a purse and you only put the things that you *want* back in the purse, and you get rid of all the junk that you don't need? This is what we do for our marriage. Typically, it is initiated by an issue that turned out to be a bigger can of worms than we anticipated. We used to find ourselves doing it reactively, but now, as one of us shifts, we realize we need to redefine the relationship, or discuss our desires from the relationship.

We're not afraid of the marriage ending, because we know we're whole and complete, so we look at our marriage now as an opportunity to continue shining our Light with each other. Many people project their fairytale thoughts on us because we're happy together: *Kim and Matt have the perfect marriage.* No, we're not effortlessly happy. It takes a lot of introspection and a lot of humility, a lot of prayer, and a lot of intention-setting using the Law of Attraction. Sometimes when we're so stuck, we both have to go back to wanting to see the highest good of the other person.

There was a time when he felt so extroverted and I felt so introverted that I couldn't imagine how we could continue to be happy together. So through Law of Attraction, I started to meditate with visualizations of us running a spiritual retreat center together—He was out greeting people and doing logistics, and I was teaching, meditating and helping them heal—We were co-creating together but off doing what nourishes both of us. I shared the image with him and he started to meditate on it. We both practiced the vibration of co-creating a cohesive marriage, and that was how it showed up in our lives.

I think people are scared to open up the can of worms, to dump out the contents of the purse, because of the fear of being *alone*, and the feeling of *unworthiness* or *starting over*. Maybe they don't think the relationship has the capacity to shift, because it started from a place of ego. Perhaps they don't know the power of the Law of Attraction ... because it all starts with a vision of what we want the relationship to FEEL like, and the energy follows. I found that I have to be clear and real about what my highest values are in our marriage, and what I feel like I need in the relationship to grow and spread my wings. This doesn't mean *he* needs to fulfill a need in me. It just means I need growth, Light, and high vibration as much as possible.

Here are some things to consider in maintaining your relationship through spiritual awakening:

- What are your deal breakers in a relationship? For me, latent anger and alcoholism don't have a place in my marriage, so if the relationship ever looks like it's heading in that direction, we tackle it before it becomes too big to handle.

- What do you want reflected or vibrated in your relationships? How do you want your relationships to feel? For example, I need independence, creativity, and freedom. Freedom with my time, freedom to express my feelings, and freedom from punishment. (Note: these are all Vata qualities!)

- What are you willing to release? What expectations are you ready to let go of because they don't serve the relationship anymore? I had to let go of many unhealthy patterns related to blaming everyone, using others as a punching bag, self-pity, and self-centeredness. In my marriage, I released my husband from being responsible for taking care of me emotionally.

Creating New Spiritual Contracts

Who knows why we incarnated this lifetime with these relationships? We may be playing out all kinds of stuff with our partner. But enough is enough. Release it and let it go. You don't need the drama anymore; fast track your way into the Light.

We can set the intention to create new spiritual contracts for our relationships. Releasing that old cycle of karma and opening up to a new intention—a new vision that you and the other person agree to. This, my friends, is the beginning of what we call co-creation. Our relationships can be *mindfully* co-created. We can have joint visions.

Sometimes when we wake up and align with our Light, we feel the density of our relationships. It doesn't mean that we have to be stuck in that density *or* bail on the relationship. If we started from the lower vibrational, deficient place in our partnership, we can mindfully and intentionally begin to redefine our spiritual contracts. We can begin to own responsibility in each conflict, recognizing that we are always projecting onto our partner, but it's hardly ever about them.

Personally, I awakened to the patterns in my marriage and realized that I wanted our relationship to evolve. I set the vision to redefine our spiritual contract. I prayed for the release of our past karmic contract the way it existed, and requested a new agreement based on our Souls' highest intentions. I specifically intended to clear the slate to have a Soul-based partnership. Here's is a prayer to get started:

"Divine, please help [partner's name] and me to release all of our old karmic contracts from this point forward. Allow us to redefine our relationship in the Light, with only high vibrational energy. Help us to create a new contract based on Soul qualities of forgiveness, love, peace, compassion, and co-creation. Please Divine, Thank you."

My husband and I are incredible manifestors because we're good at creating a cohesive joint vision, and we're good at aligning our vibration behind that vision. We were able to do this even before we were *spiritual*, before we had raised our vibrations and aligned with a higher part of ourselves. For example, we could see ourselves owning a lake house in the Adirondacks. We both got behind that vision, and then poof, we owned a lake house in the Adirondacks. We weren't clear and in alignment with ourselves because we thought a lake house would bring us peace and joy and ease, but really it just created a lot of work and didn't serve us (we could barely take care of our first house!). Within a year, we aligned behind the vision of *selling* the lake house because we realized what we got ourselves into! We were able to manifest a buyer for the lake house right before the market crashed. If we could do this at a lower vibration, imagine what is possible once we aligned with our purpose and service in the world!

We can co-create incredible scenarios when we are with another willing co-creator. Sometimes we have to lead the way and teach our partners how to do this, because we are the Light-bearers in our relationships. We can willfully accept that role to shine Light and lead the way in our relationships and community. Now, if you're in a suffering mindset, you may be saying, *Why am I always the one doing the work in the relationship? Why can't s/he lead the way?* Because it's your role! You were blessed with a magnificent connection to the Light. You can see the potential for visionary change, and now you can lead others into clarity and awareness! It is your *privilege* to do so! Plus, if we're leading people to their Light, then we have more people in the world to co-create with. Life becomes more juicy and fun.

Co-creation is: *I'm aligned with my Light. You're aligned with your Light. We get together in a combined vision and align our vibration behind it, and boom, things get really cool.*

I can go in to teach yoga with a real connection to my Heart, and I can do it as an expression of my service through a co-creative process with my Higher Consciousness. When I'm Heart-based, I go in connected to my Light, and then through the Law of Attraction, I attract people to class who have a desire to connect with *their* Light. They project their Light on me and think that I bring them Light, but it's not about me, they just love their connection to their Light and see their Light in me ... and I see my Light in them. Through the co-creative process of being in that room together, we are all uplifted in the synergistic co-creation of that class. Those who have attended my yoga classes know that every class feels different because it's co-created with different people, based on the shared vision of going inward to connect with the Heart. The way it feels when we are all together with a similar intent to connect within is pretty magical—when I'm with them I get connected to my spirit, which helps them connect to *their* spirits. By the end, it is a co-creative, euphoric, blissed-out experience that could not be created unless we were all attracting that experience to ourselves through our connection to our intuition, our Souls, our Light, and our own high vibrations.

In Summary...

Understanding your Ayurvedic constitution can help you create more balance in your body and mind. As you begin to take steps toward understanding how your unique system works, you may begin to take care of yourself in a new way. This self-care can help build better self-connection so that you work *with* yourself, rather than continuing the resistance you have *against* yourself. Soon, you will practice self-compassion because you understand how your body works, and you have tools to take better care of yourself when you get imbalanced. When you see how your lack of understanding created unnecessary expectations and judgements, you will learn to forgive yourself.

You may find that as you understand how *your* energetics work, you can watch your energetics interact with *others*. As you understand and accept others' constitutions, you better navigate relationships, and become more compassionate with them. Eventually, you may learn to practice neutrality instead of jumping into the turmoil of the air/fire/earth dynamic. Relationships become opportunities to share the vibration of love, rather than egoic *need* and deficiency. You will experience awakened partnerships based in new spiritual contracts of co-creation, versus the old battleground of deeply rooted confusions.

Journaling Practice: Balancing the Elements in Your Relationships

The following is an inner listening exercise where you're asking your Higher Consciousness questions, and allowing yourself to explore the possibility of higher states of consciousness in your relationships. If you stay connected to your breath, you may be able to access higher expressions of yourself in a relationship that's been challenging. For me personally, when one of my relationships gets stuck, I find that if I can shift into a more visionary, co-creative perspective, then I can get the momentum rolling in a positive direction. We may or may not be able to come to a place of co-creation like I imagined, but I'm able to get the positive juices and momentum flowing, which allow the relationship exchanges to be more co-creative.

Questions to Ponder

Take the following questions inward while vacillating between the mind/thought and Soul/breath. **Take ten slow, cleansing breaths before reading each question.** Identify your gut reaction, write it down, and then read the questions again to allow yourself to go into imagination so it's a fluid experience.

1. Think of a specific relationship that has caused you some challenge but is also important in your life.

2. Consider your and the other person's elements (air, fire, earth).

3. Begin to analyze the elements that are most prominent in the other person. Find their positive aspects. Vata air if they are

creative, expressive, inspired, playful, or spontaneous. Pitta fire, if they are sharp, strategic, intellectual, and clear. Kapha earth, if they are easygoing, kind, loyal, forgiving, and consistent.

4. Now look for the element's limitation in the other person. Vata air if they are worried, anxious, fearful, overwhelmed, spacey, forgetful, or inconsistent. Pitta fire, if they are angry, resentful, jealous, critical, controlling, demanding, or focused on perfection. Kapha earth, if they are often sad, depressed, lethargic, greedy, and resistant to change.

5. List the qualities that you consider their negative qualities that get in the way of your relationship. See how these negative qualities are related to their dominant elements.

6. List the positive side of those negative qualities. What are the positive sides of those elements? If the person struggles with anxiety, then look at the creative or expressive aspect of that person, the flexibility. If there's someone that struggles with anger, on the other side of that is probably passion and strength. If the person struggles with sadness, on the other side of that may be consistency and loyalty.

7. Which of their qualities attracted you to the relationship to begin with? How are/were you trying to energetically balance yourself with the relationship?

8. How can you release these old expectations for how the relationship should be, now that you understand how you are using the elements in the relationship to create balance?

9. Start envisioning a new version of the relationship:
   - How can you evolve the relationship so that you can envision it as a Soul-based contract?
   - How can the relationship shift so that it can exist without expectations, with each person having the balance of their own elements and their own path?
   - What is your individual highest expression on this earth?
   - What is the highest expression of the other person?
   - How can you envision the highest expression of the relationship?

- Where would you both resonate together in that highest expression of yourselves? (What would you be doing individually and together; what are your interactions?)

10. Begin to think of how you and the other person can be co-creators in this evolved version of your relationship. If you don't know what that means, start to play out what your highest expression and their highest expression would be like if you had a common vision of your relationship, considering their dominant elements (air, fire, or earth) and your dominant elements. How could that potentially play out to be so synergistic that it almost takes on a life of its own through the relationship?

Allow yourself to continue visualizing this co-creation that's possible in an evolved, co-creative, Soul-based relationship. Do so without any expectation or attachment. You are just conjuring up positive vibration momentum.

When you're ready, bring your breath into the chest at the Heart, tuning into Divine Source and Soul, and offer up a prayer: "Divine, please allow this relationship to release all old, karmic contracts so that the relationship may evolve as a co-creative experience of the highest expression of both of our purposes here on Earth. Please Divine, thank you, Divine. Thank you. Thank you. Thank you."

Journey the Co-Creative Path

Always be in a state of expectancy and see that
you leave room for God to come in as He likes.
-Oswald Chambers

By now, I hope that you have started to figure out how abundant the Universe is, how easy it is to manifest that which you want, and how potent you are in your ability to do so. As we practice the Law of Attraction, we begin to see how brilliant the Universe is. Have you felt it? Have you experienced it yet? I am consistently blown away by the miracles and seemingly magical experiences I've had since being on this path.

As I get deeper into my understanding about how the Universe works, I don't feel like I'm manifesting on my own. I feel like there's a team, or a co-creative matrix of benevolent energy working with me. Honestly, I haven't pinned what it is: My Higher self? God? Positive energy? Solar frequencies? Angels? I seriously have no idea, and I've become comfortable with an evolving sense of what is assisting me. Each year, I build onto the puzzle and get a clearer view of how to navigate and work with the energetic spiritual web, but the more I know, the more I realize how vast consciousness is. The more intimate I get with this energetic manifestation matrix, this web of creation, and the more attuned I can get to it's resonance, the more quickly and effortlessly I can create what my Heart desires.

The matrix of manifestation becomes a living and breathing web through which we co-create our Heart's desires. The more experience we have manifesting with this web, the more trust we have that it actually exists. We need to watch how we work with it. Observe ourselves in it. Build data about its existence and what we've co-created with it so that when we go into doubt and amnesia about our potency, we can very articulately remind ourselves how incredibly potent we are when working from our Heart.

When it comes down to it, manifestation through co-creation is very simple. There are three very important ingredients in this co-creative path: Possibility, Responsibility, and Love. We make it complex, but it can be that simple.

Visioning with Source

Co-creation can be very powerful when we are working with the Universe, with our Divine Source. Often, I will be in meditation and say, *You know what? I don't know what the highest expression of me is. Show me. Show me what I'm capable of. Please.* Our relationship with our Divine Source, our Higher selves, is an important relationship in life. We can co-create through our Soul/Source relationship. We can receive wisdom and fill in our vision, and then align our vibration with that which has been shown to us from our Highest Consciousness.

Our Higher selves can create a vision for us that we weren't able to mentally construct, that sounds and feels so right because it's part of ourselves. It's part of our intuition. We call it creativity, but it's so much more. It's intuitive wisdom. It happens when we get behind this inspiration, and when we align our vibration with the incredible vision of our Higher Consciousness.

As I've shared before, when I set my intention a couple of years ago, I wanted to **help awaken as many people** as possible, in as **little time** as possible, with the **most profound effect** possible. I also wanted to stay **lean and strong**. When the Divine showed me I could be a yoga teacher, I resisted a little bit because I was lazy! I suffered through the yoga teacher training. I acted like I had no idea why I was following this *faulty intuition*! That is, until my first day of work, when I realized that I could infuse mind, body, and spirit into ninety minutes and literally WAKE PEOPLE UP! Awaken them to their Divine spark ... into their potency!

Source can give us a vision of possibilities that are so much bigger and more beautiful than we ever imagined. If we can see ourselves as spiritual co-creators with our Higher self, our experience of life becomes blissful and aligned and so joyful. Our relationship with our Divine Source is a great relationship through which we can start co-creating.

Power of Spiritual Connection

When I'm not able to shift my vibration through my breath, yoga, or feeling into and changing my thoughts, I will reach for my connection to my Divine Source. I will ask, and sometimes downright beg, for the qualities that I am searching for. I have to tell you, I am ALWAYS given a response when I ask for one. I just need to keep my focus long enough to recognize that the response has been given!

It's important to start by feeling into Source. *Who is there for you? Spirit Guides showing you the way? Angels guiding you? A saint or goddess that bestows gifts? Is it male or female energy? Is it a connection to the energetic web or hologram? Is it the connection with your Soul? Is it your Higher Consciousness?* It's different for everyone. And it's worth finding out who your peeps are on the other side of the veil. We all have an entourage of spiritual energy supporting us, cheering us on, and aligning the physical realm to our vibrations and requests. The stronger we can feel that connection, the more potent and supported we feel.

Many of us need to re-build this connection to Divine Source. Religion may have deterred us from building our connection to *God,* or perhaps our relationships with our own father or mother deterred us from reaching for a connection to the Divine mother or Divine father energy. So maybe we need to establish new words (Divine, Source, Universe) to truly connect with that all-pervading spiritual energy.

Whatever we call Source energy, we need to *feel good* in our connection to Source. That feeling of connection with Source helps us raise our vibration to resonate with Light and love … often through the breath, the Heart, and our imaginative visualization of this high vibration Source.

Intuitive Imagination Connects to Source Energy

We can use our imagination as the way to envision and connect with our vibrations of Source. Our intuitive imagination creates a relationship with Higher Consciousness that feels good because Source maintains love, forgiveness, peace, beauty, safety, joy, harmony and truth ... always. It is a functional co-creative relationship that you can lean on since it is more resilient and dependable than our human relationships. Our intuitive imagination makes this relationship real and concrete once it is well-practiced and established. Then we can reset our vibration to it at any time.

The imagination transitions into intuition at the point when you connect this imaginative experience to your Heart. It may take time to build trust that this intuitive relationship is, in fact, real but it comes in time. The reality is that none of us really know how the Universe works or what the Divine is. (In fact, we don't concretely know much about how *anything* works.) So we go with what feels good and true to connect with our spiritual wisdom.

Our connection to Divine Source can provide us with an instant high-vibrational shift. Our faith and connection to Soul, which is guided by whether we feel good or not, allows us to tap into Source without really having to understand how it all works. Some people need to think of it as simply projecting our high vibration onto an imagined human form or deity, so we can resonate with that part of our Soul.

What's your interpretation of a Divine Source that carries the qualities that you wish to embody? What does he or she look like? What do you imagine they feel like? What would they say to you in times of need? If you know what this is for yourself, great. Incorporate it into your desires. Strengthen the connection. Play with how your Source feels. If you haven't developed it, try out a connection with Source that you feel drawn to. Doreen Virtue's book, *Archangels and Ascended Masters*, is a great reference.

Personally, I struggled with the concept of the Divine Mother, because my relationship with my mother wasn't very strong. I very vividly recall being in a meditation with my teacher, Mirabai, and her saying, *Go now to the Divine Mother*, and

I kept feeling resistance internally. I was not interested in going to the Divine Mother, but Mirabai kept saying, *Go to the Divine Mother*. And I was like, *No, thank you. That doesn't feel good to me.* During the imaginative guided meditation, I saw the Divine Mother and she merged inside of me! It was like she knew I wasn't going to go to her, so she enveloped me and there was a sense of connection, peace, and integration that has shifted my perspective personally. I was willing to go there, to face my resistance, and the Divine Mother met me halfway to help push me through my resistance.

Now, when I'm looking for resonance or comfort, I connect with the Divine Mother. She doesn't have a specific name. I just imagine her. I feel her bright, powerful, loving energy. I feel her presence when I call on her. I feel her connection and support. When I feel ungrounded, I can lean on her to find comfort, worthiness, safety, love, compassion, ease, and grace. I choose to imagine her in a yogic goddess way, because that feels good to me. I choose to read stuff about her that expresses her as an energy, as Shakti. That's *my* interpretation.

When I want to access qualities of surrender, spiritual progress, or protection, I connect to the Ascended Masters from different traditions, and the Archangels. I feel into each one to see how they feel and I talk to them to invoke their energies.

From the Yogic perspective, the Super Soul (Source) carries different energies which show up in the balanced male/female form. The Divine carries the:

- **creative force**, which holds the energy of building, wisdom, and creation;

- **sustaining force**, the energy of abundance and worldly enjoyment, which embraces the human body and the bliss that can be achieved through the human experience;

- **destructive force**, the destructive energy, which breaks down the old to make way for new transformation.

Our connection to Source, to our Higher Consciousness, has a broader perspective of our lives. It's not caught up in the prison of the ego. If we call upon it for help, **Source always delivers.** In fact, Source is waiting for us to ask!

The 5th Dimension Co-Creative Universal Matrix

As we deepen our relationship to the unseen energies with which we are co-creating, and we begin to connect with the higher vibrations of love, gratitude and well-being, we tap into what New Age spirituality would call the 5th Dimension of Consciousness (5D). This is a LOVE frequency of instantaneous manifestation, synchronicity and co-creation at a high level. It provides us with more opportunity to create from the Heart, because we are tapped into the Heart of the Universe. I like to see this as an interconnected web of opportunity and abundance ... a manifestation matrix that we all have accessible to us if we can raise our vibration to the 5D vibrational frequency of love.

We can see what this looks like by looking at that which is *not* 5D. In the 3rd/4th Dimension of Consciousness (3D), we are all SEPARATE. Here's what that looks like: I'm disconnected from all the people and opportunities that I desire. I'm on a lower vibrational frequency so I'm not resonating with the vibration of the situations that I want to manifest in my life. I'm disconnected from the web of abundance. I feel sorry for myself, and lonely, which makes me even more separate from what I want.

As we tap into higher frequencies in 5D that are aligned with what we want to manifest and attract into our lives, we tap into a greater matrix of opportunity. It is interconnected and easier to magnetize what we want. I want a new job, and people are attracted into my life to provide me with the contacts for the new job. I want a deeper spiritual community of friends, and they are within the web of interconnectedness—completely abundant and available.

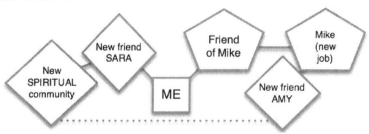

Witnessing the 5D Universal Matrix

Once we begin to attract what we desire, and get a glimpse of this 5D matrix, we tend to go into amnesia about it all. So even though we've had an experience of this miraculous 5D Universal Energy Matrix, and we have witnessed its presence in our lives, we quickly forget about it and deem ourselves powerless the next time we're ready to manifest something new. Or we never connect the dots about how _this_ '_coincidental' contact, led to that 'rare' opportunity, which led to the very thing I was working to manifest_. I'm sure this sounds ridiculous, but I've watched so many people forget their potency and ignore the miracles that occurred just months prior. I spend a lot of my time with clients reminding them how potent they are as I hold up the reflection of the last magnificent situation that they JUST manifested! The ego is full of delusion, and diluting our potency happens to be what it does best.

The Universe can put together all kinds of win-win scenarios, which synergistically benefit all the people involved in your life. The manifestations almost seem miraculous, because we don't connect the cause-and-effect of how they came about. We don't see the strings of how the _causes_ and the vibrations we've put out there create and manifest a specific _effect_. We do all this work, and then feel like the manifestation came out of nowhere because the interconnectedness is unseen.

We can begin to link cause-and-effect by being mindful of the intentions we put out there, and consciously connecting them to what is being created in our lives. When we do this, we solidify our trust in the Universe and learn to navigate the vibration of love in this 5D matrix.

Where We Get Lost

Linking cause-and-effect to see our mastery of the Law of Attraction takes practice. Sometimes we're super mindful of our vibrations and we can see the clear link between our intentions and what we've manifested. Sometimes it's not so clear, because we're zigzagging our way toward our intention.

We often forget what our original intention was because we have amnesia when it comes to what we're putting out there into the world. Our attention span is so short, and we are unpracticed at staying focused on the desire and vibration we want to manifest.

Sometimes an intention will manifest a year later, and I've completely forgotten I had asked for it! For example, I was keen on manifesting corporate yoga opportunities. I developed a few clients over the year and realized that ongoing corporate yoga didn't meet my desire to wake up many people (because the clients wanted me there every week and I wanted to be out waking up new corporations!). But I soon realized that the corporate clients kept flooding in because of all the intention setting work I did the year prior.

Maybe **the path feels zigzagged** because our expectation for *how* our intention may manifest differs from the Universe's execution of our intention. Maybe we're experiencing the process as a zigzag because we didn't understand the steps required to move us toward our manifestation. If we begin to feel lost after a few pit stops, we can forget our original intention.

When working to heal my relationship with my mother, I kept envisioning a happy, healthy relationship. I was doing forgiveness prayers and working on clearing our karma. The results I was getting were terrible, though, and the relationship was blowing up—a more angry, dysfunctional expression of both of us. This led to me setting a lot of boundaries between us (not what I had envisioned!), but two years later, with the boundaries still in place, we are able to have more peaceful time together. Not exactly what I had planned, but it was the only way for us to have a healthy relationship. You see, the blow up was the means to more boundaries and a peaceful relationship, but I couldn't see that at the time.

We could be **lily-padding to the manifestation**. Life might give a situation that looks a lot like that which we want and then turns out to not happen. When we lose the possibility of this lily pad option, we often lose our vibration, *I never get what I want*. I like to see this as a lily pad to help us build the vibration toward the real manifestation. What if the lily pad was a critical step to help us build possibility or clarity in the desire? Perhaps our manifestation is the next leap from the lily pad. If our vibration plummets, then we lose the benefit of the lily pad.

Perhaps **we're not consistent about our vibrations**, so we put something out there and begin to get it, and then our vibration drops and we lose focus. Then we stop getting what we want, so we have to start the process again. Many of us are still inefficient at maintaining a consistent high vibration for manifestation. Since the Universe is always responding to our vibrations, if we're not consistent about them, we tend to get lost on our way toward our intentions.

Manifesting our move to California has been difficult because of our inconsistent vibrations around the potential move. When my husband and I are in California, we are clear and able to set the high vibration for wanting to move. However, when we are back in our daily life in Saratoga, surrounded by friends and our Waldorf school community, it is very hard to keep a positive vibration about moving, and it begins to feel bad. So when we manifest an opportunity to move temporarily (e.g., we get a renter for our Saratoga NY home), one of us goes into fear and resistance and energetically sabotages the potential!

Logging the Miracles to Realize Our Potency

One of the most important steps in using the Law of Attraction is to witness, and keep track of, your manifestations. Not to compute success rates, but to start building awareness of how potent you are, how consistent (or inconsistent) your vibrations are, and to build trust that the Universe has your back. I never cease to be amazed when I manifest something I desired. It never gets old to witness our potency. It's invigorating and inspiring.

The self-doubt and unworthiness from the ego always seems to creep in. If you're keeping track of how you systematically manifest, you can remind yourself of your potency to build trust in your manifestation skills. Then, when self-doubt creeps in, you can remind yourself of the data proving that it works.

Working with the Universe can be an iterative process that requires a two-way conversation with our Higher Consciousness. Maybe we haven't been actively participating on our side of the communication. If we want to manifest our Soul's intentions, it helps to have a co-creative discussion with Higher

Consciousness, which takes speaking, listening, acting, and listening some more.

For example, we submit a vibrational desire to the Universe. The Universe speaks back to us through what is given to us based on our vibration. **We often aren't aware of what vibration we're putting out there until we get the messages or manifestations back from the Universe.** Sometimes, the response comes in the form of contrast, and we think we're just not getting what we want in life. But we can look at the contrast that's brought back to us and simply take it as data, and say, *Oh, wow. I asked for this and now I'm getting that. How could that be? Maybe I need to adjust my vibration.*

Often, people will say to me, *Okay, I'm working with my vibration. I'm manifesting some stuff, but now I've asked for this job and this house, and I got so close and then it fell through. What the hell? This Law of Attraction thing doesn't even work.* To this I say, *What do you mean it's not working? You got 75% of the way there and then something happened. Maybe you weren't able to keep your vibration. Maybe that which you're asking for isn't aligned with who you are. Maybe you're not understanding how things falling through is leading you to the optimal option. Or perhaps it was a lily pad!*

This is where the questioning and communication with Higher Consciousness through intuition is tremendously valuable. There's a message in your *not* manifesting your intention yet. It's kind of like a game of clues. We're not exactly sure what we're going for, so the Universe gives us some information back, and then we have to look at it and say, *Okay, what is this? Is this me? Is it an unfit job? Is it the wrong house? Is it who I'm doing it with?* We keep asking those questions to decipher what is misaligned. *Is it my vibration or the manifestation? Why?*

We tend to give up when we don't understand the cause-and-effect relationships, when we don't see *how* we have attracted the contrast that's helping us get lessons along the way toward our intention. Instead, we need to learn from it and move forward.

If you have set an intention, you can trust that everything being brought to you as contrast is there to CLEAR whatever is in your way as you work toward your intention. It may not make sense to you, but if you let the Universe guide

you and work through your life, it will all make sense in the end.

We don't need to assume that the Universe doesn't support us, or that we'll never get what we want. **We just need to learn how to work with what we are receiving.**

While you're working toward your intentions, it's helpful to go with these assumptions:

- **The Universe is giving you clues**. You and the Universe speak different languages. You want clear verbal communication, but that's not how the Universe works. So learn how your Higher Consciousness, your Source, talks to you through your experiences. Listen and watch carefully so you can decipher the clues.

- **You're just zigzagging your way to the manifestation**. This does not mean that you won't achieve your intention, or that the Universe is screwing with you, or that you're unworthy of your desires. You simply don't have the ability to see the actual path—it's not linear. You're zigzagging your way to your intention. You are following the breadcrumbs along the unknown path.

- **You may not be able to intellectually understand the process.** We get caught up in wanting to *know* the WHY and the HOW on the way to the intention. We don't have clarity, so we can't see the exact path, and we don't have the capacity to know why we're zigzagging. **We must surrender the need to KNOW.** We have to surrender to the Universe and release the resistance to the unknown, the fear.

We must build our trust that our Source (our Highest Consciousness) has our back and knows the most effective route.

The Universe knows how to get us there ... if we can just surrender the need to KNOW the WHY and the HOW, and follow the breadcrumbs on the path to our manifestation. Each time we get feedback from the Universe, instead of judging it (making it bad and saying, *the Universe sucks*), we can uncover and open the package, and feel our way in to understand the messages that are getting placed in our path. It's like a scavenger hunt, and we're just opening the packages along the way to figure out how to zigzag our way to our intention.

The way we know whether we're on the correct zigzagging breadcrumb path is based on how we feel. Our inner feeling at each fork in the road will show us whether things are going in the *right* direction.

Inner Listening

To be in a co-creative relationship with our Higher Consciousness, we have to first learn how to listen and communicate with our Higher Consciousness. There are three components to this communication.

1. **TRUST that our Higher Consciousness is communicating with us.** It's not just a one-way communication between our Soul and Source. *Why wouldn't Source respond* if a part of itself was communicating? Source is anxiously waiting to connect and communicate. We must trust that the two-way line of communication is there. A co-creative conversation can be nurtured and developed so that we can use it more mindfully. There is a response there, you just haven't learned to decipher it!

2. **Find stillness and quiet to LISTEN.** Most often, we forget about the receiving process. We have difficulty in the stillness, often because the ego fills it with noise, but if we just set a question or request out there, we will *always* get an answer. We have to listen carefully for the answers; just keep going to the meditation chair to listen in anticipation and trust.

3. **Learn to DECODE the messages we receive.** We can patiently begin to develop our ability to learn how to receive messages. **Source talks to us by delivering energy packages into our consciousness.** (I know, this sounds weird, but just go with it.) The energy packages stream into our consciousness energetically, and we need to decode them into our linear thinking. They may come in through images. They may come in through sounds. They may come in through kinesthetic vibrations or words. We may hear it through one ear. We may see it through

visualization. This is where our work and practice is critical. We have to unpack the energetic packages and learn the language. We all have intuition. Some of us can see/hear/feel it louder than others.

We may need to cultivate our intuition. Because the mind's noise is so loud, and most people haven't learned how to listen to that specific whisper, so they can't hear it. However, **those of us who are extra sensitive may easily hear the whisper from our Higher Consciousness, if we can learn how to do the intuitive inner listening and decoding.** Everyone has the ability to listen, but those of us who are extra sensitive can redirect our attention from the disturbances to the messages of our inner voice.

How do we know the communication is coming from Source, or our Higher Consciousness, versus whimsical imagination or ego? We can know whether something is based in our fear or ego, versus in Soul and Higher Consciousness, based on how it feels. If it feels bad, it's not from Source. If it feels good, it is from our Higher Consciousness. If it feels TRUE, it is from Source. If it feels uncomfortable, it may be from the mind. Words or messages from Source often feel like rock solid truth that you've known for your whole existence.

What if I listen but don't hear or see anything? This is an introspective conversation with Source. Stillness and quiet make the best environment for receiving and decoding. It may be helpful to meditate before this introspective conversation with Source, because this process bridges Higher Consciousness with present moment thinking. The way in is through connection with your breath. You will begin to bleed silent meditation with your introspective practice, so you can stay in this state while contemplating life. As you do that, you can ask questions and listen for the answers.

Everyone will have a different experience based on how their specific vibrations work in their bodies, but of course you need to be connected with yourself in order to be able to do this. We have to be in the present moment, connected to our breath and our Heart, to have the conversation and receive the communication. If we are swept up by our elements (fire anger, air worry, or earth sadness), then it's more difficult to listen. Once we ask, the receiving may come in through the physical state of someone saying something to us in that next conversation we have, or it may come in an imaginative visionary state, or it may come in hearing a whisper, or feeling a draw toward having to do something.

My Co-Creation with Source

This is all very theoretical, and it may make sense conceptually, but I'm going to share with you how this process works for me in my life so that you can begin to play with it when you are working with your intentions and desires. I ask you to follow carefully because I'm going to give you all of these scenarios that feel very unrelated, because it's the **zigzag of my co-creative process.**

My intention is to have a profound spiritual impact on the world. I have been very consistent in desiring to spiritually awaken as many people possible, in as little time possible, with the most profound impact possible. That said, it's not been very clear HOW I would do that, WITH WHOM I would do it, WHERE, WHEN, etc. So I asked for help from Source to define that further, and I co-created this experience with my Higher Consciousness.

My Inspiration: Two Hundred-Person Programs

During one of my breath-focused introspective conversations, I had a vision of doing big retreats with 200 people. It felt like the vision descended upon me, like it was being shown to me for the future. The vision kept creeping into my meditations, and when it crept in, it felt really good. I kept visualizing myself teaching a group of 200 students. I had seen a photo of Gabrielle Bernstein doing a retreat at Kripalu with this big mass of people she was working with, and I thought, *That would feel so good. That is so exciting!* I started realizing that this vision was growing in my mind, so I was concerned and asked, *Is this my ego just wanting to be famous?* The response was, *No, I don't really want to be famous for the sake of being famous—that doesn't feel good.* I wasn't interested in traveling around the world, because I had three kids and was happy with my semi-simple life. So I knew it wasn't my ego. It would feel good to be able to have that effect on that many people, in a room as beautiful as

Kripalu. So I used that photo of Gabrielle Bernstein in a room with 200 people as my visualization, to develop the vibration and desire.

Contrast: Job I Would Hate

Next, my life presented a job opportunity that I just *had to* apply for. It made sense financially for me to apply for this job, but in my preparation for the job, I felt so much resistance. I was like, *Oh my God, I would hate this job.* But I applied for it anyway because I *should*—it just made the most financial sense. In truth, that job opportunity was showing me exactly what I *didn't* want in life. It became clear that I didn't want to sit in an office with a certain group of people doing a certain type of thing. Preparing for the job interview drove me into a very strong energetic momentum toward the type of work I *did* want to do. It sent me searching for someone to help me figure out how to get into a room with 200 people. I had the job interview, and needless to say, I didn't get the job, because I can't manifest something that I have dread around. (Thank goodness!) But I gained so much clarity about how much I wanted to teach large groups.

Breadcrumb Along the Way: Write a Book

I just happened to have a friend who was an entertainment producer, and as I sat down with him, he said, *You have to write a book. If you want to get on the national scene and fill a room with 200 people, you have to write a book.* He started throwing all these numbers and scenarios at me, and frankly, it didn't feel good to think about all these marketing techniques to fill a room just so I could teach large retreats. But I got the message: I had to write a book. *Ugh, I have to write a book. Sitting at the computer for hours upon hours.* It didn't feel good for me to think about writing a book. I put the book idea on the back burner because I honored what he said, but didn't have the energetic momentum to even think about writing a book.

Breadcrumb Along the Way: Small Retreats and Programs to Build Material for the Book

Soon after that, I started teaching more retreats. I was gaining momentum around the retreats and I got into a groove. It felt good to do retreats. I also found that people wanted to do more work with me on a daily basis, so I developed teleconference meditation programs. The book was still on the backburner. My intention about teaching 200 people was on the backburner. Even though I didn't know it at the time, I was developing my teachings and materials through the small retreats and phone programs. Initially, I had clarity that I wanted to be in a room with 200 people, but I didn't have the material to deliver in the room with that many people yet! All of the retreats and meditation programs helped me to discover what I had to share with people.

After about a year of doing retreats and phone-based meditation programs—essentially developing my material—the book concept re-emerged.

Breadcrumb: California Program Transcriptions

Seemingly separately, I had this desire to go out to California for the winter because I wanted to escape the cold. I decided to write THE BOOK in California, and I didn't think much more about HOW I would do it.

The month prior to leaving for California, I had been offering a phone-based meditation program. Toward the end of the program, I was inspired to have some of the program recordings transcribed. I went through the process of learning how to get one of my teachings transcribed and posted it on my website blog. It was a bit random, but turned into a critical whim for later.

Right before I was about to leave for California, I received an inspiration in meditation. I was told to offer another meditation program with one-on-one mentoring. *Really, Source? You want me to WORK while in Cali? I want to go hang out in California and write a book and you want me to put on a program that lasts two months and requires a lot of work? Seriously? I want to naval gaze on a beach!* I went back and forth and batted it around with my Higher Consciousness, because hosting a labor-intensive meditation program while on sabbatical in California wasn't what I had planned. As I listened deeply inward, I started to visualize myself recording my meditation teachings and then getting the recordings transcribed to assemble into the basis for THE BOOK. *Whoa, absolutely brilliant! I would've never thought of that!* All of the groundwork was laid out for me, so it made total sense. My General Manager had already started preparing for the book. (Thank God I had been listening to the random inspirations!) I said, *Okay, I'll do it! I'll offer this program, and if people sign up then I know it's right and I should do it.* Of course, 27 people signed up for the program.

When I got out to California, I totally understood why my Higher Consciousness had guided me to do that. Source knew that I wouldn't be able to sit on a computer in the middle of paradise and focus on writing my book. Source knew that I taught through my voice. Source knew that I was more motivated when I was accountable to an engaged group. Source knew I would be focused and I would deliver with an expectant audience. Source knew I don't have the ability to finish a project unless there was a specific start and end to the timeline. Source knew that I needed to create all of these meditation programs and retreats in order to develop my material, so I could sit in a semi-meditative state and dictate the teachings. Source knew all of this, and set it up absolutely perfectly. Then when I was out in California, Source sent me someone who wanted to read and edit the material I put together, because my General Manager knows how to create effortlessness for me to manifest my desires.

I may not have known *why* that job interview came up, and I may not have known *why* this meeting with this producer friend came up, and I may not have known *why* I was offering a meditation program when I was about to head out to paradise. I may not have understood any of these things, so they may have felt like a zigzag. But in fact, based on the way my energy, consciousness, and mind works, the Universe put a very straight line together for me, and I followed it—like picking up breadcrumbs along the way. I listened and acted and listened and acted, and I continued through the process.

The 27 people who participated in the meditation program were part of the co-creation. They had their intentions. They communicated with me throughout the program to guide the development of the material. They would give me feedback on their experience when I mentored them, which would help inform what the next recording would be. Someone asked me, *You mean, you don't know what you're going to teach from one recording to another?* Nope, I had no idea. I sat down and I asked my Higher Consciousness what should be taught next, and then was given the material in this semi-meditative state as I was listening. The inspiration came because I trusted, because I listened. I allowed it to be a co-creative process.

Every time I get contrast, I don't look up to the Source and say, *What crap have you given me now?* I look up and I say, *Oh, what's this supposed to mean? Transcription? Okay, I'll do transcription. What do you want me to do with it? That doesn't really make sense, but okay. I trust you.* I listen and I do it and I listen and I do it. That is the co-creative process. Even though I couldn't see how the pieces fit together, I couldn't see the way the puzzle would look in the end, I trusted that each puzzle piece had a purpose in manifesting the intention.

In the end, a book was written (this book!) that I would have never been able to do in the way that I originally intended. In fact, years prior, I had tried to write a book and I got to 40 pages before I got lost in the perfectionism of it all. I wasn't able to do it. I hit the contrast of not being able write more than 40 pages, yet I kept setting the intention, and eventually when I was ready, Source co-created it with me through the high-vibrational desire to be in the room with 200 people.

More Breadcrumbs: Asked to Train Yoga Teachers

The book was 90% written, and it probably would've sat on my computer because I was getting lost in the final details, but I had been asked to train yoga teachers. As I contemplated whether to do this, *Was I qualified? What material would I teach?* I realized that I just so happened to have a practical spiritual training manual (THE BOOK) that I just wrote! So this pushed me to finish the draft so the photocopied spiral-bound version of the book could serve as the teacher training manual. The draft book became my basic material for my spiritual programs over the next year. In fact, it became so widely distributed through my programs, I was compelled to go forward with more formal publishing!

Because my intention had momentum, even when I stalled, situations in my life kept propelling the intention forward. My intention had a life and was aligning my efforts around it!

Do you see? It never felt like a lot of effort because I was doing what I loved, I was doing what felt good, and I was passionate at each step. All of my work feels like I'm playing all day long. I'm just playing with my students and having deep, fun conversations that I would be having whether I was getting paid or not. Feeling good and doing what I love were the vibrations necessary to put me in place to shift from 15-person to 40-person retreats (to eventually 200-person retreats). That's what it means to be vibrating at the level you want to manifest! Remember that my original intention was to *spiritually awaken as many people possible, in as little time possible, with the most profound impact possible*, so whether I attained 200 people or not, the book, the training, and the ongoing work was definitely achieving the original intention.

There you have it … this is how I work with my Higher Consciousness. I get clarity on what I want to manifest. I remain flexible and release all expectations for *how* the manifestation might look. I ask questions of Source. I watch for the guidance to come. When opportunities appear, I sense into how they feel, and when they feel good, I jump on them! I don't get vested in the opportunities. I remain open and know that this could just be another step in my utterly necessary zigzag. Each corner I turn gets me a little closer to my manifestation. I implicitly trust that my manifestation will occur, and I try to remain focused and clear on WHY I want what I want. I know that my General Manager is working with others' General Managers to get it done in the 5D Universal Matrix—and sometimes that takes time.

Possibility ~ Responsibility ~ Love

Having watched many *successes* as I mentor students through these Law of Attraction processes, I would say that there are three main ingredients for manifesting the life you want:

1. Recognize that what you desire is **POSSIBLE** and available to you.

2. Sink deeply into **100% RESPONSIBILITY** for everything that occurs in your life.

3. Move into the Heart for a **deep LOVE vibration** in the **present moment** to **RECEIVE from the 5D Universal Matrix.**

Let's explore each of these steps, and then look more deeply into how to incorporate this into your daily practice.

Possibility

Most of us are closed to what we want in our lives. Either we haven't defined what we want, don't think we're worthy, or think it's not possible. We have all those deep confusions that keep us manifesting exactly what we already have. By introducing the perspective that your dreams are possible—**or even inevitable!**—you'll experience a complete shift in the way you perceive the world. To go from impossibility—*I can't do it, I can't get it, I'm not able*—to possibility, *This is possible for me, It can happen!* is probably the biggest shift people need to make. It's a door opener, a game changer.

What if it IS possible to have *anything* you want? What would you want? How would you define it? What would feel good in your life? Possibility is the first step for those who are really serious about getting what they want out of life. You have to believe it's possible. Maybe you need to start with a small chunk of your dream and believe that the first small chunk is possible. Believing your desire is possible is critical to opening the door to that which you want.

A lot of people set an intention, but deep down, they don't believe it's possible. In this case, it's a non-starter. You can't manifest something if you don't think it's possible. If you are afraid of it, you won't be able to vibrate at the level of manifestation, because you are vibrating the opposite vibration. Building possibility is critical if you want to transform your life or manifest something greater for yourself.

To release the fear, simply feel through the negative vibration, work the violet flame, forgiveness prayers and Sanskrit mantras to cleanse your vibration and clear the path to possibility.

100% Responsibility

We can look at any situation from two vantage points: as a victim with no responsibility, or as potent, with complete responsibility for our participation in it. As we journey forward on our spiritual path, we recognize that the more responsibility we see in our lives, the more potent our lives become.

If I'm in a marriage and I'm not getting what I want, and I don't see any of my own responsibility in it, then I feel like I'm a victim and I basically have no potential for success in this relationship. However, if I see possibility for change *and* I see that I have responsibility for the negative patterns and exchanges that have existed in this relationship, then my putting myself in as a player and seeing my responsibility allows me to change the situation for the better.

Any experience we have in this world has been an effect of what we've attracted. If we truly embrace that responsibility, we start to recognize how absolutely potent we are in life, whether we are attracting "good" or "bad." To truly embrace our responsibility however, we need to detach from identifying ourselves with the external world and release judgment. We need to own it ALL. Not just the good that comes from us. Not just the bad. The whole damn package. This takes practice, self-forgiveness, forgiveness of others, and non-judgment. It takes a willingness to be responsible for our vibration, and the will to change it.

If we see our karma and contrast as our responsibility, as our making, then we can clear and release it, create a new path, and manifest something different. Releasing the deep confusions is key. Our fear-based attachments to feeling [valuable, worthy, lovable, etc]-enough manifests the *opposite* of what we want. We must take responsibility for our deep confusions and fulfill ourselves—with worthiness, safety, lovableness, value, and beauty—through our connection to our Heart, instead of expecting others to be responsible for these inherent qualities. This delivers us straight into our POTENCY via our responsibility for our own well-being.

All You Need Is LOVE to RECEIVE

Of course, there are many aspects we can focus on when we're manifesting, but as I listen to the success stories of what people have achieved and how they've achieved it, I consistently hear examples of how people released the need to control the intention as they sank into the vibration of love. Love is the opposite vibration of fear. If we release the resistance of fear, we settle into our natural vibration of love.

Love starts by learning to feel good in day-to-day life. This will raise your vibration so you will come into a place of RECEIVING that which you are calling into your life. You can practice the feeling of your intentions and learn to feel that way without even needing the world to change. Creating a Heart-based state of presence and cultivating a strong relationship with self through self-awareness, self-love, and self-forgiveness will pave the path for our intentions.

If we believe something's possible, we can begin to take responsibility to make the shift. In taking responsibility, we begin to release the attachments (shoulds, fears, and expectations), and recognize that an inward vibrational shift is truly critical to experiencing our potency. Then all we have to do is set that intention with the perspective of responsibility and possibility, and go into the vibration of love. Once we align with that highest vibration of love, the natural vibration of our Heart, we can achieve anything, especially when it comes to relationships. Love is the universal vibration.

Please note that if love doesn't feel good then it's our **responsibility** to FEEL through the negative vibration that we have mistaken for love. Some of us are cross-wired, so the things that we want to feel good just don't. That's okay. We just need to reach for a vibration and emotion that feels good. If it isn't labeled love, perhaps we can access it through how we feel about nature, or our children. Try not to get stuck in the negative; always reach for the positive, while simultaneously allowing the negative until the vibration goes away. No resistance. Just good vibes.

Examples of Possibility ~ Responsibility ~ Love

Now that we get this intellectually, I'm going to show you how it has worked for people. Remember how I mentioned that this book was originally a transcription of a meditation program with 27 extraordinary people? Well, I had the opportunity to guide them through the manifestation of their intentions over a three-month period. Below you will see how this process worked in their lives.

Please note that I like to be playful about this because when we step outside of our normal powerlessness, life is quite extraordinary. We're often clinging to things through the ego and our attachments. But we can look through the lenses of **anything's possible** and **I'm fully responsible for that which I'm attracting into my life**, and once I've defined that, **I can just sit in the presence of love and reception,** because love is a place of pure receiving and giving.

Put a Ring on It ~ Rachel

When Rachel started the Law of Attraction work with me, she said, *I want a ring on my finger. I've been with this man, and I love him, and I want him to ask me to marry him!* Of course, my job is to help her release her ego's attachment to the ring, so she can release the vibration of *I <u>want</u> this external situation because that will make me feel _____-enough.* As we know, wanting the ring will just push that commitment further from her.

We worked on her recognizing marriage is **possible** for her in the trajectory of her relationship. We then looked at how she is **responsible** in pushing away what she wants because of her fears and inadequacies. I asked, *Why is it so important for you to get a ring on your finger? Would it make you feel safe and secure? Would it make you feel valuable or lovable?* because any of our deep confusions will get us attached to a certain thing. We tend to feel inadequate and so we look to our relationships to make us feel adequate. She began to see that she had been attached to the ring because it would make her feel *loveable, worthy of love*. So she dug up those hidden treasures beneath the surface. She let the beach ball of unlovability pop above the surface and brought all of the related attachments to consciousness. She spent a few weeks watching herself having her *unlovable* thoughts and reactions. After watching the thoughts without judgement, the awareness took their power away. They didn't consume her like they did prior. She realized that she was in fact quite loveable! And she began to feel that way.

Once she released the attachment—the need for her boyfriend to *make her* feel lovable—she went straight into her love for him. No hidden ring agenda. No anger about what she wasn't getting from him. Just love and appreciation for the relationship. She automatically hopped straight into her high vibration vortex of LOVE. And there, she cultivated a strong, loving relationship with her man.

She let go of the ring idea for two months, just two months. The more love she poured at him, he poured it right back… because, of course, she was attracting it effortlessly from her vortex of desire! Their relationship blossomed and strengthened. At the end of the two months, he sat down and wanted to marry, buy a house, and have a baby with her. Voila! Soul-based intention manifested!

Folks, it's seriously that simple. Believe it's possible, release the limiting beliefs and attachments with awareness, and go into love. Super simple. We just get lost in the direction of what we *don't* want so we can't access what we *do* want.

Have My Cake and Eat It Too

I've had several students who get stuck on **possibility** when it comes to career.

One student didn't feel that what she wanted with respect to family and love life was even possible with the career and passionate work she wanted to do. It's a common belief to say, *If I have this aspect working well, I can't have the other thing that I love.* For example: *If I have a happy family life in place, then I can't have a passionate career. After all, we can't have what we want in EVERY area of our lives … can we?* Of course we can; as long as our happiness is coming from within, everything else will be an expression of us.

When we remember that the Law of Attraction General Manager has endless opportunities for us to fulfill our desires, then we release the HOW and go into the **possibility**. Really, she just needed to believe it was possible to do what she loved *and* still have ideal relationships in her life, and it would happen.

When we get stuck in our fears and attachments, we cling to what we have and don't see abundance. We only see scarcity. We can open to the possibility that *I can have my cake and I can eat it too*, or *I can have what I want in this area of my life and in the other area of my life as well*. Once we can see that *everything I want is possible*, we can tell the Universe to go cook it up for us. But if we get stuck in lack of possibility, we're stuck in scarcity.

Another student had a job that he really liked. It met about 75% of the things that he wanted (hours, salary, co-workers), but 25% of the passionate things that he wanted in the job (more purposeful work opportunities) weren't there. Within two months of focused intention, this individual worked every layer of his life and got to a place of both possibility and responsibility. He saw that what he wanted was **possible**, but he had to take **responsibility** for another area in his life where he wasn't being honest, and therefore was out of alignment. You see, alignment doesn't just exist in separate areas of our life. If one area of our life has dishonesty, then that misalignment exists within us and bleeds into the areas where we want to manifest. Once that person truly came to a place of brutal inner honesty, or rather *blissful* inner honesty, the possibilities for the other 25% of his career came into place (the next week!).

Soul-mate Suzy

Suzy wanted to manifest the love of her dreams. She didn't believe it was possible for her to find true love. She had committed to a life without meeting THE ONE. So we spent some time working on opening up the **possibility** of a Soulmate. She worked to open up the belief that the right match was out there and that it was possible for her in this lifetime.

Spiritually speaking, she knew the Universe is abundant because she had become quite skilled in manifesting her intentions, but she wasn't able to bridge that belief to her love life. So we played with her belief system and limiting thoughts around partnership, dating, Soulmates, and marriage. There's so many options, and the Universe is so abundant, why *wouldn't* it be possible for this amazing woman to meet an amazing man?

Once we worked through possibility, we then tackled **responsibility**. Now Suzy had some old childhood stuff to release and she needed to work some underlying fears that were programed into her mind and body early in life. So taking responsibility meant getting energy/bodywork to help access some of the deeply rooted fears stored in her body. It meant doing forgiveness prayers with the parent that she struggled with while growing up. It meant ongoing conversations about the negative vibrations that were coming up to be released because she set this life-changing intention. It also meant a daily commitment to cleansing her vibration with the Violet Flame meditation.

When you set intentions with strong desire and momentum, the Universe may first need to help you <u>destroy</u> or clear old paradigms in your life. This may temporarily feel like a crisis because old vibrations come up to be released, seemingly out of nowhere! And the only way for them to leave is to be felt in the present moment. Intense…but very cathartic!

She took **responsibility** and looked deeply at herself for two months. She felt the uncomfortable vibrations and allowed them the time they needed to release. She asked for help and support when she needed it. She didn't cover up the intensity with food or alcohol or sex … she just allowed herself to be taken by the river until it washed her up to the bank.

When the wild ride was finished, she naturally started **sending love** out to her future partner. The Soul knows, the Universe knows, who that is. She sank into trusting that. She trusted that her General Manager was hard at work hooking her up. She trusted that her General Manager was working with HIS General Manager which was working to inspire him to find her!

As it turns out, her General Manager was setting her up with a man she met four years prior. One day, during this two-month period, he just so happened to pick up her phone number that he had coincidentally kept for FOUR years, and called her up. The call came just on the other side of working through some of this deep childhood stuff that she was facing. She was in the midst of trying to manifest her Soulmate, so when he called, she accepted the first date, and of course he met every single quality that was on her manifestation list!

She saw the possibility, she took responsibility for her inner work which was revealed to her along the way, and then she just sat in the vibration of love. The 5D Universal Matrix took care of the rest. Voila!

Mom-ville Monica

Monica was a stay-at-home mom that was completely exhausted. She had poured herself into her children for 15 years and felt as if she had lost herself. She didn't want to lose herself any further, but didn't know how to get off the hamster wheel.

I helped her find the **possibility** that working herself back into her own life was actually attainable. She was skeptical at first because she couldn't believe that there was life outside of all the doing, carpooling, serving, caring. We had to build a vision of what it would even look like for her to enjoy life again. The possibility that there was a way off the hamster wheel was enough of a relief for her initially. Opening up possibility threw her into her vortex, and she instantly started having experiences of being in the flow—lots of spiritual synchronicity started occurring in her day-to-day experiences.

As she got into her flow and she took **responsibility**, we worked some of her old underlying negative vibrations about sitting still and feeling peace in everyday life. Often there's an old vibration lurking underneath the surface that keeps us from connecting with ourselves, so it just feels better to keep doing-doing-doing. We brought that negative feeling up and she simply sat with it, soaked herself in the uncomfortable vibration, until it left. And then ... it was gone.

Once she took **responsibility** for working what was underneath—the negative vibration that kept her from taking care of herself for many years—she was able to effortlessly go into a place of nurturing herself with love. She opened the pathway to be able to nurture and **love herself**, just as she had been nurturing and loving her own children.

In Summary...

Possibility is critical, because we can't open the door to responsibility and love unless we think that which we want is possible. We must believe we are worthy and that the Universe is eager to fulfill our intentions.

Responsibility takes many forms. It may take the form of visualizing and writing down what we want. It may take the form of working on forgiveness. It may take the form of mending relationships, healing our childhood, or facing any negative vibrations that are running us. We have to heal ourselves and clear the negative vibrations in ourselves. Often, we need help in doing that because it's hard for us to dig through our own stuff without getting lost. With perseverance and focused intention, it's completely possible. Just ask Source for assistance, and it will come in all forms—inspiration, healers, friends, angels … you name it.

Once we're on the path of possibility and responsibility, if we can go into a vibration of love and receptiveness, we will find ourselves in the flow, in our vortex. Getting into the place of love takes alignment, yes, but it also takes a willingness to be open to love, because as soon as we say, *Yes, Source, I'm ready to receive love* or *I'm willing to give love,* we create the situation where the Universe will start moving mountains for us to be nourished and fed with love. An open Heart is very potent.

Possibility, responsibility, and love.

Your Spiritual Practice

It's critical to start a regular practice of going inward and connecting with yourself. The simple intention to do so will change your life. But don't make it another *doing* in your life; it's not a *have-to*. In fact, once you find *your* unique practice, and get hooked on how good you feel, you will crave your inward time. Having it scheduled into your life may help you figure out where it will fit.

My Practice

My personal practice is very casual and fluid because I have three children, three cats, and a husband that works in the basement. It is not easy to get in a room by myself for any amount of time without interruption. My days are different, so some days I can spend five minutes in a car with myself, and other days I have two hours to breathe and contemplate. I try not to be rigid around my practice; it's here to serve me. Here are the steps to my daily practice:

1. Connect with Self via Breath & Heart

2. Connect with Divine Source

3. Feel and Release

4. Purify and Forgive

5. Silence

6. Manifest

7. Receive with Gratitude

Step 1—Connect with Self via Breath through the Heart

When my kids have gotten on the bus, my husband and I have spent about twenty minutes together bonding in the morning, and everybody has cleared out of my space, I will make a cup of tea and sit down in my favorite spot in the house. I'll look out the window to connect with the trees or the snow or the sunrise. I'll pull prana from looking at nature. Then I'll start feeling my breath in my body, with a focus on my Heart. That alone will take me into a very relaxed open state. It feels good and nourishing, so it gets me into a higher vibration very quickly. Feeling connected with myself and attuned to my breath feels great.

Sometimes that's enough to take me inward, and on other days I go into a visualization of pulling pink light into my Heart: *Inhaling pink Light into my Heart, exhaling it deeper into every cell of my body. Inhaling pink Light into my Heart, exhaling it until it creates a bubble of pink Light around my body.* As I breathe Light into my Heart, I merge my Heart energy through my body and energy field.

Step 2—Connect with Divine Source

Once I've established a connection with myself, to the Light outside, to my own Light through my breath, I start to feel the presence of Divine Source. I will often invoke Source by name and feel energetic connection to all that is.

Step 3—Feel and Release

I then go into my emotions and body to determine what's going on vibrationally. How do I feel? Do I feel good? Do I feel bad? *Oh, I feel bad. Okay, let me breathe into that bad feeling. When did that start? Oh yeah, when so-and-so said that negative thing. Okay, well, breathe into it and feel it. What's the lesson in this?*

Remember, we ask and then listen for our Soul's response, rather than letting the ego analysis take over. The answer is in the Heart, not in the mind. So I sit and look inward to see what vibrations I have going on, and then I **bring awareness to the vibrations. I feel them DEEPLY**, especially the ones that make me feel like I want to crawl out of my skin, because they're the ones that keep me on my hamster wheel.

Once I've felt all of the vibrations, and sat with them, sometimes the vibration just leaves. Sometimes I must do more introspection to look further into my belief systems, which may be connected to a deep confusion. Sometimes I need to have a good cry, write a letter that I don't send, or just express or release in whatever way my intuition guides me. It is a personal release and expression, not interpersonal.

Step 4—Purify and Forgive

Once I've done the feeling, releasing, and introspection, I go into a purification phase. First, I will do the Violet Flame meditation daily to cleanse my vibrational and energetic field. I feel the density lifting out of me. Then, I work forgiveness:

- To raise my vibration and release karma with someone, I may use the Ho'oponopono forgiveness prayer: *I love you, I'm sorry, please forgive me, thank you.*

- If I'm struggling in a relationship, I'll cleanse it with forgiveness: *Divine, please help me to forgive Pat, please help Pat to forgive me, help us to forgive ourselves. Please Divine. Thank you. Amen.*

- If I feel like an issue is related to my family lineage, I'll go into Howard Will's lineage forgiveness prayers: *Divine Source, for me and my entire female or male lineage, throughout all time past, present, and future: Please help us forgive all people. Please help all people forgive us. Please help us all forgive each other and forgive ourselves. Please, Divine, thank you, Divine. Amen.*

- If I'm struggling with my own issues, I will do self-forgiveness: *Divine, please help me to forgive myself completely and totally, past, present, and future. Please, thank you. Amen.*

I'll use the tool that seems like the best fit for the vibration I'm feeling at that moment. Sometimes it's just sitting and looking at my responsibility in a situation and feeling whatever emotions are attached. *Oh, I probably could've have been more mindful yesterday,* and then I'll go into forgiveness. Or *how did I create a situation for my daughter to react in that way?* More forgiveness.

As I search for the responsibility and release the emotions around the issue, I can cleanse the issue and surrender it to my Divine Source. Purification usually entails:

- On the emotional and spiritual level, Violet Flame Meditation, and Forgiveness (Ho'oponopono, lineage, Self)

- On the pranic level, Pranayama breathing to balance elements: cooling breath to release heat (Pitta), grounding breath to stabilize (Vata), or stimulating breath to energize (Kapha)

- On the energetic level, Mantra: I will pick a mantra that feels best. Or I will use my go-to mantras. If I need to remove obstacles in life, I will use the Ganesha mantra: *Om Gum Ganapatayei Namaha.* If I want to attract abundance, I will use the Lakshmi mantra: *Om Shrim Mahalakshmiyei Namaha.*

These practices help clear karma, raise my vibration, and clear the path for manifestation.

Step 5—Silence

When I've purified, the negative vibration melts away. Then I can go into a silent meditation. If my mind is busy, I just take a mantra (such as, OM, RAM, SHRIM, or HRIM), and repeat it in my head for ten to twenty minutes. I think any amount of time that allows us to clear our head, feel settled and get super connected to ourselves is perfect.

Step 6—Manifest

Once my vibration and my mind are cleared, I will go into my intentions. I will have been given the clarity of what I want based on the contrast and negative emotions I was feeling during my introspection.

I imagine my desire having just occurred. I play out the scenario visually, watching what happens. I have the thoughts associated with my desire having just occurred. I feel the vibrations and the **positive emotions** associated with it having happened. I let the movie roll until I feel like my intention already exists and I sit in those vibrations for as long as I can.

I'll just let my imagination go wild because I know my imagination is my Heart showing me all the potential. I'll sit with the imagining and creativity and play with it. Usually by the end, I'm feeling so deeply grateful and so honored to be a part of my own life.

Step 7—Receive with Gratitude

After manifesting, I sit and receive. I watch everything coming to me. I end with gratitude. Not in expectation, but deep trust that my General Manager is hooking me up. I feel so deeply thankful for the effortlessness and the wisdom of it all. I usually finish with so much motivation that my hands are trembling to go do something creative. I feel so aligned after my daily practice.

My morning practice can last anywhere from twenty minutes to two hours, depending on how much time I have. On busy days, I just make sure I'm connecting with my breath, feeling my vibrations, and purifying. Sometimes I can do this while I'm driving to my next client. After doing it for years, I can do it on the go!

Our vibrations are always with us, and we don't need to put unnecessary rules, structures, and to-do lists around our daily practice. It can simply be based on *I love myself, I feel negative, and I'm going to work toward opening to feeling better. I'm going to work toward the possibility that I can feel better, and take some responsibility to raise my vibration, and then just hang out in love and gratitude.*

Please find a guided meditation with this twenty-minute practice on my website: www.enLIGHTenWithKim.com. Click on **Community Resources** and **Book Meditations**, log in for free, and find the meditation called #7 **Daily Meditation**

Namasté, My Friends!

We make spirituality much more confusing and complex than it needs to be. It's about listening to how you feel, wanting to feel better, and allowing yourself to do so.

I leave you with the opportunity to get off the hamster wheel and awaken to your true potency. Go ahead and set your intention to work with Law of Attraction and bring *allowing* into your life so you can create possibility, take responsibility, and harness the love that is flowing toward you every second of every day.

It has been my honor to do this work with you, and I have such deep gratitude for the opportunity. It's the most incredible journey when you start putting yourself out there, in your blissful element, because what shines back at you is breathtaking and amazing. I pray that you are able to experience that in your life—that magnificence, bliss, truth, and consciousness—because it's available to us … and it's just waiting for us to discover it.

I love you all so very much, and the Light in me truly does honor, deeply honor, the Light in you. NAMASTÉ!

About the Artist

Endre Balogh, is an incredible violinist, photographer, and sacred geometry artist. I'm honored to feature this incredible work of art on my book cover. You can see more of his art and purchase prints on his website: **www.EndresArt.com.** Deep gratitude to Endre for his gifts and his generosity.

Made in the USA
Columbia, SC
03 December 2018